MAKING THE BEST OF SCHOOLS

Making
the Best
of Schools

A Handbook
for Parents,
Teachers, and
Policymakers

JEANNIE OAKES
& MARTIN LIPTON

YALE UNIVERSITY PRESS

NEW HAVEN & LONDON

Published with assistance from the Kingsley Trust Association Publication Fund established by the Scroll & Key Society of Yale College.

Designed by Nancy Ovedovitz and set in Times Roman type by G & S Typesetters, Austin, Texas. Printed in the United States of America by Vail-Ballou Press, Binghamton, New York.

Library of Congress Cataloging-in-Publication Data

Oakes, Jeannie.
Making the best of schools : a handbook for parents, teachers, and policymakers / Jeannie Oakes and Martin Lipton.
   p. cm.
  Includes bibliographical references.
  ISBN 0-300-04650-2. — ISBN 0-300-04651-0 (pbk.)
   1. Education—United States. 2. Public Schools—United States.
3. Education and state—United States. 4. Home and school—United
States. I. Lipton, Martin, 1942– . II. Title.
LA217.019   1990
370'.973—dc20   89-39035
                                CIP

10 9 8 7 6 5 4 3 2 1

To
Lisa, Tracy, Lowell, and Ethan
and their schools:

Birmingham High School
Blair High School
Eliot Eighth Grade Secondary School
Grossmont College
George K. Porter Gifted Magnet Junior High School
Grover Cleveland Humanities Magnet High School
Los Angeles Pierce College
Los Angeles Valley Alternative School
Pacific Ackworth Friends School
Pasadena Alternative School
Pasadena City College
Pomelo Drive Elementary School
Robert Fulton Junior High School
San Diego State University
University of California, Los Angeles
University of California, Santa Cruz
University of California, San Diego
University of San Diego
University of Texas, Austin
Walnut Elementary School
William McKinley Junior High School

CONTENTS

A NOTE TO READERS

We wrote this book for parents who could not easily find the information they need to feel competent and confident as they guide their children through schools. The book is also for teachers and policymakers who recognize that well-informed parents can be their strongest allies in educating children and in smoothing educational innovation and reform.

While preparing the book for publication, we found that education professionals took an interest in the book in a way we did not anticipate. Teachers, administrators, education policymakers, and educational researchers responded to the manuscript by revisiting their own intensely personal educational concerns and crises. They read as parents, reflected on their experiences as students, and only then responded with helpful professional and technical suggestions. We are reassured by this reminder of how closely educators share the parent's perspective, and we hope this book enhances that common experience.

In some ways this book takes a different approach from what is commonly supposed to interest parents. Some advice-givers cautioned us that parents did not want to be bothered by large concepts, research findings, or broad educational issues. Parents, we were told, prefer simple concepts and checklists. Others told us that parents were interested only in books that promised surefire ways to get educational advantages for their own children. But we find that parents are eager to make sense out of schools instead of just being told how to act. They want to be able to think on their feet when unique school problems arise. They believe that their own children stand the best chance of succeeding in schools where many children are successful, not just a few. We hope such parents will find this book helpful.

We believe that the goal of a high-quality education for all children is achievable without disrupting the high quality of education that only a few now enjoy. We hope this book will help parents, educators, and policymakers work together to reach that goal—for the sake of your child and everybody's children.

January 1990

INTRODUCTION

Even children who go to the "best" schools have no guarantee of getting an excellent education. Many who go to schools with outstanding reputations don't do well, and even those who do can have serious gaps in their knowledge and skills. On the other hand some children who go to seemingly ordinary schools manage to learn a good deal. We intend to explain why.

Throughout this book we address the concerns of parents, educators, and policymakers. We hope to help you make better sense of what your children and other children you care about experience at school. We argue that the same practices that make schooling better for any one child—your child—will make schooling better for all children. The best schools are those in which *all* children—not just a few—are believed to be capable, where all are offered rich learning opportunities, held to rigorous intellectual standards, and expected to succeed. To make the best of all schools, we need look no further than the schools we would want for our own children.

An inevitable tension exists between what parents want for their own child and what the community now provides for all children. This tension emerges from parents' natural determination to get the best education for their own child. If parents believe, as most do, that educational opportunities are limited—are a scarce resource—they will eventually confront the obvious: compared with other children, my child will get about the same as, less than, or more of the available resources. Of those three possibilities, getting more is the only satisfactory outcome.

Parents who can do so will position their children to receive the most of scarce opportunities. Not surprisingly, these parents tend to be among the most advantaged in our society: the wealthiest, best educated, and most socially powerful. If that description seems hard for an average middle-class parent to identify with, we can put it this way: Parents with the confidence to demand the best opportunities for their children typically are not poor, uneducated, or members of racial minorities. And confident parents will work, vote, and pull strings to get the best for their children.

Parents, educators, and policymakers who feel caught in the middle of this tension deserve both sympathy and a way out. On the one hand, protective self-interest compels parents to exert their effort and influence to get limited resources for their children (excellent teachers, curriculum, materials). And yet even those who send their children to the best schools have reason to worry. Regardless of their school's reputation, the dynamics of unfairness are likely to operate there—even if they are less apparent. On the other hand, democratic sensibilities and pragmatic concern for a secure and prosperous nation taint many parents' satisfaction with their own children's educational privileges. Parents whose children attend advantaged schools recognized for their achievements and high standards can't escape feeling discomfort when they read the miserable statistics that portray the consistent and systematic educational disadvantages of minorities and the poor. Finally, many parents and policymakers want the best possible education for all children because they care for all children—because providing such an education is a good thing, the moral thing, to do.

In the best cases, parents, educators, and policymakers struggle at the margins, not at the heart of school policy and practice to deliver better school opportunities to all children. Change is frustrating, costly, and often illusory. Tradition, inertia, and elusive public commitment discourage many; but many keep plugging away. In the worst cases, parents, educators, and policymakers combine irrational notions of meritocracy, trickle-down excellence, and blaming the victims to justify how the children who wind up with the best education deserve it, and how those who don't are less worthy. Even for the most community-minded persons, the forces of self-interest and social interest are hardly balanced. We wring our hands over mediocrity, the disadvantaged, and the lack of opportunity and equity. We convene commissions and issue reports calling for re-form. But consistently the long-range moral push gives way to the more immediate shove of self-interest.

Making the Best

We believe that the push and shove of self-interest and social interest can be aligned to work together instead of in opposite directions. Currently, many assert that one essential role of school policy is to assure an "even playing field" for all children. The metaphor means that some children shouldn't have the added burden of having to carry the ball uphill (that is, go to a school with inadequate facilities, inferior courses, and so on). The metaphor has fairness at heart but reveals some telling premises regarding the fate of those students who are not considered the brightest and are not destined to attend prestigious universities. An even playing field presumes that in the absence of gross obstacles (racist policies, hunger, physical handicaps) education is equally accessible to everyone, even if the schools are not good. A second premise is that competition for the best opportunities is not in itself a problem, as long as it's fair. Beginning with kindergarten or even earlier, one job of education policy is to distribute opportunities according to the merit, mettle, talent, and character of the winners and losers.

We need a different test of the quality and fairness of education. First, schools must qualify all children for productive and satisfying participation in the varying ways a just society requires. And second, at the end of schooling, children's qualifications to participate must not be distributed unevenly in relationship to their race, gender, primary language, parental income, handicap, or any other irrelevancy. This does not imply that schools must make all children equally competent, knowledgeable, or skilled at the age of sixteen or eighteen; democracy does not require us to deny individual circumstances and differences. However, we must look at the evenness of the playing field at the *end* of children's schooling as well as at the start and along the way.

We will argue throughout this book that, although school resources are indeed unequally allocated along economic and racial lines, no child currently receiving a good education needs to sacrifice any of that quality to improve another child's inferior experiences. A simple if not easily accomplished solution would be to spend more nearly what some other developed countries spend to educate their children. In fact, quality education can become an abundant, not a scarce, commodity without any child's receiving less education. But spending more money to equalize opportunities, while necessary, would be sufficient only if those children currently getting a *better* education were actually getting the best possible education, which they are not. Extending their educational opportunities to all children is not good enough. We worry that the "best" schools, because of their comparatively high rankings and honors, largely escape the scrutiny that would reveal that they too are seriously deficient. The provision of equal access to a mediocre education is a goal unworthy of our schools. There can be enough of the best education to reach all children only if we have the public will to pay for it *and* if knowledgeable educators and policymakers offer the leadership to reconstruct schools for all children.

The philosopher John Dewey offered a practical and elegant guide: "What the best and wisest [parents want for their] own child, that must the community want for all of its children." Dewey's view suggests that a single standard for an excellent education can be forged from parents' enlightened self-interest and civic responsibility. The first step is to ask ourselves and the community's political, business, labor, educational, and professional leaders—without any presumption that we or they are indeed the "best and wisest"—what education we all want for our own children.

Based on the likelihood that we will find widespread agreement about what constitutes an excellent education, our next step would be to provide that education to all the community's children. This differs from much current practice, in which the presumption among leaders and many parents is often that my children require a certain kind of education and their children need something else. Even if that "something else" costs as much or more to provide and even when it is designed to meet "special needs," we are certain that most children would benefit most from what the best and wisest parents want for their own child.

There are pragmatic and moral reasons to support Dewey's "best and wisest" test. First, the quality of *our* children's future will be heavily affected by the quality of education that *all* children receive. Our national welfare will demand a highly trained work force to perform skillfully and responsibly with computers, nuclear energy, genetic engineering, and more. Increasing sophistication in the business, manufacturing, agricultural, military, and service sectors will make us all dependent upon a national supply of men and women who have the knowledge and judgment to sustain prosperity and safety. Recent studies of the relationship between the quality of education and national economic growth suggest that increasing the quality of education—particularly for the most disadvantaged students—may in itself lead to increased productivity.

Moreover, the boundaries of the communities that affect our children's lives will extend beyond our present notions of neighborhood and town. In that larger community of the future, our children's prosperity and well-being will hinge on the productivity, the wisdom, and the democratic inclinations of all those who live within minutes or hours by air or electronic circuitry. In the past, many parents felt relatively secure if they could raise their children in affluent enclaves with good schools and healthy economies. Such a belief is now misplaced. In the future being better educated than one's neighbors will hold fewer advantages than living in a well-educated "neighborhood"—vastly expanded to include whole geographic regions, up to and even beyond national boundaries.

A second practical reason for having a single standard for excellent school opportunities is suggested by our corollary to Dewey's advice: "What the community provides for the 'best' of its children, that must all parents want for their own children." We know there is an uneven distribution of educational opportunities throughout the school system and even within a particular school. The fact that a high-quality education is available to, say, 10 percent of the children at a school can be of little comfort to the parent whose child is at the eleventh percentile. Even having one's child in the best class provides little assurance of quality, for "best" is a relative matter and may not be very good at all. And everyone should feel uneasy with the realization that most children do not, by any standard, receive the best education. The only way parents can be assured that their children will receive the best education available at their school is to make certain that the best is available for all the children who attend.

We also know that making the best of schools requires more than parents' steady advocacy for their own children. It requires a firm commitment to the highest quality education for all children. This is a moral and ethical commitment to one of the finest sentiments of our culture: to provide a free and equal education to all. To quote Dewey again, "Any other ideal for our schools is narrow and unlovely; acted upon, it destroys our democracy."

Perspectives on Schools and School Policy

Children need help to survive, cope, and excel at school. Parents have an immediate, hands-on advocacy role in providing that help to their children. Policymakers have a longer range community interest. But the knowledge parents and policymakers need to perform their roles is essentially the same, and it is not the technical knowledge educators need to translate policies into school activities. Clearly, the parent, the school board member, and the teacher or principal all have different jobs that require different knowledge and skills.

Yet if we are all to push and shove in the same direction—a direction that benefits our child and everybody's children—parents, educators, and policymakers need to share certain perspectives on schooling that enable them to see beyond the commonplace and act differently than they now do. The perspectives we will offer here provide a broad understanding of how the overall organization and atmosphere of a school affect children's opportunities to learn; how classroom environments affect children's self-esteem; how various kinds of lessons affect children's learning the most important subjects; how the home environment affects school success; and much more. These perspectives enable parents and policymakers to ask tough questions that are sure to bring tricky and controversial answers: How do schools use tests to judge children—that is, to determine who needs a special program or who might not be ready for the next grade? Are these tests fair and accurate? What is really important to learn in school subjects like English, art, math, social studies? Why do schools think it so important for young children to learn to read "on time," even though many would be better served by learning to read later? Why do schools make it possible for—even encourage—some high schoolers to take easy courses? Why are so many children assigned to classes in earlier grades that almost guarantee they will not be in rigorous programs in high school? Why do parents gradually back off from their involvement with their children's school?

We've applied the following test to the perspectives we offer in this book: Are they anchored both in democratic values and in evidence from educational research? For reasons of space, we omit much supporting data and citations of relevant studies. Nonetheless, what we offer is a more complex, demanding, and knowledge-based approach to helping children and understanding schools than what we found in many how-to pamphlets and guidebooks. Ours is not an approach that lends itself to recipes, formulas, or lists of do's and don'ts for making your child a genius. Neither does it suggest ways of blackmailing or pestering schools into giving special advantages, favors, or privileges to your child. We do include many specific suggestions from our own research and experience, but these are offered more to illustrate a perspective than to prescribe specific actions.

When parents, educators, and policymakers are eager and willing to understand schools from broad and more theoretical perspectives and when they know the limits of piecemeal, hurried responses to individual crises, they can better scrutinize consequential school events that at first seem trivial. Armed with such perspectives, policymakers will be more effective in safeguarding and promoting the public interest. Educators will be more professional in making immediate and long-range plans. And parents will be able to keep a more watchful eye on their children and intervene with confidence when necessary.

The remainder of this book sets forth the perspectives, knowledge, and values that we believe are necessary to make the best of schools.

Chapter 1—The Culture Perspective

To sort out what goes on at school, parents, educators, and policymakers must place day-to-day school practices and events within a complex and interrelated context—the school culture. The school culture is nothing less than the shared history, habits, traditions, values, and practices that shape the meaning of each and every event at school. The school culture is the "glue" that holds together sometimes disparate and seemingly random school practices. Some school cultures help make children's learning experiences exciting and challenging; other cultures make schooling lifeless, boring, or worse. A cultural perspective helps us notice if there is a feeling or environment at school that makes it seem inevitable that all children will succeed. Are the opportunities to learn, expectations for learning, and professional conditions for teaching clearly in evidence? Do you wish that you could be a student or teacher there? By asking these questions and others, you will come as close as possible to evaluating the quality of the school fairly.

Chapter 2—The Learning Perspective

Chapter 2 introduces the real business of schooling, children's learning. Much is known about how children learn, but parents and schools often don't pay enough attention to it. Those who believe that children learn best according to a stimulus-response, behavioral, or training model deny children many valuable learning experiences. In contrast, when parents and schools encourage children to make sense of their experiences, children feel themselves to be in charge of their learning and become eager to learn. This chapter presents theories of learning that schools rely on and suggests how they often limit children's opportunities to learn.

Chapter 3—The Classroom Perspective

Children learn the knowledge and skills that schools teach in classrooms; here also they receive information from other students and from teachers that exerts a powerful influence on how they view themselves as learners. The classroom is where most children form their first impressions of themselves as either highly capable or unsuccessful students. Later, again in classrooms, these impressions are cemented in place. The best learning and the most positive self-perceptions seem to develop in classrooms in which children emulate real-life problem solving that requires knowledge that is complex and rich in meaning. Children learn best when they have some opportunities to work cooperatively instead of exclusively competing. They learn best when their hard work brings rewards and when slacking off is neither satisfying to them nor supported by classmates. Chapter 3 presents information adults can use to determine whether a particular classroom is a good place for children to be.

Chapters 4 and 5—The Valued-Knowledge Perspective

When scientists, artists, historians, accountants, and others look inside classrooms, they are often amazed that school subjects bear so little resemblance to what they actually do in their jobs. They recognize the vocabulary of the subjects, but they also notice that children often miss the essentials. Each subject has at its core a unique set of fundamental principles or basic concepts that escape children's attention in many schools (even if the children appear to be succeeding and are getting good grades). Can't we all remember passing—even getting good grades in—courses yet later finding that we retained very little understanding of what was really important about the subject? Chapters 4 and 5 describe the basic school subjects children learn and how they might be taught in rich and meaningful ways.

Chapters 6 and 7—The Evaluation and Sorting Perspective

The commonly accepted reason for testing, grading, ability grouping, tracking, and repeating grades is that these practices help schools address children's individual learning needs—that they identify a child's ability or knowledge and/or make it possible to assign the most appropriate lessons or classes. But, as we describe in chapters 8 and 9, these practices can also be destructive. And because they are nearly universal (it is hard for most people to imagine schools without them), the potential for damage to your child and others is great. Understanding these practices should enable parents, educators, and policymakers to monitor carefully what happens to children and to begin chipping away at some of the most damaging effects.

Chapter 8—The "Special Needs" Perspective

Chapter 8 surveys how schools define special needs and what resources are made available to children with physical, emotional, social, and learning problems. A critical dilemma for both schools and parents is how to provide these children with the special attention and resources they need and deserve without isolating and alienating them from the mainstream of school life.

Chapters 9, 10, and 11—The Parent-Involvement Perspective

Today, nearly all parents have difficulty bucking the social forces that can be far stronger than their own influence or confidence. On the other hand, modern families—whether two-career, single-parent, or dad-works-and-mom-stays-at-home—are or can be smarter than past generations. Chapter 9 describes the fundamentals of home support for learning—those aspects of family life that can help a child be ready to succeed at school. Chapter 10 covers the knotty business of homework. We suggest some general principles for keeping homework independent learning and avoiding the homework battles many families wage nightly. We also offer ways to help children get assignments done, ways that are consistent with broad learning goals. In Chapter 11 we outline strategies for working with your children's school when difficulties arise. We suggest ways that parents who are advocates for their children can, by working with teachers and administrators, make a difference in what happens at school.

Chapter 12—The Reform Perspective

The conventional approach to school improvement is to do what schools have always done only do it better, work harder, and next time try to get it right. But this course of action only gives children more of the same—the same school practices, organization, and beliefs that now fail to meet children's needs. Our inescapable—if embarrassingly simple—conclusion is that if we want schools that are very different, we will have to do schooling very differently. Each of the perspectives we develop throughout the book suggests a marked departure from the conventional ways of conducting school. In chapter 12 we examine public policy directions that will enable communities and school professionals to make the changes that make the best of schools.

MAKING THE BEST OF SCHOOLS

CHAPTER ONE

Wrestling with Tradition: An Introduction to the School Culture

If you walked into a school today, you'd know just what to do. Schools haven't changed much since your time or your parents'. Bells still ring, rules are posted on the walls, teachers take roll. Children still drop their textbooks on their desks, if they haven't forgotten or lost them, and they do the assignments on the chalkboard. They still work quietly enough to hear the clock, and they manufacture enough noise so they can't hear themselves think. They misbehave, create, and get sick; they act mean and hurtful, and they offer generous acts of kindness. Now, as then, profound and ridiculous experiences leave lasting impressions. Much of what children learn they forget, but never as much as they remember. Schools have carpeted the floors, installed computers in the classrooms, and found teachers who look younger than most of ours did. Yet you would still recognize the frustration and exhilaration of this place. You'd recognize them from your memory and from the pit of your stomach.

We ask you to return with us to schools and view them differently. As T. S. Eliot put it, we hope "to arrive where we started / And know the place for the first time." We hope that a fresh perspective will help you look sharply at school practices that are so familiar they are rarely examined. This perspective looks at schools as cultures steeped in history and beliefs that often have little to do with learning.

Taking this cultural view, we ask you to look at schools as places that needlessly limit learning and almost always defy change. Yet, we'd also like you to recognize that schools don't have wills entirely their own. Despite well-deserved accusations of mediocrity and demands for reform, schools mostly give society what it wants. Are schools doomed to carry out social expectations that limit learning and frustrate change? We don't think so. Parents, educators, and policymakers who view schools from a cultural perspective can decide to what degree schools persist in honoring counterproductive traditions. And they can begin to help their children and schools break loose.

ASSUMPTIONS AND CONFLICTS

The American public's expectations exert tremendous influence on the school culture. That list of expectations has been growing ever since colonial times, and it shows no sign of getting shorter. Consider your wishes for your own child and the children in your community. You want them to be healthy and emotionally strong, to feel confident, be ambitious, and have integrity. You want them to appreciate the aesthetic work of others and to be creative themselves. They must have the knowledge and commitment to be fully participating citizens. They must experience the richness and heritage of diverse cultures as they come to understand their own. You want children to understand and appreciate the skills they need to work and live harmoniously with neighbors and family. You want them to be sound, curious, and critical thinkers. And of course, they must be competent in the basics, able to read, write, compute, and find information in a variety of resources. As John Goodlad succinctly put it, "We want it all."

Sure, we might quibble about schools trying to do too much, but few critics seriously consider shortening the list. These goals are like motherhood and apple pie—too good to be criticized. However, as schools work toward achieving them, they run headlong into conflicting beliefs and traditions. Conflicts among various goals and expectations shape schools as much as the expectations themselves:

■ We want rigorous and demanding schools in which children can't simply get by or slide through. And we want serious and committed students who are respectful of their schools and teachers. Yet, society constrains these goals, with its low regard for hard intellectual work. Many parents complain if the demands of schoolwork make students feel uncomfortable or interfere too much with their lives outside of school.

Movies and television typically portray schools as boring—with little to offer beyond sports, friends, and a showcase for fads.

- We want schools to prepare a work force that will ensure national prosperity and strength. Yet, long-standing prejudices keep schools from making some of the most necessary jobs seem attractive to all children. Few minority children and girls, especially, believe that they can attain careers in science and mathematics.
- We want local control of schools so that they can provide for the unique needs of each community's children. Yet, many local decisions clash with regional or national sensibilities. For example, local districts who may want to censor library books are usually overridden by state or federal authority. Some neighborhood people object to a high school health clinic that offers family-planning information.
- We seek educational equality to ensure that all children have opportunities to get to the top in an upwardly mobile society. Yet, we find innumerable ways to give educational advantages to children from families that are socially and economically advantaged. And when less privileged children don't succeed, we often blame the children themselves— or their parents and teachers.
- We believe that education is among the most important of national responsibilities. We insist that teaching our nation's youth is among the noblest professions. Yet, we try to fulfill this responsibility with a smaller percentage of our national income than most other industrialized countries. We refuse to pay our teachers as well as many other countries pay theirs.
- We cherish our diverse cultural heritage and take pride in our national melting pot. Yet, we can draw an unmistakable conclusion from over thirty years of desegregation attempts: Americans respond very nervously when their own schools become the pot for mixing the cultural ingredients.

The list could go on, but the point is clear. Americans expect a lot from their schools, and many of these expectations conflict with social realities. Not surprisingly, schools have developed cultures that accommodate and juggle expectations and conflicts—cultures that in the process often compromise learning.

THE COMMON SCHOOL

Historically, Americans have incorporated their hopes for education in the *common school*. In the 1830s, Horace Mann conceived of the American common school to complement what families taught their children at home. These were not charity schools for the poor, but rather free public schools for the sons and daughters of farmers, businessmen, professionals, and the rest. Mann intended common schools to teach the knowledge and habits citizens needed to function in a democracy. He envisioned the common school as the "great equalizer" and the "creator of wealth undreamed of" and hoped it would eliminate poverty and crime and shape the destiny of a wise, productive country. From the beginning, however, schools fell short of Mann's vision. Even so, we continue to pin our hopes on the public school. Americans see it as the ideal place in a democracy for all children to get a free and necessary education.

Over the years, society's idea of an essential, basic education has changed. So has its definition of a child. A century ago, Americans thought that five years of school were what children and the country needed to be well-governed and prosperous. Five grades seemed sufficient to learn reading, writing, and arithmetic. It was enough time to indoctrinate children, especially immigrant children, in the rudiments of American culture. They could learn the habits of citizenship (including a heavy emphasis on work) necessary for social harmony. Policymakers did not think adolescents needed supervision other than what families and the workplace provided. Only those children interested in a gentleman's education or heading for the professions needed schooling beyond the age of ten or eleven. They could get that in less widely available public or private schools.

We now see a twelve-year education as the minimum requirement for instilling in students the knowledge and good citizenship required to promote the social welfare. We have extended schools' supervisory and social responsibilities to age eighteen, when students choose employment or higher education. We have also redefined the fundamentals of a common education. A familiar example is computer literacy, named in the 1983 national report *A Nation at Risk* as one of the new educational basics.

Over time schools have shifted away from providing a common *set of learnings* for all students. Now schools focus more on offering a common *place* that all students attend. We expect schools to prepare children differently—some for jobs or technical training, others for universities and the professions. Do different sets of learning prepare students equally well to benefit society? Do different learnings prepare all children equally well to benefit themselves? Society often dodges these questions, even as it maintains its commitment to the common school.

How will we define and redefine common schools in the future? We can be sure of conflicts, but little else seems certain. One trend that seems likely to continue is the extension of public schooling to include college or technical training. Yet, we may find it increasingly acceptable for the content of education to diverge before age eighteen. Perhaps some children will be leaving high school earlier—opting for job training, early college admission, or community service. Some educators look to a day when preparation for work and rigorous intellectual development are complementary—not contradictory—elements of common schooling.

A major challenge to the common school in the years ahead is the increasing geographic bifurcation of the nation into poor inner cities and more affluent outer-urban and suburban communities. As middle-class families—minority and white—have moved away from central cities, the remaining residents face problems of unemployment, poverty, and racial isolation. Unemployment among blacks has steadily increased, and currently black youth unemployment is more than double that for young whites. Many city smokestack-industry jobs have moved to the suburbs or disappeared entirely, and few inner-city residents qualify for urban white-collar jobs. Most must settle for irregular, part-time work lacking security or benefits. Recession and declines in earning have kept large numbers of inner-city residents below the poverty line. Accompanying these trends has been an overall increase in the number of children being raised in single-parent, female-headed households and a decline in government programs supporting poor children (for example, reduced benefits from Aid to Families with Dependent Children and more stringent eligibility requirements). Today, most Hispanic and black students attend urban schools with nonwhite majority enrollments. In 1988 only seven of the nation's twenty-five largest city school systems had white enrollments greater than 30 percent.

These urban changes are a part of two major shifts that have profound implications for the future of the common school. Overall, larger proportions of poor and minority children enroll in public schools each year. At the same time, middle-class whites—often older and more affluent than earlier generations of parents of school-aged children—increasingly choose private education. Some of these seek the status and privilege of private schools. But many worry that racial integration has precipitated a decline in school quality, and many others fear for their children's personal safety in schools where crime and violence are increasing.

In the face of these changes, the question of whether government should allow parents greater choice of where their children can go to school has become more salient. Some policy analysts contend that if parents could choose their children's schools, the ensuing competition would increase the quality of all schools. In recent years the discussion of choice has included the idea of vouchers—funds that could accompany children to whatever school their parents chose. However, if vouchers extend to private schools, they raise issues of state support for private enterprises and the separation of church and state. More likely, parents will increasingly choose among public schools.

Plans for providing parents with choices within public school systems were spurred initially by efforts to voluntarily integrate urban schools. Now, public "magnet" or theme schools proliferate, even in areas in which racial integration is not an issue. Magnet schools, by definition, emphasize different rather than common experiences. Some stress the humanities, science, or other academic disciplines more than regular schools do. Others emphasize the performing or fine arts. Some are vocational, such as the new urban academies that teach academics in the context of occupations. Conservative or liberal philosophies distinguish others, such as fundamental and alternative or open schools.

Choice in the public sector has complex consequences for common schooling. The long-term contribution of specialized schools will depend, in part, on who attends which schools. It will depend on whether all children, regardless of their race, class, or gender, feel welcomed in the finest schools the community provides. Magnet schools may simply alter our definition of the common school. They may replace nearly identical neighborhood schools with a variety of high-quality, theme-oriented programs open to any student who wishes to attend—commonness of a different sort. However, if magnet schools become highly selective in the hopes of retaining white or affluent families in public schools, they will probably cater to separate rather than common interests. If that happens, children may have academic and social experiences only with others like themselves, and we will have lost the dream of the common school.

Some seem willing to give up on the idea of the common school, especially as national demographics shift. Others become increasingly committed to its central role in preserving our national community. Can the common school survive the inevitable conflicts that lie ahead?—or, rather, can we achieve Horace Mann's dream of such a school? We can't predict how long the nation's commitment to the common school will last. We do know that today's schools continue to struggle to balance the interests of those who prefer a separate education against the value of equitable common schools.

SCIENTIFIC MANAGEMENT AND
THE FACTORY MODEL

If schools' goals have been shaped by lofty idealists, their management practices have come from hardheaded types. Schools have inherited the factory model of production from business and industry, which stems from turn-of-the-century theories about how to manage factories scientifically and efficiently. During the change from small, community manufacturing to large-scale industrial production, theories about organizing people and jobs efficiently revolutionized the workplace. These theories also exerted their influence on schools.

Industrial efficiency caught the public imagination through the writings of Frederick Winslow Taylor and the example of Henry Ford. Taylor recommended time-and-motion studies to set standards of performance. Basing their practices on careful record keeping, managers established the "best methods," which replaced the rule-of-thumb approaches that workers had developed over time. Managers trained and supervised workers and were themselves trained in techniques of scientific control and efficiency. People called the techniques scientific because they were systematic and precise and allowed few individual judgments and little variability. Factory owners and managers centralized decision making and authority at the top, divided labor by specializing tasks, and governed every aspect of the enterprise with rules, regulations, and an impersonal (more efficient) attitude toward the individual. Ford's assembly line became the apex of scientific management. His auto workers, easily trained and supervised by managers, used standardized methods to perform small tasks.

At the same time that scientific management was solving production problems, schools were seeking solutions to other problems. Not unlike today, demographic changes caught educators and politicians unprepared to provide eight to twelve years of education for rapidly increasing numbers of children—many of whom were immigrants. As schools grew larger and more expensive, politicians, industrialists, and social reformers criticized them for their inefficient methods and dubious success. Many critics suggested that, like all large enterprises, schools could achieve greater success with factorylike management systems. The factory model appealed because industries were dramatically increasing their productivity and profit. If *they* could raise their productivity by becoming more efficient, why not schools?

Most educators of the day were not far removed from the dusty school-masters of earlier times. They undoubtedly knew something about knowledge and about children from farms and small towns. Yet they were unprepared to run large, cost-effective operations involving hundreds and thousands of students. Industrial efficiency seemed to provide an answer. Many educators were staggered by the diversity of newly arrived southern and eastern European immigrants and viewed them as having educational and social needs far different from those of other Americans. Some educators embraced scientific methods, believing that older models were incapable of bringing order and uniformity to schools that faced such diversity.

It's not surprising that educators, especially those in urban areas, quickly began to relish the role of the expert and the personal status and political clout that came with scientific management. Knowing management principles, they could stand on an equal footing with the increasingly prestigious lay school board members—usually businessmen. Applied to schools, scientific management brought the appearance of efficiency to the educational enterprise. As in business, the function of the efficiency movement was to produce school products (educated adults) at the lowest cost. The *quality* of children's education was often of secondary importance.

Scientific management methods helped create the school bureaucracies we have today. We can hold these management styles and attitudes as much responsible for promoting educational mediocrity as we can credit them with remedying inefficiency. The legacy of scientific management is schools that are rule-dominated, slow to change, and top-heavy with administration.

Progressive businesses today realize that they must modify their assembly-line mentality if they are to produce high-quality, competitive products and services. Schools have been slower to catch on. Despite growing evidence that factorylike schools produce mediocre education, most schools continue to fine-tune the factory model. When children don't learn well, too often blame goes to the raw material (children themselves) or the workers (teachers). The possibility that the school culture works against children's high achievement escapes notice.

THE CULTURE OF SCHOOLS

The typical American school is subject to a multitude of expectations. It is also caught between the often conflicting forces of idealism, diversity, and efficiency. How have schools responded to these expectations and conflicts? Almost paradoxically by trying to respond to all demands while resisting fundamental change.

Seymour Sarason, a psychologist at Yale University, studied schools' largely unsuccessful attempts in the 1960s to improve children's learning. He recognized the power of the school culture when he showed that schools rarely took reforms seriously. Their traditional ways of organizing classes, teaching subjects, and going about day-to-day activities blocked change. Instead of changing to fit the reforms, schools made the reforms conform to the way the schools had always been.

These fixed ways of conducting schools—Sarason called them "regularities"—are so ingrained in schooling that we hardly notice and rarely question them. Almost never does anyone consciously say, "Let's do it this way." For example, at one school the faculty stays late to give children extra help. At another the parking lot empties shortly after the last bell. Very likely, a teacher who moved from one school to the other would soon adopt the habits of the teachers at the new school. At one school the principal freely drops in at classrooms and participates in lessons. The children love it, and it pleases the teachers that the principal knows about the class activities. At another school the principal tries stepping into classes and gets a cold reception. Here, the teachers feel the principal is nosy and doesn't trust them. At some schools teachers follow the required curriculum to the letter; at others they don't. Some schools don't expect children from certain neighborhoods to do well. At some schools teachers pitch in to help their colleagues. We may never be able to trace the origins of such informal regularities. New teachers receive no explicit instruction in such regularities, but they don't take long to learn.

Other regularities are formal policy. Children go to school five days a week and have summer vacations. Schools put children into classes by age, about thirty to a class. History teachers start at "the beginning" and work their way up to the present. Each subject has its textbook with questions at the ends of chapters. Teachers grade children A, B, C, D, and F and send home report cards about four times a year. Schools give children tests to measure their achievement, and the public judges the quality of a school by the scores of its students. Educators sometimes have as hard a time explaining and justifying the formal regularities as the informal ones. Most people assume that they rest on rational pedagogical principles. Typically, they do not. Sarason suggested that a visitor from Mars might ask, "Why do you do it this way?" He also suggested that few people at school would ask. If they did, fewer still would be able to answer. And those who propose changes risk an uproar of protest. Regularities exert their power precisely because we cannot imagine schools without them.

School cultures work. Most schools are not anarchic, crazy, disorganized blackboard jungles. Neither are they cold and dehumanized brave-new-world factories. Some schools are worse than others. Some are even dangerous. However, most schools have quiet halls, busy students, and teachers who feel in charge. Adults supervise children in safe places. Children learn to read; they graduate; they go on to college or work. While Americans worry about declining school quality, national polls consistently find that most parents are satisfied with their own children's schools.

Do we paint a rosy picture? Hardly. Rather, we offer a lukewarm acknowledgment that many schools try hard and that many schools may be as good as they ever were. Children's successes—learning to read, graduating, finding employment—assure us that something happens at school. On the other hand, many children don't learn to read, don't graduate, and don't get jobs. And among those who do, there are countless who *can* read and don't bother to. Many graduates feel only partly educated. Too many adults who have jobs hate their work. These lost opportunities point to the large gap between a school culture that simply works and one that promotes high-quality learning.

A cultural perspective pushes us to look beyond schools' most obvious features. We need to ask how principals, teachers, and students think about their work. How do they relate to one another? What is important to them, and how do they determine that? The answers to these questions reveal as much about a school as its test scores, science equipment, or buildings. To examine a school's quality we have to look at its entire culture.

In this chapter, we explore two dimensions of the school culture. First, the social context of American schools, which includes the history, traditions, assumptions, beliefs, and conflicts already described. These shape all schools. Schools rarely stray far from the boundaries set by these American educational traditions. Second is the immediate culture of any school in particular. Despite the sameness of schools, their immediate institutional environments differ from school to school and community to community. This immediate culture includes the *opportunities* to learn that schools provide, their *expectations* for how well children will learn, and the *professional conditions for teaching*. These characteristics provide a framework for both criticizing and reconstructing schools.

THE HEART OF THE SCHOOL CULTURE: OPPORTUNITIES, EXPECTATIONS, AND TEACHER PROFESSIONALISM

What do parents and policymakers find when they look critically at schools? They may gain few insights if they do not penetrate the familiar, hardly noticeable regularities. Most observers simply rely on their own school experiences as a standard for judging excellent, mediocre, or truly awful schools. Classes that match their preconceptions usually satisfy parents and policymakers, and many educators. If classes and preconceptions don't match, they often resort to limited options for improvement. For example, policymakers can try to raise standards for teachers and curriculum, and parents can try to switch their children to better classes and schools. At best, these reactions are narrow and limited and accomplish little. They consider only the point of delivery of knowledge (the teacher and child in class) and ignore the larger school culture. As Sarason pointed out, much more matters than just the teacher and the child. The remainder of this chapter places the teacher and child within the school's cultural context.

Opportunities to learn are what children have access to at school. Do they have well-qualified teachers? Do they attend classes in which the teachers believe children can learn high-quality knowledge? High expectations for learning encompass the extent to which a school encourages, cajoles, and sets the tone for serious, energetic learning. The professional environment of the school refers to the adults who work there. Do the teachers and administrators have the support, resources, and processes to help children learn? Schools that provide ample opportunities, press for rigorous learning, and enable teachers to act professionally won't allow social expectations to overwhelm the central, academic mission. In such schools enthusiasm for organized sports, popularity contests, and the display of expensive or distracting clothes or toys doesn't deflect attention away from learning. And such schools are not bogged down in bureaucratic routines.

Opportunities to Learn

If a school has no French class, no one will learn French at school. No music? No computers? Then no one learns about music or computers at school. These are obvious examples of lack of opportunity. Most are more subtle. For example, all third graders receive reading instruction. Even so, the quantity and quality of that instruction vary. Likewise, every high school offers mathematics, but not all schools offer the full range of advanced math classes. And not all students have a chance to take those classes. When looking at opportunities, we need to pay attention to the most outstanding classes schools offer. Whether math, art, or physical education, we want to know whether rigorous classes are available, how many the school offers, and which students have access to them.

Opportunities and Teacher Quality All teachers should have full state certification. Elementary school teachers should have a college degree either in education or in one of the subjects they teach. They should hold a state-issued generalist certificate that covers all elementary school subjects. Secondary teachers should have a college degree with a major in the principal subject they teach. These are minimums. Many teachers hold advanced degrees and specialist credentials.

From time to time schools must hire teachers with emergency credentials or employ substitutes on a long-term basis, particularly in areas like science and mathematics, where teachers can find better paying jobs in the private sector. For example, estimates from 1984 show that as many as 30 percent of secondary science and math teachers were not fully qualified. Some districts with severe shortages regularly hire unqualified teachers. Minority and poor students suffer the most from poorly qualified teachers because their schools have a difficult time attracting qualified and experienced teachers. The proportion of unfilled teaching vacancies is about three times larger in central cities than in other areas.

Credentials don't guarantee that teachers have had good training or teach well. However, other factors being equal, teachers with degrees and credentials stand a better chance of exhibiting those other characteristics that do matter. Is the teacher an intellectually curious person? someone who loves to learn and gets excited about ideas and experiences? Does the teacher really know the subject? Can the teacher communicate intellectual curiosity and subject knowledge to the children? The importance of teacher quality can't be overestimated. All the beautiful school buildings and newly purchased texts and materials can't replace a teacher who makes learning come alive.

Opportunities and Resources First, there should be enough teachers. Too few teachers means classes will be large and difficult to manage. Some research shows that fifteen students or fewer is optimal at the elementary level. Unfortunately, classes that small are nearly unheard of in any but the wealthiest private schools. Secondary school classes should probably not exceed twenty-five students, although most do. Smaller classes do not cause more learning, but they may strongly affect how teachers design and carry out lessons. Further, class size not only affects the time teachers have available to spend with individual children, but also influences teachers' flexibility in experimenting with teaching strategies. If teachers are responsible for unmanageably large classes, their morale will suffer, and eventually low morale translates into lost opportunities for children.

Materials, equipment, and facilities also matter. If children are to become readers, they need classrooms and libraries full of books. Science requires equipment and laboratory space. Physical development requires things to climb on, toys and sports equipment, and open space in which to play. A good way to judge the quality of school resources is to ask the teachers about them. They will have a clear, practical sense of what they have and what they lack to do a good job. Few teachers long for luxuries. Books, audio visual equipment in good working order, hands-on materials, a decent copy machine, access to a telephone, and fewer students per class are typical needs.

Opportunities and Time Spent on Learning In some elementary schools considerable time gets used up with recesses, lunch, unstructured playground activities, and special events. For example, one national study found that elementary schools scheduled from eighteen to twenty-seven hours per week for instruction. This range reflects an important difference in learning opportunities. Additionally, the study found that most classrooms spent only about 70 percent of the scheduled time on learning activities. The rest went toward getting ready and cleaning up, discipline, and socializing. This means that in some schools children spend as few as three hours a day actually learning.

Some junior and senior high schools excuse children from class for all kinds of reasons. Their sports team may need to get ready for a game or the gym may need decorating for a dance. The whole school may get to watch cartoons as a reward for having met their candy-sale goal. There is no end to the ways in which schools can spend time on routines. Taking the roll, tardy checks, lining up properly, and practicing good behavior are just a few. Children can lose as much learning time in the pursuit of quiet and orderliness as they lose because of noise and disorder.

It's a mistake to think that schools can easily limit these time-consuming activities. Each has its roots in school traditions and societal expectations. Americans see social activities and athletics as ways for common schools to help children prepare for community participation. Schools view athletics as a vehicle for teaching fairness, competition, and cooperation. We sometimes justify sports as opportunities for poor, minority, and academically unsuccessful children to find their niches in school (even though the only reliable payoffs for schooling come from academic achievement). Bureaucratic routines and record keeping are often a response to legal requirements schools can do little to change.

In spite of the cultural obstacles, a few schools engage children in learning nearly all the time. Learning doesn't need to be entirely quiet and serious, and it doesn't even need to be orderly. As we describe in chapters 2 and 3, what counts most is the time children spend making sense of ideas and experiences. The loudspeaker should not interrupt, and messengers should not be running in and out of the class. Extracurricular activities should not be so intrusive that students spend their class time just waiting for the next special event.

Opportunities and a Rich, Balanced Curriculum Most schools teach the same subjects. They differ, however, in whether children learn the most important knowledge in those subjects. (We describe this important knowledge more fully in chapters 4 and 5.) Whatever the subject, important knowledge is challenging, complex, related to real life, and rich in meaning. But again, the culture of schools interferes. Complex lessons don't fit nearly as well with the traditions of efficiency as do simpler, standardized, easy-to-manage assignments. Simpler lessons help teachers meet accountability requirements such as monitoring, checking, recording, and grading. The practice of using standardized test scores to judge student and school quality pushes many teachers to teach to the tests. Testing practices further reduce the richness and complexity of knowledge—often to simple true-false facts (more about this in chapter 6). Signs of a trivial curriculum are children spending lots of time memorizing, filling in blanks in workbooks, doing the same arithmetic problems over and over, and spending little time reading books, writing compositions, and solving complex problems.

A former French minister of education supposedly boasted about the efficiency of the French educational system. He claimed that on any given day, at any given hour, he could tell what topic French children were studying. He knew what book they were reading and what page they were on. To many Americans that sounds pretty good. However, a rich and balanced curriculum runs counter to rigid standardization. It weaves together large units of knowledge rather than string along bits and pieces of facts; it mixes abstractions with concrete experiences and children's informal knowledge of the world. The teacher offers a variety of ways for students to learn complex ideas. Teachers who respond to the richness of their own experience and knowledge as well as to the diversity of their students will not all be on the same page at the same time. When the teacher breaks down complex ideas into simple, easily managed tasks, children get a false notion of learning. They think that knowledge must come in easily digestible chunks that fit into logical sequences of small ideas. They may come to distrust their abilities if they don't get the simple answers quickly.

Parents and policymakers should not confuse long lists of "behavioral objectives" or scientific-sounding "diagnosis and prescription" methods with a rich curriculum. Ask what books children read and what math concepts they will learn. Ask them what scientific principles they understand and apply. Ask children about the big ideas behind their lessons.

Opportunities and Access to "The Best" Earlier, we stated the obvious: If the school does not teach a subject, no one learns it at school. When some children take a subject and others do not, the limits on opportunity are just as obvious. All children may study the same subjects, but those children the school identifies as having more ability receive superior knowledge and instruction. Children the school thinks are less bright get less. Typically, schools that group by ability do not provide equal opportunities to all children (as we will discuss in chapter 7). These limits on opportunities seem to make considerable common sense—appealing to people's sense of efficiency. However, equally good sense tells us what will happen when a group of able readers reads stories and a low group does only worksheets. The latter will have fewer opportunities to read stories. Likewise, if the advanced history class requires a research paper and the regular one doesn't, some children won't get to practice research skills. Schools use elaborate rationales—based on outmoded notions of ability—to explain why some children should have access to better knowledge.

Considerable research substantiates the educational losses that occur when all children don't have high-quality opportunities. For example, the Carnegie Foundation found that schools, assuming that most teenagers will not benefit from the most challenging classes, provide a wide array of high school classes based on their low estimation students' abilities. They also found that most students were enrolled in mediocre and easy classes. Our own earlier research confirms these conclusions.

Opportunities and Extra Help Good schools don't let students fall behind. They provide extra help, and they keep parents informed if children need more support outside of school. Ideally, extra help comes within the classroom during regular class time. A special resource teacher, a paid aide, or a parent volunteer may provide an extra boost. Or a peer tutor, either in the same class or from a higher grade, may provide one-on-one assistance. On the other hand, programs that pull children out of the regular classroom to offer extra help may actually limit their learning. Extra help should supplement classroom lessons and should not substitute a remedial program for the regular one. Programs that tutor children in the regular curriculum are much better. (More about programs for children needing special help appears in chapter 8.)

Helping children keep up with the regular curriculum, despite its undisputed benefits, conflicts with standardization and efficiency. It may disrupt schools' orderly progression through the curriculum. It may cost more. On the other hand, *not* helping children keep up is also costly and inefficient. The consequence is that children must repeat grades and schools must provide additional easy classes.

Opportunities and Parent Involvement Many effective schools involve parents in instruction. Children learn more when parents help them with their lessons. When parents volunteer in the classroom, they lower the ratio of children to adults. Some schools develop helping strategies for working parents to use at home. Many are similar to the suggestions in chapters 9 and 10 for developing supportive home environments and helping with homework. Joyce Epstein's research suggests that parents and teachers should share some instructional responsibilities. When they do, homes become more schoollike, and schools become more familylike. This home–school linkage helps children develop academically, socially, and personally in two complementary environments. When schools integrate parents into the work of the school, parents gain confidence and competence. That translates into children's success—even among the most disadvantaged families.

Expectations for Learning

All schools say that learning tops their list of priorities. However, schools differ in how much they stress students' accomplishments. A few schools nurture and loudly applaud learning as special and central. They spend most of their time and energy on learning activities. And learning, rather than a multitude of other activities, provides children with their most important success and rewards. Most schools have lower expectations. Many focus their attention on "keeping the lid on." Rewards from social life, sports, or neighborhood gangs can overwhelm learning. School pride may focus on quiet halls, high attendance at sports events, or a well-decorated campus.

Consider the following description of a fairly well-off suburban high school. This school is *not* "at risk," yet its expectations for learning seem quite low.

The bell has rung and the last few eleventh graders are sauntering into their second-period class. Several present absence slips to the teacher, confessing truancy or documenting their real or invented illness or family emergency. Three others present passes, respectively, from the school nurse, the counseling office, and the student government advisor. Another has forgotten her pass, and the teacher sends her to the office. There are seven students absent. A couple might arrive late. Others will receive summonses from various corners of the school. Only two-thirds of the students actually attend the entire class two days in a row.

Over the public address a student recites the Pledge of Allegiance—without error today, though that is not always the case. Another student reads announcements. The senior class advertises, as it will each day for two weeks, its fund-raising computer-dating dance. Two students perform a hastily written skit. They are too close to the microphone, and their garbled speech is nearly unintelligible. However, a few adolescent sexual innuendoes manage to get through, and the class receives them with exaggerated, uproarious appreciation. A single academic announcement arouses no apparent interest: the scholarship society will offer tutoring at noon. An announcer praises a winning sports team and commends the losers for a great effort. The vice principal issues a warning about lunch passes. He adds that makeup testing will take place in the library and therefore the library will be closed for the next two days. Announcements over, instruction begins.

The students at this school score well on standardized tests. They gain admittance in good numbers to top-rated colleges. Some, particularly those in the highest college-preparatory tracks, undauntedly pursue outstanding education. The youngsters held in highest esteem by their peers are better-than-average students. They are also as notable for their good looks, cars, and general sociability as for their academic achievements. We also find some disdain for many of the top students, especially those with less social appeal. Even the adults at school exercise caution about spotlighting their achievements. All students, particularly the large group that simply gets by, would achieve more if their school made its real business seem more important.

Elementary students, too, benefit when their school expects them to achieve. When high expectations are present, students' satisfaction is *part of,* not a *break from,* learning. The most satisfied students, parents, and teachers report that their schools have a highly academic atmosphere.

Schools can't fake high expectations—not for long. In response to pressure for higher test scores, some schools try to motivate students through hoopla, pep talks, and prizes. Often, teachers and students perceive these campaigns as attempts to manipulate them rather than as support for genuine learning. Initial bursts of enthusiasm can quickly erode to schoolwide cynicism. Recently, seniors at a high-achieving California high school intentionally lowered their scores on state achievement tests. The student body president told reporters that students were angry that school officials emphasize publically reported test scores over learning. Parents and policymakers can look for more authentic signs of high expectations at a school. They can start by asking these questions:

Is Learning the Top Priority? Is learning recognized and rewarded? Or do sports, clubs, and social events always get the attention? Which students get recognition at school assemblies and over the loudspeaker? athletes? contest winners? academic achievers? Academic contests can be misleading. Some city- or nationwide academic competitions do much to generate attention for schools and enhance civic pride. However, these contests rarely involve more than a very few children, and they often require significant time and other school resources. Just as sports often place too much emphasis on winning instead of on playing, academic contests such as the nationwide Academic Decathlon may emphasize winning over learning.

Does the principal spend her time on paperwork, meetings, and building maintenance, or does she fit a bit of time for teaching? Does she visit classrooms frequently because she loves to watch learning, or are her visits limited to the teacher supervision requirements? Listen to the principal talk about what makes him proud—is it the clean campus? high attendance at the baseball game? the achievement of a prizewinner? Or does the principal describe in detail the rich learning experiences going on in classrooms?

What is discipline like? Educators who are serious about learning control misbehavior and promote a calm and orderly atmosphere. Some of the most amazing examples of such schools can be found in the most unlikely urban neighborhoods. When determination is in place, neighborhood crime and violence can be kept outside the schoolyard and classrooms. Accounts of principals and faculties who have worked together with parents, community organizations, and the police to keep schools free of assault, weapons, and drugs have become increasingly commonplace in big cities. Heroic principals like New Jersey's Joe Clark, who keeps order and discipline by expelling many students and threatening others with a baseball bat, may make good press, but the sustained and thoughtful involvement of parents and the community is just as likely to make schools safe. At the same time, such schools stand a better chance of bringing about a rich academic climate as well as a safe one. For example, a principal in San Diego convinced the school parents to lobby the board of education for a new fence to prevent drug peddlers on the street from entering the school grounds. She persuaded the local police to "adopt" the school and thus provided a deterring presence that was not lost on potential troublemakers. Concurrently, the faculty revamped the instructional program to provide richer learning opportunities. The combined efforts had a powerful effect on the academic climate of the school.

Do High Expectations Extend to All Children? When schools assign children to demanding classes and expect them to perform well, children get the message: "We believe you can do it." They learn how smart the school thinks they can be.

Most school cultures foster the belief that only some children can learn a great deal. They also promote the assumption that most will be average and some will not learn much at all. Educators and the public find these expectations reasonable, given their understanding of children's differences in intelligence. Sometimes a caring faculty intentionally maintains low expectations, thinking they are being kind. We discuss these beliefs further in chapters 2, 6, and 7; in chapter 3 we discuss how teachers act on them in classrooms.

If a school staff believes that all students *can* learn challenging subject matter, then they will work very hard to provide conditions that will enable them to. These efforts pay off. However, some schools simply apply more pressure for high grades or better test scores. Classes may pile on more homework and more minutes per day of the same low-level curriculum. This distorts the notion of high expectations.

The following are some questions that can reveal a school's expectations: Are all children—girls as well as boys, minorities as well as whites, poor children as well as more affluent ones—expected to study rigorous subjects like algebra, a foreign language, and advanced science? What percentage of students does the school expect to go to college? (A good question for elementary schools as well as high schools.) Does the school keep records of how many complete college (or even high school)? Do classwork and homework include long-term projects, papers, and research activities? Can children get by without trying very hard?

Is Student Progress Regularly Reported to Parents? Schools should keep parents informed about what's being learned and how well. Report cards should communicate what children have learned. Lists of check marks or letter grades tell little. Schools with high expectations use back-to-school night and open house to tell parents about the curriculum and students' progress. Regularly scheduled parent conferences and written reports keep parents informed of good progress. And when a child has difficulties, the school acts immediately. A teacher or a counselor calls, and strategies to treat potential problems begin soon after.

Professional Environment

How do we get schools to provide ample opportunities and hold high expectations? To develop cultures that enhance children's learning and don't limit it, parents, policymakers, and the public must support professional teaching conditions. Only then can educators themselves work to change the day-to-day regularities in schools. Absent professional teaching conditions, other reforms will have limited effects. Raising teachers' salaries to attract more highly qualified people would help schools, as would making major changes in the training of teachers and school administrators. So might other reforms such as lowering class sizes, upgrading textbooks, stocking libraries and laboratories, and buying computers. However, professionalism in schools means much more.

First, the community must value and trust teachers who act according to their considered professional judgments. They must perceive teachers as having skills and knowledge that are neither widely held nor easily gained. When looking for professional teaching environments, we might ask, Do teachers work with and learn from their colleagues? Do they have a chance to think and plan? Do they influence schoolwide decisions? Do they help train new teachers? Are teachers *trusted* to work, think, plan, and influence?

Parents and other members of the community should not underestimate the power of their role in supporting a professional teaching environment. Schools often act timidly, anticipating community criticism if they give teachers time outside the classrooms for professional, but nonteaching activities. Many teachers have trouble looking beyond their own classroom walls. They are accustomed to pinching every penny and every moment. They need considerable encouragement from outside schools if they are to grow and participate fully as professionals.

Professional teaching carries with it the burdens of its history. The earliest schools rarely demanded that teachers have more than basic literacy skills. Often a high school education alone fulfilled preparation requirements. Later, many teachers attended normal schools or teaching colleges, which lacked the rigor and prestige of other colleges and universities.

Teaching also suffers from the low status society gives to its clients—children. Historically, society has not valued children highly. Neither has it valued those who spend their lives with them. Servants, not professionals, cared for the children of the middle and upper classes. And for most of this century teaching has been women's work and, in segregated schools, minorities' work. Community leaders saw women as being dependent on their husbands or other male authorities for leadership—not suited for making important decisions. The feminization of teaching fit nicely with scientific management theories. Women and minority teachers provided schools with a class of low-status employees—those who occupied the bottom positions on the organizational chart. They carried out the decisions made by those at the top—male administrators. Finally, society did not consider women the proper source of a family's income. Married women were often deemed unfit for teaching. While doctors, lawyers, and other professionals have made significant strides in this century, teachers' status, authority, and pay have remained very modest.

The low esteem of teaching prompts schools to apply efficient, technological procedures that further deprofessionalize teachers. An example is the steady trend toward regulated, "teacher proof" lessons. Some lessons are even scripted. In theory, anyone who can read can teach them. Should we wonder why fewer highly able people now choose teaching as a career?

What's Wrong with This Picture?

Most people have seen the puzzles in children's activity books called "What's wrong with this picture?" The pictures seem okay at first glance, but on close examination we discover something is wrong. Perhaps the farmer is wearing two different socks, the bull has udders, the apple tree has a pineapple growing on it, and so on. Similarly, schools at a glance seem like pretty smoothly functioning places, with nothing much wrong. Yet keep in mind all those regularities—the habits, the ways of doing things, and the blinders that protect the school from chaos. They also insulate it from change and innovation. The following anecdote portrays real events. We include it here as a cross section of what can go wrong with the professional environment within a school culture. You might look for evidence that the teachers in the story lack contact with one another, have little autonomy, are stuck in the bureaucracy, and have too little influence over school decisions. They have no important role in orienting new teachers to the profession or to the workplace. Once hired, they are left to sink or swim without the time to think, plan, and collaborate. Here is the story:

A parent asked why her fourth grader could not use a calculator at school. The teacher, new to the school, did not realize that several of his colleagues allowed children to use calculators. He explained to the mother that the curriculum did not introduce calculators until the sixth grade. The parent, an engineer, felt that the use of a calculator could enhance mathematics learning. The teacher agreed that calculators could be put to good use in earlier grades but felt his hands were tied. The parent inquired further. Sure enough, phone calls to the principal and the school district's director of curriculum (who checked on the matter with the district's mathematics specialist) confirmed the policy. Children were not to use calculators until the sixth grade.

No one the parent spoke to thought the policy was a good one. The director of curriculum did not express an opinion but suggested there were probably arguments for both sides. The parent, more persistent than most, contacted the assistant superintendent for instruction. He personally saw no problem with using calculators in earlier grades. He repeated what the principal and the director of curriculum had advised as the next step: the parent should contact the parent representative of the school district's Curriculum Advisory Committee, which reviewed the math curriculum on a three-year cycle. The representative on the committee could bring up the matter of using calculators at that time.

This story does not end well, although it is not a disaster either—just like most of what happens in schools today. Predictably, the parent was discouraged from following through. At an Administrative Cabinet meeting, district administrators and principals discussed the importance of being consistent in following the mathematics curriculum. Someone said he had heard about a fuss regarding the use of calculators in the earlier grades. A principal in attendance—not the one at the school in question—took this to be a serious problem. Upon returning to his school he wrote a memo to his teachers about complaints over not adhering strictly to the math curriculum. Specifically, some teachers were inappropriately allowing children to use calculators. In fact, some of the teachers at this second school had been allowing children to use calculators for some time. In their individual ways they disregarded the memo. One "lost" it. One read it to her class so she could claim that she told the children not to bring calculators. However, she did nothing further to discourage children from bringing them and continued to answer children's questions about how to use them. One teacher who had forbidden children to use calculators felt vindicated. The teachers did not discuss this issue with one another, and the principal never mentioned another word. Two years later, when the district committee revised the math curriculum, they did not change the calculator section. No one present had the time, concern, or perhaps knowledge of mathematics instruction to raise the question, "What's wrong with this picture?"

Are Teachers Autonomous? The use of calculators is not the most important issue in this story (although most mathematics educators and mathematicians approve of their use, and some school districts issue calculators along with textbooks to every child). A major concern is whether schools allow teachers to make professional decisions about their classroom teaching. Over the long run, most teachers' decisions will be at least as competent as decisions made by others. Teachers who make decisions will definitely feel more competent, valued, respected, and professional. That counts for quite a lot.

Teachers need flexibility to adapt the curriculum to their own classes. They need to try ideas and methods that extend beyond the formal policy for the entire school. Such autonomy empowers teachers to enliven instruction and make teaching less like working in a factory where someone else prescribes each step. For teachers to be effective they must also make use of expert knowledge and, at the same time, adapt that knowledge to make it appropriate for their own classrooms. Without autonomy, some teachers learn to distrust their own inclinations and knowledge. If teachers are not supported in their efforts to try out new methods, they may decide that learning new methods is a waste of time.

Of course, schools must place some limits on independent actions. They need to coordinate curriculum among teachers and grades. They need to control inappropriate classroom practices. In this sense, operating a school is certainly a team effort. That is precisely the point of professionalism.

Do Teachers Have Time to Prepare, Think, and Work Together? No profession is immune from the charge by outsiders that its members enjoy excessive idle time. In fact, the time a surgeon spends operating, a musician spends performing, or a lawyer spends in court represents only a fraction of their work. These are times when they are performing the tasks that the rest of us erroneously assume comprise their entire professions. Similarly, teachers' primary visible task is teaching children in the classroom. This typically occupies five to seven hours a day, five days a week, but teachers must also spend time grading, completing administrative paperwork, supervising, tutoring, preparing for classes and parent conferences, cleaning, and telephoning parents. These activities must take place when teachers are not teaching.

If attending to children and simply keeping up with lessons consume all of a teacher's time, little time or energy remains for professional activities. A professional school environment requires that teachers have time for creative, energizing lesson preparation. They need time to read, to work with colleagues, and to participate in decision making. Unfortunately, even school districts that value professional work can provide little time for it.

Time itself, however, like other school resources, is necessary but not sufficient. The school culture must also allow teachers to use the time well. Most school cultures resist teachers' influence on school policy. The dismal financial condition of schools and the intransigence of the school culture keep most schools from providing teachers with the time to be professionals.

Do Teachers Influence Policy and Curriculum? Establishing school goals, selecting new programs, setting staff development priorities, and devising processes for teacher evaluation require teachers' long-range participation. Of course, teachers won't always make the best decisions. Nonetheless, when they participate in policy and curriculum decisions, their teaching becomes more closely aligned with school goals and with widely accepted views of good practice. We know from studies such as Sarason's that teachers may easily ignore or subvert policies about which they have had no say.

When they don't help to decide policy, some teachers follow regulations to the letter. Others give the appearance of doing what administrators tell them but behind the scenes do what they like. The best of these teachers will see their work go unnoticed, even by their colleagues, and the worst will go unchecked. Neither situation provides a strong foundation for professional teaching.

If the teachers in our calculator story had been empowered to make decisions, they might have informed themselves further by consulting research, exemplary practices, and reports of mathematicians. They might even have arrived at a schoolwide agreement, and even if some had disagreed and gone against the common practice, the divergence would not have exceeded what exists now. Teachers need an environment that encourages critical scrutiny of accepted practices. In such an environment they would learn more about their colleagues, gather more information, discuss their views more, and challenge current practice.

Are Teachers Buffered from Nonteaching Tasks? Schools should keep to a minimum paperwork and bureaucratic requirements that do not require teachers' special skills. Nonteaching personnel should supervise playgrounds, lunchrooms, and bus lines, keep records for the candy drive, and so forth. Schools should see student behavior problems as problems requiring the attention not just of teachers but of child, parent, and school. A widely held impression is that the teacher is a jack-of-all-trades—part educator, part janitor, part babysitter, part secretary. A more dignified and more productive conception would include professional components of teaching—part educator, part executive, part psychologist, and so on.

Are Working Conditions and Salaries at Professional Levels? School professionals need easy access to work space, offices, a lounge, phones, and secretarial services. Additionally, classrooms should be suited to the work the teachers try to accomplish. Children themselves should have suitable workspaces: clean, well-lighted, well-heated or air-conditioned classrooms with plenty of room for productive activity are minimums. Teachers need professional-level salaries; in their absence low staff morale can undermine commitment. Moreover, lacking adequate salaries, many teachers moonlight and thereby sap the energy they need for teaching. Average salaries for experienced teachers in 1988 barely topped $30,000, including summer work.

Given the new career options available, teaching attracts fewer candidates from its traditional pool. Smart women and blacks go elsewhere—into business, medicine, and law. Many experienced teachers leave to take higher paying jobs. Put bluntly, teachers feel poor, and poor people find it hard to feel professional. People resentful about being poor find it hard to act professionally. And everyone else finds it hard to take poor people seriously as professionals.

Who's in Charge of the Profession? All professions need specialists who have management training and talent. School administrators must be responsible for the daily running of schools, just as hospital administrators are responsible for their facilities. Moreover, professions must also be responsible to their clients. In education, these "clients" are children and the public.

Nevertheless, in any professional workplace the most potent force for high levels of performance is a close association and identification with one's peers. Isolated teachers who do not share responsibilities for school-wide and professionwide decisions will be less responsive to standards for best practice. Administrators, policymakers, teachers, and the public all agree that something is quite wrong with teacher training, entry standards, and procedures for monitoring teacher competence. Even so, widespread reluctance to give teachers themselves a greater professional role stands in the way of developing a high-quality profession.

The increasing involvement of professional teachers' organizations in shaping the direction of educational policy represents a very modest step in the right direction. Teacher unions are increasingly advocating changes in school structures and teaching practices. Additionally, teachers have a role in the new National Teachers Certification Board, which is working to develop standards by which teachers can be "board certified."

At schools that enjoy professional working conditions, teachers have energy and enthusiasm. They have permission to teach well, and they are eager to develop their skills. Effective in their work, they believe that their efforts result in their students' learning more. And working hard makes sense to these teachers because they know that their efforts will not be undermined. Administrators and policymakers welcome the problems these teachers identify as opportunities to improve the school—not as the complaints of malcontents. Such schools (to the degree that external conditions permit) attract high-quality teachers and encourage them to remain.

Nonetheless, a professional environment, like opportunity to learn and expectations for learning, requires more than cheerleading and saying, "We can do it!" Parents, policymakers, and teachers should not underestimate the degree to which professional teaching conditions fly in the face of tradition. All should appreciate the essential role of community-wide support in establishing their legitimacy.

Necessary But Not Sufficient

Are the best teachers those with the highest salaries? Not necessarily. Will a school that has lots of laboratory science equipment have students who learn science better? Maybe, maybe not. Will a faculty that tries to keep its expectations high for all children have the smartest students? There are no guarantees. In this and the chapters that follow we identify conditions in the home, school, and classroom that research shows are necessary for a high-quality education. However, any one of these conditions, especially one standing alone, does not *create* high-quality education.

Take, for example, the conflicting claims about lower class size. Some research suggests that smaller classes do not result in more learning, especially if nothing else in the classroom changes. Should we therefore stop worrying about large classes? Absolutely not! Smaller class sizes may be *necessary* for improved education, even though they may not be sufficient to overcome all the rest of what ails schools.

We find another example of the necessary-but-not-sufficient principle in recent responses to children's poor mathematics performance on standardized tests. Research as well as common sense shows that the children who spend the most time studying math learn more math. In response, many schools have increased the time spent on math or have required additional math courses for high school graduation. But these steps may not produce significant results if the culture of schools stays the same—if teaching methods don't change or if new classes are no more challenging. And if math teachers do not receive better training, they will not use the added time to advantage. If children (particularly girls) continue to associate high math performance and academic achievement with being unpopular, the time the school adds to math classes will accomplish little. Furthermore, an increase in math time may take time away from other subjects. Increased teaching time may upset teachers and trigger a salary dispute. Under circumstances like these, the move to improve math education could actually lower overall achievement. Clearly, spending more time on math may be a necessary ingredient for improving math learning, but it is not sufficient in itself.

We're convinced that each of the school conditions we have discussed is most powerful in combination with the others. When the school extends important knowledge to all students (opportunity) and focuses its resources and energy on high-quality learning (expectations), more students learn better. However, schools cannot sustain lasting opportunities and high expectations unless policymakers, strong administrators, the community, and teachers support a professional environment. Together these new regularities can create a school culture that fosters all children's learning.

Parents need to make the best of schools today for their own children. Policymakers want to make schools better for all children, now and in the future. To understand the obstacles and appreciate the possibilities, they must look critically at common school practices and schooling traditions. They need to consider how the school culture limits or enhances children's learning. Only then can they decide how to react to current school conditions and shape improvements for the future. The remaining chapters tackle these difficult issues.

FOR FURTHER READING

Raymond Callahan, *Education and the Cult of Efficiency.* Chicago: University of Chicago Press, 1962.

Lawrence A. Cremin, *The Traditions of American Education.* New York: Basic Books, 1977.

Michael Cole, *Educating for Equality.* New York: Routledge, 1989.

Linda Darling-Hammond, *Beyond the Commission Reports: The Coming Crisis in Teaching.* Santa Monica, CA: The RAND Corporation, 1985.

John I. Goodlad, *A Place Called School.* New York: McGraw Hill, 1984.

David Labaree, *The Making of an American High School: The Credentials Market and the Central High School of Philadelphia, 1838–1939.* New Haven: Yale University Press, 1988.

Jeannie Oakes, *Improving Inner-City Schools: Current Trends in Urban District Reforms.* Santa Monica, CA: The RAND Corporation, 1987.

Arthur Powell, Eleanor Farrar, and David Cohen, *The Shopping Mall High School: Winners and Losers in the Educational Marketplace.* Boston: Houghton Mifflin, 1985.

Seymour Sarason, *The Culture of the School and the Problem of Change.* Boston: Allyn Bacon, 1971.

Theodore Sizer, *Horace's Compromise.* Boston: Houghton Mifflin, 1984.

David B. Tyack, *The One Best System: A History of American Urban Education.* Cambridge: Harvard University Press, 1974.

Arthur E. Wise, *Legislated Learning: The Bureaucratization of the American Classroom.* Berkeley: University of California Press, 1979.

CHAPTER TWO

Learning: The Business of Schools

Imagine a sculptor working a rough block of stone. She marks the stone with a grease pencil, makes notations on a pad, stands back and envisions what the stone will become. Imagine a waiter wending his way through tables during the lunch-hour crush. He keeps track not only of orders, but of items the kitchen is out of, the preferences of a generous tipper, and much, much more. Imagine, too, how this waiter manages to be efficient without seeming hurried, and friendly but not ingratiating. Consider the last time a child made you feel guilty because you didn't buy him that candy on the store shelf. Picture the last time you marveled at a craftsperson, scholar, physician, clerk, store owner, full- or part-time homemaker, business executive, or *anyone* who was doing a complicated job exceptionally well. How did they *learn* to do that? And how did they learn to learn?

In this chapter we discuss learning. As we do, keep in mind that learning is among the most complicated processes imaginable, and we still don't know much about it. However, we have increased our knowledge dramatically over the past few decades. This new knowledge generates tremendous optimism about the ability of all children to learn. Unfortunately, most schools have not woven this knowledge into the fabric of the school culture. To do so would require them to change much more than their perceptions of how children learn. Other regularities such as how teachers teach, test, grade, and organize classes would have to change since they match older ideas about learning. The way schools are organized into grades and subjects would also need to be changed. Schools would have to take a new look at knowledge itself and, perhaps, at what constitutes an education.

TRAINING AND SENSE MAKING

One important type of learning, *training,* enables us to respond appropriately to events and needs. Some behavioral responses are physical, such as when children are toilet-trained or when we react somewhat automatically to the shout, "Watch out!" or when a surfer negotiates a wave. This physical response can be internal. Stomach rumbles at the smell of a favorite dinner cooking and heart-rate increases before an important meeting are two familiar examples. At other time we express our trained behavior in language or with social conventions: we memorize a phone number or say, "Yes, please."

We use the term *sense making* to refer to a second type of learning. Sense making is the mental process by which we construct individualized meanings and responses to our experiences. We figure out causes and effects, we apply knowledge gained from one experience to a different one, and we solve complex problems. Whenever we identify a problem, think about it, and solve it, we make sense of our experiences. We learn.

Humans take quite naturally to both training and sense making. Often there seems to be no clear-cut distinction between the two. People almost automatically respond appropriately in situations that reward some responses and punish others—training. Also, they can't help making sense of their environment—trying to understand Why? and Under what conditions? and What if?—sense making.

Training—and Its Limits

Psychologists have studied training ever since Pavlov taught his dogs to salivate at the sound of a bell. Pavlov's turn-of-the-century studies led to the development of behaviorism, a branch of psychology that focuses on how humans and animals change their behavior in response to pleasure or pain. We are all familiar with the fundamental principles of behaviorism. Pleasurable consequences strengthen behaviors, and undesirable consequences weaken or extinguish them. The effects of rewards will last longer than the effects of punishments.

The behavioral approach to learning is appealing because it often works easily, conforms to common sense, and uses time-tested methods. Most parents and teachers apply behavioral theory intuitively. They train children by rewarding desirable behaviors and by punishing or ignoring unwanted ones. Of course, the ever-present challenge is to be sure that children think of the rewards as pleasurable and the punishments as something to avoid. The child who continues to behave in ways he knows will bring punishment reminds us of how behavioral training can miss the mark. The child probably continues to act badly because he wants the reward of attention (even if it's negative) more than he fears punishment.

Behaviorism (known also as behavior modification, stimulus-response learning, and reinforcement theory) pays most attention to events *before* learning (stimuli, input, causes) and actions *after* learning (responses, output, effects). Behavioral psychologists pay somewhat less attention to what goes on at the moment of learning. Many of them think it is too unscientific to try to account for hidden processes, since they cannot observe or measure the actual learning as it takes place in the brain or mind.

Training conditions people to adopt behaviors that relate directly to their physical survival and to social conventions. This is necessary for children and adults to fit in or even be tolerable to the rest of their fellow humans. Children need to brush their teeth long before they can *reason* about the concept of prophylactic tooth care. They need to stay out of the street before they have sensible notions of how cars can damage bodies— before they understand human mortality or the physics of space, speed, and distance.

One advantage of training is that it may not require a high degree of understanding or cooperation. A baby doesn't need to understand why he should drink from a cup before he accomplishes the feat. To get him to use the cup we take advantage of his developing muscular control and coordination. We rely on his ability to focus on a task and his response to rewards. He receives pleasure from pleasing his parents, and he likes controling objects. Likewise, toilet training makes very clear sense to parents, but a child can be successful simply by doing it. He's not required to understand.

At home, we train children to hold a spoon, pick up their socks, and not to slam the door. We train them to call home if they're going to be late. "If you pull Daddy's beard, you'll have to get off my lap." "If you are gentle, you can hold the puppy." "Stay close or you might get lost" are words young children hear when they are being trained. Adults use training programs to help them stop smoking, lose weight, read faster, or think positively. "I better slow down or I'll get a ticket." "I'll buy that dress as a treat when I lose five more pounds" are thoughts adults have when they train themselves.

Schools also rely heavily on behavioral theories of learning. Memorization of spelling lists and multiplication tables emphasizes training aimed at eliciting automatic responses. These practices might be in part a response to the view that the mind is a muscle and learning is mental exercise. Memorizing is a favorite workout for the mental-exercise folks, who think if thirty practice subtraction problems are good, sixty are better. If the child is a strong student, have him do one hundred in half the time. Schools also train children in routines such as lining up before class, freezing on the playground at the sound of the whistle, and quieting down when the teacher raises one hand. Success brings rewards—praise, good grades, happy faces, extra time for play, public recognition. These rewards and punishments follow the principle that positive reinforcement establishes behavior and punishment extinguishes it.

To be sure, training works. Children do memorize lists, learn the multiplication tables, and behave on cue. At home they develop table manners and occasionally pick up their socks. Many adults quit smoking or even lose weight. Although today psychologists don't use the metaphor of the mind as a muscle, some do think of the mind as being like a computer that processes some information automatically. Computers have rapid matching abilities, systematic organizing powers, and extensive memories. Training results in the computerlike automization of some processes like adults learning to drive a car and children learning multiplication tables—knowledge that would be impossible to use unless it was automatic. Although these are important learning processes, schools overemphasize them and need to recognize that the brain is more complex than a computer, and the training process explains only a fraction of learning, in school or out. Think about the work of the sculptor, the waiter, and the physician we mentioned earlier. And think about the knowledge that enables you to make decisions.

What does it take to decide to replace a car; to serve wine with dinner; vote for the incumbent; return the overpayment; give the drooping plant less or more water; or hold your tongue when you are angry? These decisions require us to *make sense* out of a very confusing and disorganized world. No list to memorize, no training program, no simple decision-making guide (gather the facts, list the pros and cons, and so forth) prepares us to make those decisions.

There can be important differences between the results of training and of sense making. Training is often limited to particular situations. In contrast, when we make sense, we more easily generalize our knowledge and experiences. For example, the trained child keeps his distance from a stove because his parents warned him about it or pulled him away from it. Perhaps he has a vivid memory of burning himself. Another child may be cautious around stoves because he understands how and why stoves can be dangerous. The first child may have good stove habits; he may act properly around stoves. If quite young, he may have the only response for which he is ready—stay away. Nonetheless, no matter how well we have trained him, we had still better keep an eye on him. On the other hand, we can have greater confidence when the second child is around stoves in his own kitchen and probably around a fireplace or campfire as well. Caution makes sense to him.

Training and sense making work together. It is neither desirable nor possible to eradicate all behavioral elements of children's education, at home or at school. However, we know unequivocally that schools rely too heavily on behavioral approaches to learning. This major problem in the current culture of schools limits what and how well children learn.

Social Learning

Social-learning theory partly bridges the gap between training and sense making. Social-learning theorists note that children observe and copy others' behavior. As they observe, children notice and internalize the rewards and punishments that others receive for their actions. Then they monitor their own behavior and compare it to that of others in similar situations.

Children, like adults, want the rewards they see others get, and they try to avoid the punishments others receive. The effect of a reprimand an older sibling receives for playing with matches won't be lost on a young child. Knowing the consequences may not stop him from playing with matches, but he will surely know that he, too, should not do so. Similarly, children who grow up around adults who turned their own achievements in school into good jobs with high salaries see firsthand the rewards they can expect from school success. Social-learning theory helps explain the impact of adult role models and peer pressure. It also suggests a more deliberate role adults can play in shaping what children learn. Teachers and parents can structure what children observe. They can guide children's interpretations as they make sense of the consequences of others' actions. For example, simple questions can guide children's learning from their observations: "Why do you think Johnny got elected?" "What might happen to Mary if she keeps acting that way?"

Social-learning theory considers the child's own observations, judgments, and reflections. It acknowledges that sense making within the learner is just as important to learning as rewards and punishments. Contrast this view with the strict behavioral one that sees people more as objects acted upon by their environment. With its emphasis on observation and interpretation, social-learning theory helps explain why children adopt particular social behaviors, even if they have not personally experienced the consequences.

Cognitions: Making Sense of Experience

Cognitive psychologists pay most attention to what takes place within the learner. They see children as active agents—making sense, understanding, and creating knowledge. Children are doers of learning rather than passive receivers or observers of outside events that cause behavior changes. Cognitive learning theories emphasize the mental processes humans use to take in new information. These processes combine new and old information in ways that enable people to understand and reinterpret experiences. Many educators and psychologists call these sense-making processes high-level, critical, or executive thinking. When schools attempt to teach critical thinking, they are—or should be—concerned with cognition. Cognitive processes permit us to do difficult and sophisticated learning and generate new knowledge.

It is often easy to see the *results* of learning. We can watch our child sloppily bake a cake, multiply, or excel at an after-school job. And we can probably identify some of the stimuli for his learning: We might credit the modeling we provided when he watched us bake a cake, or point to our own instruction when we taught him to drive. But recognizing such stimuli and results tempts us to describe learning with formula-like precision, even if we can only guess at what might be going on inside the child's brain as he bakes or drives. Meaning-making (cognition) is less precise in the describing because it is the invisible "figuring out" that takes place between the stimuli and results.

Yet, a cognitive view does not discard the idea of stimulus and response. Whatever prompts a child to act on a problem and whatever the child does or concludes are part of the figuring out. Children turn both ideas and physical sensations into meanings that are compatible with what they learned previously. That explains why different people interpret even the simplest things so differently. Whether a room gets too warm or whether a waitress pours enough hot fudge on the ice cream depends on the *meaning* we give these conditions. These meanings matter more than the actual room temperature or quantity of fudge. We might give a different meaning to the same temperature if we were lying on a sunny beach. And a child might not reason that he had too little fudge if his brother didn't appear to have just a tad more.

The mental images we hold—the pictures, patterns, and scripts of how the world operates—influence our cognitive processing. So does our capacity to retain and recall information, to reason, and to determine what is logical. Cognition allows children to apply what they already know to novel situations. It also allows novel situations to affect what children already know. This dynamic process means that children don't simply recall whole, preformed meanings. They alter meanings to suit new circumstances, even if the circumstances are very different.

Like most of real life, thinking is complex and disorderly. Sometimes we take years to make sense of ideas and experiences. Sometimes making sense happens literally overnight. That's what we really hope for when we tell someone to "sleep on it." Sometimes understanding happens in a flash. "Aha!" is a sure sign that someone has suddenly made sense out of confusion.

Cognitions also depend on age and development. Consider a child's experience in the sandbox—pouring sand back and forth between a small pail and a larger one. This experience adds to his growing understanding of what cognitive psychologists call *conservation*. The conservation principle explains a fundamental physical law: altering the shape or position of something does not change its volume or quantity. A younger child will conclude that a small pail filled to overflowing contains more sand than a large pail only partly filled. This child will not conclude that the amount of sand remains the same whether it fills one container of half-fills a larger one. Only later, when he is old enough and experienced enough, will he develop the concept of conservation. And as he does so, he will seek out and pay attention to related experiences. Most important, he will make sense of them in new ways. He will become more curious and more inclined to experiment. He will not only take advantage of learning experiences, but create these learning opportunities by himself.

Making new meanings requires a complex interplay among broad concepts (such as conservation), small bits of information (sand filling or not filling the pail), and sufficient age and development. An eighteen-month-old will not understand the concept of conservation. He needs time, and he needs experience with sand and pails, water and buckets, getting into a full bathtub, trying to squeeze an extra toy into a suitcase, and the like. He probably also needs to feel all the possible attendant emotions—playing with sand is fun, approved by parents, feels good, and so on.

Schools and Cognition

Most educators know less about theories of cognition than they do about behaviorism. Every teacher's repertoire includes rewards and punishments, but not all use strategies intended to encourage cognitive development. Policymakers and educators show increasing concern about critical thinking and problem solving, yet few understand the learning model that helps explain how those processes work.

Even when individual teachers or the principal have studied cognitive theory, they may not be powerful enough to change the school culture so that it encourages sense making. Traditionally, instruction, testing, and grading rely on observable behaviors for proof that learning occurs. Cognition is more difficult to observe and measure than behavior. Teachers have a harder time documenting that a child has made meaning of a concept than demonstrating that he can correctly, if superficially, answer a test question. Unfortunately, when policymakers and educators use test results as evidence of teachers' and schools' effectiveness, they may unwittingly be promoting behavioral approaches to learning.

Children have a much richer learning experience when teachers consider cognition. For example, the arithmetic problem Divide 25 by 7 has a correct answer—3 with a remainder of 4. From a behavioral perspective, the child is successful if she produces this answer. However, the correct answer is only one element in a learning cycle of increasingly large ideas. From a cognitive perspective, any of the following questions can enrich arithmetic instruction and evaluation. Listening carefully to children's responses to these questions can provide a window into their sense making. Furthermore, when children explain their reasoning, teachers can discover and correct children's misconceptions.

- What are you thinking as you do the problem?
- Why does your answer make sense?
- Can you draw a picture that illustrates this problem?
- Can you and your friends write a story question that requires solving this problem?
- Can you write a story problem that is mathematically correct but logically absurd? (Here's an example: If 7 people fit in a van, how many vans will you need to take 25 people to the ball game? Answer: 3 and 4/7 vans.)

- Why do we call this process division?
- What is a remainder, and why do you have to have one?
- How is a remainder like a fraction and how is it different?
- How can you see this problem to illustrate the principle of conservation?

The concepts embedded in the answers to these questions foster mathematical thinking. In real life, using mathematics requires far more complex and concrete procedures than the ability to produce the abstract correct answer—3 with a remainder of 4. For example, a recent survey of mathematics skills did ask children to figure out how many vans they would need to transport a given number of passengers. The most often chosen answer included a fraction (remainder) of a van. While the answer showed that they had computed the numbers correctly, it was wrong because the children didn't round up as they would have to do in real life. But real life didn't enter their mathematical thinking. Events like these fuel the concern of mathematicians that schools are teaching children to apply rote formulas rather than to think practically or mathematically.

LEARNING: SCHEMES, ASSIMILATION, AND ACCOMMODATION

Over the past several decades, Jean Piaget has influenced cognitive psychology more than any other psychologist. Piaget's interrelated ideas of *schemes, assimilation,* and *accommodation* explain basic features of cognitive functioning. His concept of *equilibration* explains the energy, tension, sense of balance and imbalance, and even the motivation that drives the whole cognitive process. These concepts describe the complex interplay among new and previous experiences. Others continue to modify and refine Piaget's work. Even so, cognitive psychology—a combination of theory, common sense, and rigorous experiment—continues to reflect Piaget's observations about fundamental mental processes. Piaget's ideas are complex. Each needs cautious qualifying because we are looking at *models* for development—not rules. However, the following broad explanations should help convey their significance.

Schemes

We can think of schemes as the mental frameworks we use to organize our perceptions and experiences. Cognitive psychologists also use the terms *models, conceptual structures,* and *networks* to describe these frameworks. We use the word *schemes* to refer to the ideas that underlie all of these terms. Like categories or models, schemes enable us to bring our prior knowledge to bear on new experiences. Schemes allow us to recognize objects we have never seen before *if* we can connect them with our past experiences.

For example, we all know a category of furniture designed for people to sit on—chairs. We expect to find this kind of furniture in houses. We have experiences sitting and resting in these objects. In short, we have a sense of "chairness" that relieves us of the need to do elaborate figuring before we take a chance and sit down. Each time we have a new chair experience—say, with a rocking chair, a backless chair, a leather or a green or a broken chair—we fill out our sense of chairness a bit more. At the least we confirm and probably extend our chair scheme. When we encounter a new chair we know at a glance what it is. We know what it does, and we understand its limits. We can estimate its social significance (this chair is an expensive though tasteless addition to the living room), and much more.

The concept of conservation—that quantities remain the same even when they assume different shapes—is also a scheme. It, too, helps us make sense of a large category of experiences. For example, our first inclination might be to buy a large box of cereal. We don't, however, when we find out that it weighs two ounces less than a smaller box that costs the same. Here, we rely on measurement in part because we have internalized the principle of conservation. This is information that helps us not to get fooled by appearances. In the late 1970s, when gasoline prices skyrocketed, some gas stations switched to pricing gas by the liter. Many drivers reported feeling better about what appeared to be a lower unit price until they reminded themselves that it still cost more to fill up the tank. Small children who have yet to grasp conservation will usually prefer the larger box of cereal.

We don't automatically transfer basic schemes from one situation to another. It often takes a conscious effort to do so. A science student may correctly find the mass of an irregular object by measuring the volume of water it displaces. However, she will probably not consciously relate the physics principle she applied in the laboratory to her real-world experiences—such as when she gets into the bathtub and the water overflows. Instruction that calls specific attention to the relationship might help her understand the principle at work in the bathtub. Such instruction would foster her cognitions. Unfortunately, much science instruction is based on behavioral principles. Exploration usually goes no further than the right or wrong answer in the lab.

We increase the depth and richness of our current schemes with each interaction among smaller ideas, tasks, and experiences. When we asked those many questions about the division problem, we promoted such interactions. We encouraged the child to mix specific division tasks with other kinds of thinking that were not directly related to division (the social skills of using division processes while working with others, for example). This broadening and mixing helps children not only to learn how to divide, but also to think a little more like mathematicians.

Schemes and the Processes of Assimilation and Accommodation

We typically see learning as adding information that builds on existing knowledge. When we ask children, "What did you learn today?" we usually want to know what new facts they added to their existing store. Piaget called this adding on or blending assimilation.

It's much less common for us to ask, "How did you change today?" And of course this is a much harder question to answer. For example, compare these two questions and the answers you are likely to get: (1) "What did you learn about the Civil War?" and (2) "How do you understand the Civil War differently?" The first question asks, in effect, for added knowledge. The second question presumes that additional knowledge requires alterations in the knowledge and understanding the child already has. This second process—the changing or altering of schemes to accept new experiences—Piaget called *accommodation*.

These two processes are interdependent. Nothing new gets added (assimilation) without schemes changing (accommodation), and schemes don't change without new experiences. Importantly, experiences may include one's own thoughts. Just sitting and thinking can generate new (mental) experiences and force accommodation.

Humans can get very set in their mental ways—and this can erect barriers to further learning. Firmly fixed schemes do not easily change to accept new experiences. For that reason people often alter their perceptions to make new experiences compatible with their existing schemes. For example, most children *and* adults have incorrect but fixed schemes for many of the physical laws of the universe. They naively experience the sun as moving across the sky instead of attributing the apparent motion of the sun to the earth's rotation. Schemes extend to social as well as physical phenomena. For example, adults (teachers among them) who have not related to educated blacks or other minorities often conclude that minorities are intellectually less capable than whites. Just giving them the information that all groups contain the full range of abilities probably won't correct their misperceptions. Once people form misconceptions they require considerable evidence and impressive experiences to shake loose their faulty schemes.

Schools, Schemes, and Curriculum

Schools typically treat children as if they were born with intellectual blueprints. They act as if the school's job were to lay down layer after layer of bricks, build walls, and fill up the mental rooms with facts. In contrast, the idea of accommodation allows us to imagine that we constantly rearrange the walls and change the shape and contents of rooms. Sometimes it seems that we start over from scratch. Yet, after each addition and reorganization we still have the original materials, which we put to new, broader uses.

Schools overemphasize assimilating new information (filling up children's heads with facts) and pay too little attention to building and rebuilding schemes. They overlook (or don't recognize) the complementary nature of accommodation and assimilation. Because schools emphasize new information instead of making sense, they make learning more difficult than it needs to be. Children have more trouble remembering isolated facts—names, events, and dates—than remembering those same facts when they relate to larger ideas.

For example, Civil War facts are more likely to stick if children link them to the politics of the time or to the context of the Northern and Southern economies. Children will find it hard to remember facts about the Trent Affair (the names of the ships, the date, and so on) unless teachers connect these facts to their larger context. To make such connections, a teacher might encourage children to discuss how the Trent Affair related to the South's lack of industry and its dependence on markets for cotton. She might ask the children to consider the concept of alliances and what motivates countries to form them. She might ask how the children themselves form alliances—designing activities in which the children observe the range of social, political, and personal associations they enounter in their communities. The class might speculate about the significance, then and now, of Abraham Lincoln's apology to the British for the North's mistake. And she might extend that question by exploring the children's ideas about the difficulty individuals and nations have with apologies. In such a lesson, children could learn many important concepts without neglecting the facts that support them.

Likewise, if we expect children to memorize grammar rules without extensive writing experiences, they are almost sure to miss the purpose of learning those rules—to be better writers. On the other hand, if children write a lot, they need very little formal grammar training apart from their writing. Besides, without lots of writing, grammar won't make much sense or be of much use. A cognitive approach would ask children to think differently about writing *while they are writing*. Of course that would include paying attention to the rules that apply to their work.

Knowledge in the real world does not arrive in full bloom at the end of a lesson or semester. Our schemes evolve as we recycle, reconsider, recombine, and revisit them. Certainly, to help children acquire schemes, schools must pay considerable attention to the orderly development of their learning. The recycling and reconsidering should be not random. Schools must present knowledge and experience in ways suited to children's development and prior experiences. But, as we described in chapter 1, schools favor the apparent efficiency of one best method at one best time. When they try to teach and test children in a fixed sequence, they make the tacit assumption that all children have had similar and sufficient prior experiences. They also assume that all children learn at the same rate and in the same way.

We wouldn't want schools to stop asking children to memorize facts, learn specific attributes of democracy (such as voting and representative government), and know essential grammar rules. We wouldn't want them to give up many of their other traditional tasks. However, when lessons focus too heavily on adding bits and pieces of information, they pay little attention to whether and how children assimilate that knowledge into old schemes or accommodate their old schemes to accept new knowledge. In the process they offer few opportunities for children to struggle for new meanings.

The Struggle for New Meanings

Assimilation and accommodation are rarely in perfect balance. We don't establish schemes and cement them in place. Rather, the more we know, the more we need to know. Each new experience doesn't complete an idea or close a mental door. Rather, it creates new empty places that push us to look for more information. Sometimes we get the new information from our own store of knowledge—facts and experiences that we had all along. Perhaps we reinvestigate old schemes, and perhaps we ask a question we hadn't thought of before. Piaget referred to the rare balance as a state of equilibrium and to the more common imbalance as disequilibrium. The whole process of moving from imbalance toward balance, only to be disrupted again, Piaget called *equilibration*. Who hasn't felt, "That makes perfect sense!" (equilibrium), only to back off from that perfect solution a few moments later. Often, we must acknowledge that, although we may understand things better, we have more work to do (disequilibrium).

School, parents, and children themselves often neglect the importance of equilibration in learning. They notice tension and uncomfortable delays between the time children receive instruction and when they genuinely understand. Often they interpret this tension as a sign of inefficient learning rather than as an essential part of understanding. Rather than being inefficient, equilibration motivates children to make sense. Well-intentioned parents or teachers who try to construct fail-safe learning experiences may hope to minimize frustration. They want to guarantee that the child will master a particular learning objective easily. Yet doing so may actually suppress the very process children need to be active sense makers.

For example, under pressure to teach reading skills, schools often rob children of time for reading real books. Yet children need books that give them complex, troublesome experiences that can throw their old schemes into disarray and cause new learning to take place. To be sure, children must master basic reading skills. But children become committed readers only when teachers, books, and ideas nurture their broad intellectual disequilibrium. Books create a tension, a hunger, that children can satisfy with more reading.

Similarly, parents and teachers want children to understand complex ideas (democracy, the theme of man against nature, and so on). However, the school culture can obstruct lessons that sustain intellectual struggles. The culture can prevent children from reworking schemes or having enough firsthand experiences to make sense of these ideas. Too few children participate in activities that require them to think and act democratically or actually experience nature in ways provided by the Outward Bound programs. Especially as they grow older, a blizzard of facts and drills can overwhelm children.

LEARNING AND MOTIVATION: WHO'S IN CHARGE HERE?

Consider this: That infant in the crib, that upside-down six-year-old on the jungle gym, that fourteen-year-old in front of the mirror in a very short time will be full-fledged adults. By their late teens they will have lots of adult experience, knowledge, skills, and wisdom. During childhood they will learn nearly all the language, values, talents, and social and learning skills that will serve them for the rest of their lives. And they will have learned most of this on their own—like scientists—experimenting, observing, and making sense of their world.

One of the wonders of being human is that we learn so much so easily and have so much fun doing it. Children naturally feel competent. They tackle difficult tasks on their own and have no natural inclination to feel discouraged by mistakes. Just think of the number of times small children try new and difficult tasks. From climbing stairs to buttoning clothes to making sentences, they keep plugging away until they get it right. Indeed, patience seems far more natural than impatience. A child's face lighting up spontaneously as he masters a task reminds us of the sheer pleasure learning brings, and how learning can be its own reward.

Sense-making processes begin at birth. A newborn learns naturally and spontaneously. He learns from his own body as he responds to light and sound, as he sucks and cries. The sound of his cry, the sensations of his mouth, the motion of his body all increase the baby's awareness of himself. Much of the baby's learning is interactive. With his responsiveness, he encourages parents to hold, rock, touch, speak, and sing to him. All the while, the baby is learning to be more in charge. He makes sense out of all those events, slowly at first, but gathering momentum after the first months of experiences.

Motivation and Children's Eagerness to Learn

We can't separate children's feelings about themselves—feelings that we label self-concept—from their thinking and learning processes. And these feelings are inextricably linked to their feeling in charge of their learning. Here, we use the expression "in charge" to mean feeling capable, competent, responsible for, and in control of one's own thinking and decision making.

Consider your own reactions when someone asks you to be in charge of something. Most people would have some of the following thoughts and concerns:

Have I done this activity before?
Will I be successful?
I must be capable if they asked me to be in charge.
They asked me, but there has been a mistake.
Does someone want me to succeed? to fail?
Will it be rewarding?
Do I feel confident?

If I am not successful, will I feel hurt? look foolish? be poorer?
Who will know?
Can I learn the parts I haven't done before?
How curious am I to find out what will happen?

These questions remind us that we don't automatically leap into being in charge. In fact, some adults prefer others to take charge. Yet even when we follow another's lead, we feel better and we learn most if we attribute our actions to our own decisions. We have strong personal, social, and cognitive needs to be *willing* participants in whatever we do.

While practically all children possess the capacity to learn what teachers expect, each child's willingness to be in charge shapes her learning results. We can never separate learning results from a child's willingness to pay attention, to receive instruction, and to participate with others. Learning relates to how committed the child feels to the ideas or activity. It interacts with her willingness to risk understanding more slowly or differently from peers, to seek out materials and information, to ask for clarification, and to alter previous ideas to assimilate new information. This willingness to act and eagerness to leap into learning is what we call *motivation*.

Beliefs about Motivation

Adults often explain children's failure by stating that they lack motivation. Sometimes we assume that motivation comes and goes, as when we say, "I don't feel motivated today." Some see motivation as an action, like spanking or encouraging: "What can I do to motivate that child?" Clearly, motivation is a flexible and useful idea for referring to the unseen energy and determination that drive people to take charge of their actions. However, two people using the term may have very different premises about what it describes.

How people use the term *motivation* reveals much of what they believe about learning. The behavioral view of motivation rests heavily on reinforcement (reward and punishment). We can easily understand its appeal. Rewards and punishments affirm our commonsense observations of how the world works. They can stop behavior that we don't want and sustain behaviors we do want, at least temporarily.

Long before first graders have a well-developed scheme for proper classroom behavior, teachers can motivate and train them not to talk while others are talking and to raise their hands before speaking. Teachers who are skilled classroom managers can accomplish this after a relatively short period of rewards and possibly punishments. However, they run the risk that, if the rewards and punishments stop, so will the desired behavior. Often, maintaining good behavior requires increasingly large rewards or punishments.

Sometimes we distinguish between extrinsic motivation, which comes from someone or somewhere else, and intrinsic motivation, which we generate from within. Rewards and punishments often provide extrinsic motivation, and they can be efficient in starting or stopping simple, routine acts and habits. But as behaviors become more complex, systems for rewards and punishments must become equally elaborate. Rewards and punishments become harder to keep convincingly aligned with the behaviors they must influence. Moreover, outside rewards and punishments are not well suited for influencing the most complex and valued behaviors.

In contrast to behaviorists, cognitive psychologists emphasize intrinsic motivation. They see this motivation as tension, a sense of imbalance, the drive or desire to make meaning. If such tension is present in lessons, children will work hard even in the absence of consistent outside reinforcement. Learning European history, keeping oneself studying hard day and night while some classmates are not, working with others cooperatively, and so on require resources from within. External rewards can help, but they can't carry the whole motivational load. Rarely can children draw on their full measure of internal resources if they attribute their success to conditions beyond their control. They do far better when they see success as a result of their own volition and efforts.

DEVELOPMENT

Can you bring to mind medieval paintings that portray children with adult faces on top of chubby child bodies? If so, you have an idea of how people understood learning well into the twentieth century. Historically, society thought children had the same mental capabilities for learning as adults—they just weren't as good at it. Even today adults look at children and see miniatures of themselves.

In fact, a four-year-old does not think or learn in quite the same way a nine-year-old does. A nine-year-old's thinking differs from a teenager's. Piaget corrected the child-as-miniature-adult conception by outlining a series of distinct developmental stages. Each stage appears to be the optimal time for particular kinds of learning. The concept of conservation we described earlier is part of stage-related learning. Piaget observed that children must reach a certain developmental stage before they stop thinking that a tall one-quart container holds more liquid than a shorter one. Today's psychologists prefer a much less rigid view of development and have softened the distinctions between stages. Today's psychologists think that development may appear to be stagelike because children's ease of learning and the learning strategies they use are affected by their prior knowledge, experience and maturity. But most depart from Piaget's view that the actual structure of thinking changes as children progress through stages. Even so, the broader principle holds: children's thinking develops.

The concept of development points to fairly predictable learning sequences—with successive stages incorporating and extending the accomplishments of previous stages. The concept helps us understand which activities children may be ready to learn. It also underscores the futility of pressing children into activities for which they are not ready. Laws of the physical world, complex operations such as reading, and mathematical abstractions such as subtraction all involve more than careful and methodical teaching. They require a developmentally ready child. After several centuries of trial and error, schools teach developmentally appropriate tasks to most children most of the time. However, many of children's school problems result from instruction that is too narrow or inflexible to accommodate even slight differences in children's development.

Schools need to pay more attention to development. But they can also err in the opposite direction by using stages as if they were scientific diagnostic tools. In particular, schools and parents often think that the child who develops earlier is more intelligent and a better prospect for academic achievement. Developmental levels are too imprecise to be used to diagnose individual children. Since children follow different developmental clocks, it's extraordinarily difficult to pin down the age at which a particular stage should begin. Adults can do considerable damage when they try to assess children's intelligence or predict their futures according to the age at which they acquire a particular skill. When schools hold back a slower developing child because she is not ready at the same time as her classmates, or when they push ahead a precocious child, they often create frustration or failure.

Maturation, Experience, and the Influence of Others

Development relates, in part, to physical *maturation*. Children are not born with completely developed nervous systems. Young children gain new information at different rates based on their developing vision, hearing, and other physical capabilities. Just how and when these factors affect learning is not completely understood. Some mental processes do not fully develop until children are physically mature.

Development also depends on *experience*. A child who has enough experiences with conservation of volume (playing with water in the tub, with sand at the beach, and so forth) will understand conservation when he is otherwise developmentally ready. His experiences may help him learn it somewhat earlier or more completely than a child with few experiences. However, few advantages accrue from *training* children to do tasks before they are ready. A rich play environment with lots of opportunities to explore and invent is all that most children need for normal development.

The *influence of others* also shapes development. Most immediate and obvious are face-to-face interactions the child has with her family and friends. But the total social environment also contributes to children's self-concepts and the way they make sense of the adult social world. And, of course, the school culture influences development, particularly children's acquisition of social concepts such as sharing, cheating, competing, and making friends.

Finally, we simply can't predict who will do what and when. Children surprise. History abounds with stories of early-blooming Mozarts and late-blooming Einsteins.

Personal, Social, and Moral Development

Just as we find little precision in the predicting of children's stages of intellectual development, we see even more uncertainty about how children develop personality, relationships with others, and moral awareness. But we cannot separate children's thinking about knowledge and skills from how they think about themselves, how they think about others, and how they think about right and wrong. Two prominent psychologists have contributed to the idea that personal, social, and moral development also proceed in stages. Both emphasize how the developing child makes sense out of experiences.

Erik Erikson identified eight stages of personal and social development, five of which take place before the age of eighteen. Like the stages of cognitive development, these stages are flexible and overlapping, and they vary considerably among individuals. Erikson's stages help us observe children's social growth. They portray many of life's growing-up struggles as healthy development instead of aberrations that alarm parents and annoy schools. Of course, most parents gain some confirmation that their children's struggles are normal from observing other children and talking to experienced parents and teachers. However, families today seem to have fewer opportunities to observe their own children and check out their doubts with others in the community. More parents feel isolated from family, neighbors, or the school and have trouble distinguishing between normal developmental hassles and serious trouble. The typical struggles (which we might interpret as the normal developmental work of the child) that Erikson includes in his stages should be familiar. Erikson's stages consider children's maturation, experiences, and social interactions. When combined with an understanding of intellectual development, his stages help fill out a picture of the whole child.

During the child's first eighteen months, more or less, his essential developmental task is learning to rely on his mother. He also must learn to trust himself not to disappoint her. When mother cares for her baby and responds to him with pleasure, he trusts both her and his own worthiness. If mother is uncaring, her child will not trust others and, inevitably, he will lack confidence that others will care for him. Trusting oneself is closely linked to trusting others at this early age. As in all of his childhood stages, Erikson connects developing personality with social interactions, and the earliest interactions are among the most important.

In the second stage children explore possibilities for acting on their own. During the "terrible twos" power struggles frequently take place. Children slowly learn that sometimes they get what they want and sometimes they don't. During this stage, Erikson suggests, too few adult-imposed limits can cause children to feel out of control or have an unrealistic sense of their own autonomy. In contrast, too firm a hand can cause them to feel powerless and incompetent. The essential struggle between risk and security parallels children's needs for both autonomy and guidance.

Between ages three and six, children act and talk vigorously and spontaneously. They are full of energy and initiative. They develop a sense of comfort with their ability to make things happen—to be a force in the world and have others pay attention to them. But they may also feel unsure of their natural urges and guilty about them. This can happen if worried parents become too restrictive or punitive—afraid that their children will become uncontrollable.

During children's elementary school years, their developing self-concepts take on important new dimensions. Some children begin to define themselves as learners, workers, and as people who accomplish things. Successful experiences promote such positive self-perceptions. Failure, on the other hand, can lead children to doubt their learning capacity. They may place responsibility for failure on circumstances beyond their control. Or they may attribute their success to the teacher or to luck rather than to their own efforts. Neither belief helps them learn.

Teenagers struggle to resolve both the old conflicts of childhood and new trials of adulthood. They must assert themselves as independent individuals; at the same time they crave support and acceptance. In the process they may test, challenge, and shock others, especially their parents. They try to imagine themselves as adults. As they do they will often idolize adults (or even slightly older teenagers) whom they fantasize as having perfect or at least conflict-free lives. Many teenagers feel emotionally battered by their own conflicting wishes—security vs. independence; recognition as a humanitarian vs. power over others; intimate but undemanding social and sexual relationships. The resolving of these conflicts helps generate very rapid development and makes these years both joyous and painful for adults to watch.

Lawrence Kohlberg studied stages of children's and adults' moral decision making. He focused primarily on reasoning—the process by which people make ethical choices. Like Erikson's, Kohlberg's distinctions line up in fairly recognizable ways. The simpler, more concrete moral reasoning appears earlier in life; the more sophisticated and abstract reasoning develops in adulthood, if at all.

Kohlberg relied on Piaget's ideas of cognitive development to identify stages of moral decision making. Anyone who has tried to play checkers with a three-year-old knows that the child's concept of rules is different from that of most adults. Young children can learn to state the rules. However, they may not be able to act upon them if losing a point or a game doesn't make sense. Kohlberg did not produce a scientific hierarchy of moral decision making that we can apply to individuals. Rather, he offered a wide range of processes (we might call them moral schemes) that people use to arrive at their moral choices. The following list shows the variety of logic that is possible. Note how difficult it is to assign a child to a single stage and how even adults make decisions in each or most of these ways:

- Children make their early moral decisions out of habit or fear of punishment. They follow the rules made by authorities. These decision-making processes have a decidedly behavioral flavor—that is, children don't make sense out of the rules. They follow them because "that's just the way it is."

- Later, children interpret externally imposed rules to make them consistent with and satisfy their own needs. Children practice their developing understanding of fairness, especially when it does not conflict with their self-interest.
- Later still, children learn to override or reinterpret self-interest to make decisions that please others and gain approval. They attempt to make sense out of what other people define as right.
- For some people maintaining the social order and respecting authority define what is right and good. They obey laws, not out of blind acceptance, fear of punishment, or desire for social approval, but because they understand rules to be essential for a moral and orderly society.
- People reason that rules need to serve society, and they believe that reasonable people can decide on what is best. Values and ethical principles take precedence over tangible gains and losses to the individual. Laws may be disobeyed if they conflict with one's highest principles.

A few implications of Piaget's, Erikson's, and Kohlberg's work warrant emphasis here. At each stage of their development, children have particular learning and growing-up work to do. Much of the time they experience a natural state of struggle, conflict, or disequilibrium. Adults must participate in these experiences at times, and at other times they should keep their distance. Sometimes children's struggles are obviously painful; sometimes children seem inappropriately blasé. Aside from not allowing self-destructive behaviors, there are few hard-and-fast guidelines to help adults decide whether to step in or hold back. We feel comfortable with the following rules of thumb: First, parents and teachers nearly always act appropriately when they listen nonjudgmentally as children explain their reasons and tell more about their feelings. Second, parents and teachers nearly always act inappropriately when they look for quick action that will speed along children's development.

WHAT ABOUT INTELLIGENCE?

During this century, the Western world has invented a peculiar way of thinking about and measuring learning ability. IQ—the intelligence quotient—is firmly entrenched as a symbol of intelligence. People consider IQ to be an attribute, substance, or quality that defines the upper limits of learning ability. Those who have a lot of this quality have a high IQ, those with less a low one. Further, conventional wisdom holds that children are more or less stuck with the intelligence they are born with.

Another common belief is that families quickly influence how children will apply their intelligence to learning. Therefore, a high-IQ child born to an intellectually impoverished family will supposedly develop personal barriers to learning. All these beliefs account for the common notion that by the time children reach age five or six, schools can do little to alter their intelligence or ability. These beliefs also contribute to parents' and educators' interpretations of children's school success. Chapters 6, 7, and 8 describe how schools act on these interpretations.

Cognitive and developmental theories depart dramatically from these traditional views. Rather than as a property, substance, or attribute, cognitive psychologists view intelligence as *process*. They believe that the processes that make people intelligent are not uniform or of a single type, but rather are multiple. For example, the Yale psychologist Robert Sternberg describes three types of intelligence: one that promotes analytical and critical thinking; one that leads to the development of creative new ideas; and one that enables humans to respond quickly and productively to everyday events and experiences. Sternberg suggests that people may have strengths in one or the other of these intelligences.

Similarly, Howard Gardner, a psychologist at Harvard University, discounts a *single* intelligence and emphasizes the many mental abilities—intelligences—he suggests we all have. His theory of multiple intelligence stresses the flexibility and variety of children's proclivities for learning. How one comes to know and use language—one of Gardner's intelligences—may be quite different from how one develops skills in music—another intelligence. Gardner also defines logical-mathematical intelligence, visual-spatial intelligence, bodily-kinesthetic intelligence, and an array of personal intelligences.

Gardner suggests that all humans inherit the capacity to develop each of these intelligences. However, within a society individuals will vary in their particular strengths and preferences. Some cultures stress certain kinds of intelligence over others. In schools survival and success depend heavily on language and logical-mathematical abilities, while other less literacy-bound abilities are less valued. Out of school, people with strengths in these other domains make important contributions. Since success out of school depends upon far more than technical skill in reading, writing, and computing, it is clear that schools undervalue other types of intelligence.

These emerging views of learning challenge the belief in fixed intelligence. They force us to consider the strong likelihood that children learn new ways of processing information as they experience the world. In short, children learn to be intelligent.

LEARNING AND THE SCHOOL CULTURE

We have argued here that teachers pay too little attention to children's cognitive processes and interpret intelligence too narrowly. But the culture of the schools supports these views, and even well-advised teachers may not be able to alter their instruction.

Schools' recent history of striving for industrial-like efficiency has led to tightly organized systems for teaching that mesh with behavioral views of learning. These systems fit the belief that students learn best by mastering sequences of short-range problems and isolated, easily tested facts. Consistent with the factory/production model, the school culture often treats unresolved or untestable problems as inefficiencies. But real life and real learning are filled with ambiguities. Typically, parents and educators have firm notions of what learning looks like. They want to see children working quietly and producing correct answers in orderly and sequential ways. Most believe that these behaviors, even if they are not learning itself, are good stand-ins for it.

Many children quickly learn to identify the behaviors that adults want and the school culture supports. Those who can, learn to listen carefully for the answers that please adults. They become skilled at selecting and repeating correct answers and disregarding the information they don't understand. They avoid the rigorous thinking that schools don't reward. These teaching and learning regularities are at the root of many learning problems—even for those children who succeed at school. Behavioral approaches do not reward thinking that leads to the real dynamics of scholarship. Such thinking often entails searching for, rather than avoiding, additional problems and unresolved conflicts. Children get little support when they identify dilemmas they cannot wrap up quickly. They may receive little encouragement to revisit ideas that passed by the year before as if on a conveyor belt.

Unfortunately, if children learn to state correct answers without learning the underlying concepts, they may have trouble when they try to build on their missing or incomplete understanding. They may be among those who have a rude awakening when they suddenly do poorly in a demanding course or enroll in college. Schools see children who are less adept at producing the behaviors the school culture values (rapid recall, motivation for grades, sitting still, neatness) as being less capable. They will usually assign these children different (that is, slower) learning opportunities. Children rarely have the chance to reinvestigate concepts that they couldn't master earlier. Most school cultures make it inevitable that some children fall behind.

Still other children may give their studies considerable thought and effort that adults fail to acknowledge or miss altogether. Ironically, sometimes children are so captivated with the conceptual underpinnings of a problem, so engaged in the process of figuring it out, that they miss hearing the answer. In fact, they may be learning a lot. Sadly, they often feel discouraged and foolish when they do not produce the kind of work that earns rewards.

A more recent cultural regularity is that learning should come easily. That is, some people believe that having to work very hard is a sign that too much pressure is being placed on the child. This leads many children to interpret having to work hard as a sign that their thinking or their talent for learning or both are inadequate. So they identify difficult, complex problems as unnecessary or unfair burdens, and they associate the energy and tension of learning with something to be avoided.

Some years ago George Leonard's influential book *Education and Ecstasy* helped create the impression among careless readers that all learning should be blissful. Adults coached children to reject learning that wasn't fun, and they attributed a child's disinclination to work hard to faulty curricula or teaching or to a mismatch between the lesson and the personal tastes of the child. Nonetheless, Leonard's book was a welcome response to the earlier widespread denial of affective (feeling) factors in learning.

Learning, however, *is* hard work, even as it is satisfying and pleasurable. The movement between equilibrium (the state in which there is no problem and no learning is taking place) and disequilibrium produces tension. This equilibration is essential learning energy that propels children to alter concepts when they confront new information. It is a creative process that makes children inventive, constructive, and active learners. It can also cause discomfort. Successful learners welcome the tension and associate it with their previous success at solving problems. That, too, is the ecstasy of learning.

Intellectual, personal, social, and moral development by definition are disturbing. Development implies change, and change requires undergoing experiences for which we are not completely prepared. For adults and children alike growth requires challenges to moral certainty or complacency. It requires social interactions for which we are not ready and baffling intellectual challenges that demand considerable patience. We don't want to rush children into situations for which they are not intellectually, personally, or socially ready; neither do we want to protect them from disturbances that lead to learning.

The Real Learning Essentials

In spite of the limits and intransigence of the school culture, recent developments in the psychology of learning provide parents and policymakers with reason for optimism and with some guidelines for making the best of schools:

Children are more alike than different in how they think and learn, even though these processes are far more complex than previously thought.

Children who are free from serious neurological disorders can learn the important knowledge and skills schools attempt to teach.

Children exhibit developmental differences in their learning abilities. Rarely are these differences large enough to explain the increasingly large achievement differences as children move through school. That some children perform so well and many others never achieve what is possible tells us as much about how schools work as about how capable the children are.

Parents who hold firmly to these principles can feel confident that their advocacy for their children will stand a good chance of benefiting their children's classmates. Policymakers intent upon improving schools and school systems can be more confident that their reform efforts will serve the interests of all children.

FOR FURTHER READING

Jerome Bruner, *Toward a Theory of Instruction*. New York: W. W. Norton, 1966.

Erik H. Erikson, *Childhood and Society*. New York: W. W. Norton, 1963.

Howard Gardner, *Frames of Mind: The Theory of Multiple Intelligences*. New York: Basic Books, 1983.

Stephen J. Gould, *The Mismeasure of Man*. New York: W. W. Norton, 1980.

Peg Griffin and Michael Cole, *The Construction Zone: Working for Cognitive Change in School*. New York: Cambridge University Press, 1989.

Lauren B. Resnick, *Education and Learning to Think*. Washington, DC: National Academy Press, 1987.

Alan H. Schoenfeld, "On Mathematics as Sensemaking: An Informal Attack on the Unfortunate Divorce of Formal and Informal Mathematics." In J. F. Voss, D. N. Perkins, and J. Segal (eds.), *Informal Reasoning and Instruction*. Hillsdale, NJ: Erlbaum, 1988.

Robert E. Slavin, *Educational Psychology: Theory into Practice.* Englewood
Cliffs: Prentice-Hall, 1986.

Robert Sternberg, *Beyond I.Q.: A Triarchic Theory of Human Intelligence.*
New York: Cambridge University Press, 1984.

————, *The Handbook of Human Intelligence.* New York: Cambridge
University Press, 1982.

R. Sund, *Piaget for Educators.* Columbus, OH: Merrill Publishing, 1976.

J. S. Vargas, *Behavior Psychology for Teachers.* New York: Harper and Row,
1977.

James V. Wertsch, *Culture, Communication, and Cognition: Vygotskian
Perspectives.* New York: Cambridge University Press, 1989.

CHAPTER THREE

Classrooms: Where Children Learn

Disappointment awaits most parents and policymakers who step inside classrooms. They probably won't see children experiencing the exhilaration of meaningful learning or the energizing belief that they are capable. Nationwide studies of schools draw a discouraging picture of the average classroom: Teachers are clearly in charge; they talk or watch while students sit in rows and listen, read, answer questions, daydream, or fill in workbooks or dittoed sheets. Children nearly always do the same assignments, and they almost always work alone. Their lessons usually lack complexity and connection with the real world; often they are simply boring.

Classrooms don't have to be dull or out of sync with children's natural ways of learning. Educators can create environments in which enthusiasm for learning and self-confidence are commonplace instead of occasional, precious moments. And, to be sure, some now do. But, for most teachers, creating complex, meaningful classroom learning experiences isn't easy. The school culture supports commonplace practices—lecturing, book work, working alone, and so forth. And most teachers' traditional, behavioral view of learning further constrains their lessons. Even those who would like to apply their understanding of cognition and development to classroom activities have few genuine options in most schools.

They must abide by state, district, and school mandates that govern curriculum and instruction, and their classes must coexist with the school culture.

As a result, most classrooms develop cultures that match school norms, complete with conventional procedures for keeping things running smoothly and efficiently. Traditions dictate how classes should look and set expectations for the relationships between children and adults. Unfortunately the most common rules, traditions, and expectations lead to what researcher Kenneth Sirotnik has called "consistency, persistency, and mediocrity" in American classrooms.

At a gut level, we all recognize those rare classes that stretch children's minds and imaginations. Often we attribute their specialness to the efforts of an extraordinary, charismatic superteacher. This rare individual creates memorable schooling experiences despite the press of the surrounding culture. But most teachers are not miracle workers, and we should not expect miracles from them. What we should expect, however, are classes that apply our growing understanding of children's natural learning processes to the formal learning at school. And we should expect the kind of teaching that sets these learning processes in motion.

What might such classrooms look like? This chapter describes five characteristics of classes that help children become confident, skillful learners who use their meaning-making capabilities to be successful at school. Two of the characteristics relate to beliefs about success that guide the development of learning activities and shape children's responses to them:

1. Teachers believe that *all* of their students can succeed academically.
2. Children believe they can succeed and, when they do so, they attribute success to their own effort and persistence.

Three additional characteristics put teachers' beliefs into practice and promote children's confidence and willingness to work hard. Together they add up to what Elizabeth Cohen, a sociologist at Stanford calls a multidimensional classroom:

3. Lessons present knowledge as rich, complex, and meaningful.
4. Activities require children's active participation and promote their working together.
5. Evaluation and grading systems communicate progress privately and encourage hard work.

All five of these qualities interact strongly with one another, and, as they do, they support children's self-concepts. They are consistent with a cognitive view of learning, and they help make schooling fair.

TEACHERS BELIEVE THAT ALL
CHILDREN CAN SUCCEED

Insights from cognitive psychology support the belief that all children learn very well. They suggest that we can expect all children to master most of what schools want to teach. (A few children with dramatic neurological handicaps may be exceptions.) A productive school culture must foster this belief in all children's intelligence and capacity for high levels of learning. Supported by such a culture, teachers can create classroom conditions that enable all children to learn.

Be forewarned, however. The belief that all children can succeed differs from the conviction that all children are valuable, lovable, and talented in their own ways. We share that conviction, too, but it does not substitute for the belief that children can learn intellectually challenging knowledge and skills. For example, it is one thing to recognize a child's special artistic strengths, but it does not serve that child well to make him the illustrator for a group science project and excuse him from research and writing. He should still be accountable for learning the same science principles. Unless teachers believe all children are smart enough to learn, they will expect less from those they judge to have lower ability. Low expectations are nearly always self-fulfilling. Children accomplish less when adults expect less from them.

Differences and Expectations

Many educators (and parents as well) act as if the differences they see in children result from inherent limits in their ability. Many think that only a few students are really intelligent. Many believe that intelligence is either inborn or fixed quite early in life, that it is neither teachable nor learnable. This belief often leads both adults and children to conclude that only those blessed with superior intelligence can do well in school.

Formal tests support these views of intelligence. However, as we noted in chapter 2, the established traditions of studying and measuring intelligence often mislead educators and parents. Newer theory and research support a more flexible view of ability: Differences don't imply limits.

The beliefs teachers hold about ability have power. They lead teachers to act in ways that can make those beliefs real. Rosenthal and Jacobson's landmark study in 1968, "Pygmalion in the Classroom," was the first to propose self-fulfilling classroom prophecies that begin with teachers' beliefs. Rosenthal and Jacobson told a group of elementary teachers that a few children in their classes were late bloomers. They said that, even though these children weren't exceptional at the moment, they were likely to make substantial strides in the future. In fact, the researchers randomly selected children who were neither more nor less ready to bloom than the others. Nevertheless, at the end of the year, those identified as late bloomers and expected to shine academically outperformed their nonidentified classmates. Considerable subsequent work has substantiated Rosenthal and Jacobson's main conclusion: teachers' expectations influence how well students do.

However, teachers' expectations don't automatically create high achievers out of some children and low achievers out of others. Self-fulfilling processes happen in subtle and complex ways. Researchers Tom Good and Jere Brophy suggest one way. The teacher expects particular results from certain students. As a result, he behaves differently toward students according to his expectations. Differences in the teacher's actions communicate quite clearly what he expects, and these actions influence what students expect from themselves. They affect students' motivation and effort, their actual achievements, and their aspirations. Teachers then respond to students' subsequent effort and achievement in ways that reinforce initial expectations, and the cycle continues. Consistent expectations that children see as accurate and deserved have long-term effects.

By now, nearly every educator knows about the self-fulfilling-prophecy phenomenon. Nonetheless, school and classroom cultures still stress children's different abilities rather than the belief that every child can succeed. This emphasis on differences (and the self-fulfilling prophecies it promotes) may be the most limiting factor in classrooms.

Allowing Children to Be Both Different and Capable

Educators must believe that students can do well, but this is not enough. They must create learning experiences that permit them to do well. The task is difficult since children do differ in development, style of learning, and prior experiences. Because of these differences, some children find learning at school painful and some breeze along. Yet struggling or breezing also depends to a large extent on whether school conditions provide children with the time, opportunities, and resources appropriate for them.

Schools don't routinely provide appropriate conditions for all children. When *some* children do well, many educators mistakenly assume that the right conditions are available for everyone. Too often they conclude that those children who don't do so well are themselves to blame. The easiest explanations are that some children are not capable or that they are lazy.

However, Benjamin Bloom's research largely discredits such assumptions. Bloom achieved impressive results with all children when he provided them with one-on-one teaching and teachers who tailored instruction to their needs. That is, the teachers gave each child enough time, opportunities, and resources. Eighty percent of Bloom's experimental students achieved at a level reached by only 20 percent of the students in typical classrooms. Because of its high cost, one-on-one is not a practical solution for schools. Nonetheless, Bloom's findings support the belief that, when conditions are right, all children can learn more than they usually do. Bloom's results provide an incentive for educators to seek group methods that come close to the one-on-one tutoring results. At the very least, schools can use Bloom's findings to set goals for themselves and their students.

Of course, some teachers, school administrators, policymakers, psychologists, and educational researchers do believe that all children can succeed. Even so, most frankly admit that they don't know how to create classrooms where this happens. Many educators have searched for techniques that have the effects of one-on-one teaching. Mastery learning strategies and computer-based instruction are prominent attempts that have had mixed success. For the most part, the search has been somewhat disappointing. Practical, low-cost classroom strategies that ensure every child's success remain elusive.

Part of the difficulty is that many school regularities make it hard for teachers to allow children to be both different and capable. Teachers may know their students for only a brief time—usually four and a half to nine months. That's too short a time to notice large changes in children's development. Lockstep curricula, fixed time limits, and customary grouping practices reinforce teachers' beliefs that children's learning patterns are unchangeable. Under these conditions, *relative* performance in classes rarely changes. The best students at the start of the year usually finish on top at the end as well, and the poorest beginners typically end up at the bottom. This phenomenon reinforces teachers' beliefs that only students who are now successful will succeed in the future.

The belief that all children can't succeed at high levels leads teachers to group children for learning according to their different expectations. For example, teachers assign young children to ability groups for reading and mathematics depending on how quickly and well they expect them to learn. Later, schools sort children into different course sequences depending on how well teachers and counselors expect them to learn and what they think the children will be suited for after graduation. These ability-grouped classes help set in motion the self-fulfilling prophecies we described earlier. Teachers and others match low-ability classes with low expectations and high-ability classes with high expectations. Sure enough, that is how children usually perform in those classes.

Students don't miss the significance of being in a high or low group, either. To illustrate, one high school we know added an honors calculus class to its math program. After one semester, the math teachers reported that, overall, students lost more than they gained. Previously, teachers and students had thought that everyone taking calculus was a top math prospect. Now, both students and teachers expected only those in the honors class to attain the highest level of mathematics achievement. They expected less of those in the regular calculus course.

Another factor is teachers' own sense of efficacy (teachers' expectations for themselves). Teachers cannot risk believing that all children can succeed if they have little confidence in their own ability to make success happen. This may not reflect a poor attitude as much as teachers' realistic appraisals of what they can actually accomplish in the school culture.

Teachers, school administrators, and policymakers often tout high expectations as a means of improving student performance. However, talk about high expectations may not reflect a genuine belief that nearly every child can find academic success. Thinking positively about children and well-meant campaigns promoting high expectations don't substitute for actions that support high achievement. Slogans and pep talks by themselves only frustrate teachers and children. Schools must back up high expectations with fundamental changes in school organization and classroom practice.

CONFIDENT CHILDREN WHO WORK HARD

It's common knowledge that when children feel good about themselves, they are happier and more successful. We know less, though, about the dynamics behind the intuitive sense that self-concepts influence learning. What we know is that children's self-concepts include the conclusions they draw about whether, how, and why they succeed at school and that children rely on these conclusions to predict success. They also use them to avoid feeling bad and wasting energy over probable failures. Children's self-concepts direct them to make sensible decisions: for example, why work hard at something if you know you will fail?

To be successful at school, children themselves must believe they are capable, and they must act on that belief with the hard work and persistence it takes to succeed. Children learn to work hard when hard work makes sense—that is, when their efforts pay off in some valuable way. Children who feel competent and in charge expect valuable successes, and they exert the time and energy to learn.

Children who don't feel competent often assume that no amount of effort will lead to success. They often display a learned helplessness. That is, they decide before even trying a task that they can't succeed. Many such children eventually turn specific negative self-judgments about their effort into global negative judgments about their overall worth. They may begin by saying, "I don't do well in math when I don't study as much as others study" and end up believing, "I'm not smart at math" or "I'm not much of a student."

Self-Concepts in the Classroom

Clearly, schools don't have sole control over children's self-concepts, which begin developing well before the children reach school. Nonetheless, classroom experiences do influence children's confidence, effort, and persistence. Confidence and willingness to work hard partly depend on how likely children are to gain rewards in the classroom, and whether they think those rewards are valuable. They also depend on how publicly the teacher judges a child's attempts to gain rewards, and on how classmates react to his efforts—whether they conclude that the child is a competent person.

Children daily risk their confidence in classrooms. Nearly all schools require teachers to cover a standard curriculum at each grade, and teachers usually plan lessons so that all students in the class do the same tasks. Because children differ in their prior experiences and development, classroom tasks can be effortless for some children and quite difficult for others. Usually the rewards go to the children who find lessons easy.

In addition to causing them to miss out on rewards, many children's difficulty with lessons becomes public knowledge that others use to form negative conclusions about their ability. Public displays of children's performance may be as innocent as the posting of quiz scores, or they may be as mean as a teacher calling on a student when the teacher knows that he doesn't know the answer. Regardless of the teacher's intent, the class uses mounting public evidence to conclude that some students are not endowed for success.

Children receive a steady barrage of messages about what others think about their prospects for success. As time goes on, children's views of themselves correspond more and more to their classmates' and teachers' opinions and responses. In the best cases, the messages children receive add up to a positive, attractive package. The child, his teacher, and his classmates form a consensus that he can do tasks competently and gain valued rewards. We can count on such a child to put forth the hard work that success requires. Few children quit trying if everyone expects them to succeed.

On the other hand, children find it nearly impossible to sustain confidence, hard work, and persistence if everyone expects them to fail. For example, a child whose friends respond to his A grade by exclaiming, "I can't believe you got that grade!" will consider his achievement a fluke. Eventually, negative judgments lead many children to give up. The investigations of social learning theory by the psychologist Albert Bandura demonstrate this quite convincingly. When people must play subordinate roles or take on labels that imply inferiority or incompetence, their effectiveness and performance nearly always decline.

Fostering Positive Self-Concepts and Motivation

Teachers and the classroom activities they plan should help children become confident and willing to work hard. This means that teachers must create learning activities in which all children find the conditions they require for success—no small task. Teachers must try to design lessons that provide evidence that working hard and sticking with it will pay off. One key is whether children take charge of their learning. When children take charge, they learn that their effort can bring rewards. If not, they may credit luck, an outside influence, or some native gift.

The teacher's task is complicated by the fact that lessons that are too difficult or those that children can master without trying often lead children to disassociate their own control and energies from success or failure. In either case, children often attribute the results they get to the magical quality of ability. Like adults, they believe people are either born with lots of ability or not. Indeed, by the time children reach high school, being gifted with ability is usually admired more than hard work and persistence.

Moreover, if teachers always emphasize results—always getting the predetermined right answer—they may foster children's belief that self-worth comes from those results rather than from the level of effort expended to achieve them. They may discredit their own hard work. At the other extreme, some classes communicate that results don't matter. They may convey that trying hard is enough, and that it's less important if a student doesn't learn or finish a task. Neither type of class helps children feel in charge because neither matches effort and persistence with achievement.

However, when teachers design lessons that allow children to connect what they do with what they learn, they feel in charge of their learning. When children succeed they are likely to attribute that success to themselves. When the next opportunity arises, they may work even harder because of their experience that hard work pays off. More important than the specific success of the moment will be the growing evidence that their hard work (which they take charge of) has meaning. Such evidence can translate into competence and intrinsic motivation to do the hard work learning often requires. Intrinsic motivation sustains a child's willingness to work hard even when he must wait for rewards. It can keep a child going on a long or difficult project or when temporary setbacks create frustration.

Teachers who allow students to participate in classroom decisions, plan learning strategies, and design assignments also foster children's positive self-concepts, since these activities place children in charge. When children have some say over how they will learn, they can experience the satisfaction of following their intrinsic desires rather than the demands and instructions of others.

When teachers put children in charge, adults don't abandon their responsibility for the instructional program or, in the words of one worried teacher, "put the monkeys in charge of the zoo." It does not mean either that children are transformed into fully independent learners, though that is always an important goal. Rather, it means that they see themselves as increasingly capable as they take on greater responsibilities for organizing their own learning. They actively figure out what they need to do, determine consequences, evaluate their resources, and the like. They get help from others, and others rely on them. Children function less like workers carrying out orders to learn than like executives setting personal learning goals and policies. We have, then, these classroom learning paradoxes:

- Mature, independent learners are, of necessity, interdependent. They must learn with each other, and they must do it themselves.

- In each child there is a sense maker or learner. There is also an organizer of learning opportunities—a teacher or executive.

What Stands in the Way?

In most classrooms teachers want to stay in charge of learning. Their reasons are more complex than the obvious explanation that it makes sense for grown-ups to tell children what to do. In fact, as we described in chapter 2, outside of school children learn most by acting and deciding on their own, not by following adults' instructions. Why, then, in classrooms do we so often find the near opposite of what works so convincingly outside?

Once again, the culture of efficiency emerges as a powerful obstacle. It lies at the core of many conventional classroom practices. Teachers carry the burdens of little time, few resources, and many responsibilities. They must teach subject matter and cultural values. They must keep children safe, happy, and busy for at least six hours a day. And they must prepare children to be responsible citizens and skillfull workers. To meet these extraordinary demands, teachers rely on standardized, factorylike systems to get it all done. Putting children in charge could wreak havoc with teachers' tightly organized lessons and timetables.

Worldwide, businesses and industries are recognizing important inefficiencies in the old factory models. They are also exploring ways of creating interdependent work tasks and of giving their personnel greater responsibility over work decisions. But teachers still lack autonomy and inclusion in professional decision making, and they almost always work in isolation. They may find few examples in their own worklife for the delegating of authority and sharing of responsibility that could work so well in their classrooms.

Furthermore, many educators simply don't believe that children learn best if they take charge. In the last chapter, we described how schools typically favor behavioral approaches to learning. Perhaps the most important consequence of that tendency is that adults tightly control what knowledge students learn and how they learn it. Training, memorizing, and habit formation require that control be firmly in the hands of adults. The ideal student acts like a sponge that sops up knowledge quickly and efficiently. Schools expect that skillful adults, in charge of the inputs or stimuli, will *cause* children to learn.

Finally, adults like to organize and keep things tidy. It suits our sense of order to have all children start school at the same age, learn reading at the same age, and march en masse through the K–12 curriculum. Efficiency pushes teachers toward allowing all children the same time to learn. Few of these classroom regularities foster in children the feeling of being in charge. None fits particularly well with a cognitive view of learning.

Classrooms do not need to follow these discouraging patterns. Counter to the norms of the school culture, some teachers do create classroom environments in which children develop confidence and a willingness to work hard. These teachers believe that all children are capable, and they find responsible ways to put children in charge of learning. The remainder of this chapter describes what such teachers do:

- Teachers provide children with access to complex knowledge that is rich in meaning.
- Children work cooperatively as well as alone. Competition plays a minor role in motivation or achievement.
- Teachers treat evaluation as a sensitive and private matter. When they grade and evaluate, they don't publicly compare one child with another.

KNOWLEDGE THAT IS COMPLEX
AND RICH IN MEANING

The teacher assigns a short story to the class. The children read silently at their seats. Some shuffle and whisper, and a couple of the poorer readers lose interest when they notice the fastest readers finishing. Two other children have read the story before. One child makes quite a show of telling everyone she knows how the story ends. The other child scrunches down, hoping no one will notice while she doodles on her tennis shoe. At the end of class the teacher tells the children, "Those who haven't finished, finish for homework. Quiz tomorrow."

Tomorrow comes, and the children take a ten-point true/false quiz. The teacher gives the quiz partly to check their memory for detail (the main character's name, who shot whom, and so on) and partly so she can be sure that they actually did their homework. The children exchange papers and mark each other's answers. The teacher reads the question and calls on volunteers for the correct response. She encourages children to ask questions about the story, and she elicits conflicting opinions about the answers. She shrewdly works in literature concepts that she introduced several days before. She talks about plot, rising and falling action, foreshadowing. She summarizes the best discussion responses and settles disputes about answers. When they've finished, the teacher assigns the children to read the next story. Tomorrow there will be another quiz.

If we were to place school assignments on a continuum from the complex, meaningful, and intellectually challenging to the superficial, trivial, and fragmented, this story assignment would lean toward the latter.

Contrast it with the following scenario. The teacher took the class to the library. Once there, the children selected books from among many mystery stories that the librarian had pulled from the shelves. Each of the children read several stories—sometimes together with other children, sometimes alone. After a few days, the teacher asked the children to talk about the stories they read with small groups of their classmates. She asked them to pay particular attention to how the stories were alike and different. The groups made lists of some of the common elements in their stories. Each of the groups then shared its list with the other groups. The children discussed differences in their lists and tried to reach agreement about which elements were specific to mysteries and which they might find in all types of stories. At the end of these negotiations, each student wrote his or her own mystery story. The group helped revise all the stories. They wanted them to be ready for a public reading at the Mystery Festival the class produced for the students in the room next door.

Or consider this contrast. The math teacher explains to the class how to add feet and inches and demonstrates at the board. She then assigns a page of twenty practice problems ($6'\ 4'' + 2'\ 10'' = 9'\ 2''$). An alternative? Down the hall another math teacher follows her explanations by giving small groups of children rulers and building materials. She asks them to draw a plan and construct a class project. During the course of planning and constructing the children enthusiastically add and subtract feet and inches. This second lesson requires that the children understand *and use* measurement skills. It also allows the children to work with mathematical ideas in a practical context. The mathematician Alan H. Schoenfeld notes that in teaching such lessons, the teacher allows the children to become members of a "mathematical community." As members of that community, children see themselves as math-using specialists in a real and practical math-using world.

The second math assignment is also more concrete and hands-on. The first only allowed the children to deal with the abstractions of numbers on paper. The second lesson is not low-level (a common mistake observers often make when children are constructing things). Rather, it treats mathematical knowledge as far more complex and rich in meaning than the first. More children could succeed with this challenging lesson—constructing the building *and* adding feet and inches—than could succeed with the twenty drill-and-practice problems alone.

In chapter 4 we develop more fully the idea that teachers should expose children to complex knowledge in each subject area. Here, we want to stress that rich, complex knowledge is an essential component of multi-dimensional classrooms, classrooms where all children stand the best chance of learning very well. The presentation of knowledge as being rich and complex is quite different from what schools typically emphasize—knowledge divided into small, disconnected chunks of facts and skills. To summarize:

- Lessons based on complex knowledge treat thinking and learning as active, self-motivated processes. Such lessons are complex, interrelated, and social. They are contingent on knowledge connecting with the learners' individual styles, strengths, experiences, and beliefs.
- Lessons based on complex knowledge require children to confront life's real and complex problems—for example, finding and doing useful work, understanding one's culture and traditions, creating art, enjoying life with others.
- Lessons *not* based on complex knowledge disadvantage children in these ways:
  —They don't match the complexities of real life.
  —They're incompatible with cognitive learning processes.
  —They devalue working with others, since simple, short-range problems don't require complex interactions and alternate approaches.
  —They encourage comparisons among children: Who learns the most the fastest?
  —They discourage hard work and persistence by breaking difficult-to-learn knowledge into successively simpler pieces until children master it. Children who don't succeed at making sense out of fragmented knowledge may assume that they are less well suited for success than others and quit trying.

ACTIVE AND COOPERATIVE LESSONS: THE SOCIAL ORGANIZATION OF CLASSROOMS

Human beings are social. So the fact that learning is both an individual, mental process and an interactive, social one shouldn't surprise us. In chapter 2 we described how social factors influence children's learning. Here, we describe how social interactions in the classroom help determine how well children succeed at school.

Classroom social interactions extend beyond conversations among friends and acquaintances. They include all the ways children and the teacher relate to one another about academics, behavior, and social matters. Even when children are not talking or working together, they interact. They listen while one person in the class speaks; they observe; they make or avoid eye contact. Everyone in the room has a nearly constant awareness of the others.

Classroom interactions are rarely random. When children talk, whom they can sit near and talk to, and what they talk about follow highly organized routines. These routines shape the classroom's social organization. Classroom activities can connect children with one another or keep them apart by requiring them to work alone toward an individual objective. Activities determine whether children compete with one another for the best performance on the same tasks or work cooperatively toward a shared goal. Classroom organization can either provide children with a single route to success or allow them a variety of paths. It can ask them to take in knowledge passively or generate it actively. Taken together, classroom social interactions can allow children to take charge of their learning or make them feel as if they are always taking orders.

Organization that Can Inhibit Learning

In most classrooms, teachers try to avoid problems that might arise when children talk or work together. They strive for quiet classrooms and establish rules to govern relationships and manage the class efficiently. However, quiet classrooms are not free of influential interactions. Teachers talk to the whole class at once, and they walk around the room giving individual help. They call on students to read aloud to the class, answer questions, or write something on the board. Those students who are quick to catch on wave their hands eagerly and are noticed by everyone. Others sit quietly hoping that no one will notice them and that the teacher won't call on them. Often they feel embarrassed about their relative lack of knowledge or their shyness. Some create a ruckus to distract attention from the fact that they are unprepared. Some students, bored, lapse into daydreams. Most whisper among themselves whenever they have the chance.

Many classrooms fill entire days and years with such stifling interactions. The researchers Ernest Boyer, John Goodlad, and Theodore Sizer have found these patterns in classroom after classroom in schools across the nation. Only occasionally do classroom activities make it necessary or appropriate for children to talk and work together. And teachers consider much of that time as "free" or optional. Most important classwork gets done when children compete against one another or work alone.

Most students only occasionally get a chance to practice the interactions that can promote learning—articulating, explaining, offering reasons. The times when children do talk in class are likely to be performances. As performers, they are quickly judged by others right or wrong, smart or dumb. Some children cope in such environments by being quick to figure out the right answers and by gaining the status of being smart. However, few children, even the quickest ones, can use such classrooms to explore and make sense of new ideas and experiences. The risks of self-exposure are just too great to forget oneself and become immersed in the knowledge at hand.

The sociologists Elizabeth Cohen and Susan Rosenholtz call these classrooms *unidimensional* because they nearly always assign all children to the same task. They point out that when a single task dominates, children need to use only a limited number of skills to be successful. And because children differ in the skills in which they excel, such classes also limit opportunities for success. Further, a unidimensional structure robs children of the opportunity to make choices about what, how, and when they will do particular tasks. They lose that essential feeling of being in charge. Because of the high visibility of their successes and failures, children (and their teachers) may make global judgments about their competence, and these judgments easily translate into self-fulfilling prophecies.

Organization that Can Enhance Learning

We have far more confidence in *multidimensional* classrooms, which display a radically different social organization. Multidimensional classrooms provide a variety of learning tasks that require a broad range of skills. Students often cluster in small groups. They exchange ideas, work on separate but interrelated tasks, and help each other learn. Teacher talk does not dominate, and neither do whole-class sessions of questions and answers. Teachers in these classes function more like orchestra conductors than lecturers. They get things started and keep them moving along. They provide information and point to resources, attend to the social skills children need for learning (asking one another questions; offering help; not putting others down), and coordinate a diverse but harmonious buzz of activity.

Teachers in these classes pursue both the social and the educational advantages of children's talking and working together. Sharing, talking, and working with others are central to the lesson, not by-products or violations. As they work together, children can take charge of the assignment. They help divide up the lesson into tasks and decide how, when, and by whom each task will be done. Each child has an opportunity to make valuable contributions to classmates' work. Everyone can have his own work appreciated by others. Despite (or perhaps because of) all the interactions among children, any one student's strengths and weaknesses seldom become fodder for comparison or embarrassment. On the contrary, while working *with* others, children can safely watch and learn how others become successful. Not surprisingly, children in these kinds of classrooms learn more.

Productive Working Together

Considerable research documents the advantages that come when children work together. However, organizing children for productive group work presents difficulties since it's complicated and different from what most children, parents, and teachers expect. For four or five children to work together they need to cooperate, but most children, accustomed to competing against their classmates, have few skills for cooperation in classrooms.

To work with others productively, you can't keep your ideas a secret. You can't be wishing that your neighbor will fail so that your efforts will look better, and you can't insist on personal victories. You can't keep offering excuses if several others hold you accountable. You have to help others and be able to receive help from them. Moreover, you have to find value in what others offer and view your own success as interdependent with theirs. This means you have to experience some of the personal risks involved in sharing. Without doubt, you need the social skills to resolve the inevitable conflicts that occur.

Teachers cannot simply tell children to move their chairs and work together. They must gradually help students develop social skills, and they must design lessons carefully to take advantage of those skills. Absent these steps, group work may not be an improvement over working alone.

Cooperative Learning

Educational researchers have identified many of the academic and social conditions necessary for children to work together. They have developed strategies called "cooperative learning" that teachers are increasingly using in classrooms. Cooperative learning is strikingly consistent with the conditions that promote children's sense making.

Cooperative lessons offer a variety of tasks and paths to success. In this way, they accommodate students' differences. Such lessons are nearly impossible, however, unless the knowledge they contain is complex and rich in meaning. Productive cooperative groups must seek rewards from achieving a group goal—a goal that students cannot reach unless each group member does his own best work. Such lessons challenge better-skilled students more than competitive lessons do. Simply doing better than others no longer brings easy rewards. All students, regardless of skill level, are able to contribute in areas of their strength, and all can receive help in areas in which they do less well. In cooperative lessons, students have the opportunity to elaborate on the ideas that come easily to them. They can explain and demonstrate their knowledge to others, and they can ask specific questions when they don't understand. All these opportunities help children master difficult concepts.

When lessons include these opportunities, the commonly expressed fear that working with others will slow down the progress of better students is unwarranted. Even the strongest students make considerable intellectual gains when they work with children of all skill levels.

What might such a cooperative lesson look like? No single lesson can cover the entire range of possibilities, but a literature unit—briefly sketched here—illustrates some essentials. In a ninth-grade English class groups of four children had worked together for nearly ten weeks. They had practiced the necessary social skills: how to ask for help, give explanations, not dominate, not put down their classmates and others. While certain groups still had problems to work out, most had achieved easy familiarity. They behaved like any group of people who work together over time and experience successes. The teacher had balanced each group as far as possible, mixing students who differed in race, boys and girls, highly skilled and less skilled students. She mixed high-energy social students with shy, quiet ones.

The class read *To Kill a Mockingbird,* an engaging and intellectually demanding book. The novel includes themes of racism, justice, early education, one-parent families, small-town life, courage, sexism, maturation, assuming the perspectives of others, and more. Soon after the class started the novel, the special-education resource teacher (who had several students "mainstreamed" in the class) arranged a lunchtime showing of the movie adapted from the novel. Most students didn't want to give up their lunch periods, but several did—including all the special-education students. These children had an easier time reading the book after they had seen the movie. Furthermore, because they had an overview of the novel, they could make valuable contributions in their groups.

After reading about one-third of the book, each group member adopted a different character to follow. As they finished reading, the students wrote short compositions describing their characters and linking them to the book's themes. They took notes on their reading and exchanged ideas with "expert groups." That is, they conferred with their classmates from other groups who had chosen the same character. Although the students could get help and ideas from their classmates, the teacher held all students individually accountable for their brief composition.

The next part of this assignment emphasized group interdependence. That is, no student could successfully complete his own work without the participation and cooperation of his group mates. The children wrote a longer composition, "Exploring Themes in *To Kill a Mockingbird* through Four Characters." They used the short pieces that each of the four group members had written as source materials. In the longer assignment, the most skilled students found sophisticated differences and commonalities as they explored the characters and themes. They practiced research conventions by attributing ideas to their sources—quoting both from the novel and from their classmates. Less skilled students stretched beyond their first inclination to simply summarize their group's four papers. They attempted to do what their more highly skilled classmates did.

Throughout, the interaction was intense—questioning, explaining, arguing. The students had pragmatic reasons for engaging others and expecting good work from their fellow group members. As the individual compositions neared completion, the students grew increasingly interested in what their peers were writing. After all, their own ideas were being represented. It's hard to squelch your curiosity when you see your own name in the text or footnote!

When they had finished their compositions, each group wrote a skit loosely based on their characters. Each picked a common conflict at school that concerned them. The groups selected such problems as social cliques, dating, drug use, grade pressure, intimidation and violence, and parent–child trust. Then each student conjectured about how his or her character would fit into the school conflict. (The teacher permitted them to take liberties with the characters' age or gender.) Each student wrote the dialogue for his own character.

Finally, the groups performed the skits for the class. Because the skit had a group rather than an individual goal, the group shared a single grade. As with the compositions, each student achieved something by working with others that he would not have achieved working alone.

Certainly, there are times in class when it is most appropriate to take a test while sitting quietly and alone. There are times to listen to the teacher, especially one skilled at lecturing or telling an engaging story. There are times to watch a film. When writing a composition, students need some time to be alone with their thoughts. And teachers can be most effective when they teach some low-level skills to the class as a whole. Even so, children should not spend most of their time working alone. Working alone is especially counterproductive if lessons provide limited paths to success and set a single criterion for rewards.

Work in small cooperative groups won't solve all the problems that ail typical classes. Nonetheless, successful cooperative groups *enable* learning to take place while presenting the fewest limits to students and help assure many essential conditions for learning. They make it more likely that teachers and students will believe that all can succeed. They work best with rich and complex knowledge. Cooperative lessons provide multiple paths to success, and they promote evaluations that lead to more learning.

What about Individualization?

Teachers individualize instruction when they design a special program of study for each child in the class. The concept of individualized instruction became the rage in the 1960s and is still popular in some places. Individualized instruction sounds like the ideal arrangement for allowing students to maximize their learning. However, few classrooms ever reach complete individualization. Teachers find it virtually impossible to create a truly distinctive set of learning activities based on each student's needs.

In most individualized classrooms, children differ only in the pace at which they go through learning tasks. Most of these tasks come from commercially produced programs—perhaps a kit or, more recently, a computer program or, occasionally, instructions for a project. What nearly always happens with these programs is that slow students get slower. They become more and more distanced from those who race through. Skilled students may finish quickly, but often they don't spend the time to make sense of what they are studying. Few individualized programs engage students in rich and complex ideas. Perhaps the greatest drawback to individualized instruction is the tight control imposed by preplanned, sequenced tasks. Students almost never make choices or interact with each other in ways that enhance learning or promote positive social relationships.

PERSONALIZED EVALUATION

Children inevitably use classroom evaluations such as tests and grades as evidence of their own capability. In chapter 6 we discuss the technical side of evaluation and testing in greater detail. Here we consider the meaning adults and children give to classroom judgments about learning.

Public Judgments about Ability

Individual comparisons loom large in the school culture. Nearly every aspect of a child's academic and social behavior stands a chance of being evaluated, counted, and ranked. As we noted earlier, many classrooms make evidence of children's capability a matter of public record. Children's performances are highly visible, and so are the good/bad judgments about their performances. Easy comparisons encourage children to judge their own knowledge and skills against those of their peers. As that happens, the risks are high that some capable students who are making a good effort will judge themselves too harshly if they think they are below average or not the very best. Others may be too generous to themselves. They may reason that they learned as much as they needed to because their scores were better or even the same as those of their classmates.

How are judgments made public? Teachers post grades and other symbols of students' progress: letters, numbers, stars, smiley faces, racehorses, and halos, along with sad faces and zeros. Teachers sometimes read scores aloud or permit students to return graded papers to their classmates. Results of aptitude, achievement, and other standardized tests become public when students or their parents share scores voluntarily. Teachers also routinely display student work on the bulletin board. Most often, teachers mean well and make an effort to show the best examples. Some may display good work to motivate other children. And by keeping poor assignments off the bulletin board, some hope to protect the child whose flawed work might embarrass him. Display only the best examples? Display all examples, including the best and worst so everyone can know and compare who are the best and worst students? Display no work at all? None of these choices is completely satisfactory, since the issue goes far beyond showing examples of student work.

Teachers seldom consider privacy because it is so contrary to the school and classroom cultures. Indeed, comparisons are an integral part of lesson design, instruction, grading, and the thinking of adults and children.

We would be foolish to presume that teachers can easily avoid comparisons and their bad effects. Furthermore, most students expect these public routines. Consequently, protests about the public nature of student evaluations run the risk of increasing public attention to the complainer.

Grades and other written evidence of evaluations are not the only fodder for public comparisons. There are countless informal but equally public opportunities to form judgments. The teacher's approving tone of voice, her condescension, or subtle gradations in her level of enthusiasm send clear evaluation messages. Classmates act out and reinforce evaluations. In competitive classroom games, children are spontaneous and obvious in their approval of some children and disdain for others. Children scramble for seats next to the best students or next to the class clown. They often conspicuously avoid other children.

Children advertise their own scores and thereby reinforce their status. Some children cope with low scores while preserving the appearance of dignity by communicating that they don't care. They are likely to exclaim, "Hah! I got three out of ten!" as others are to tell their neighbors that they got 100 percent. Being disruptive, not studying, and getting additional poor grades provide evidence of not caring. All are a defense against being judged not smart. To put forth great effort and get a (comparatively) low grade is too humiliating for many children to risk. Some reason that it's better to put forth very little effort and in that way preserve the possibility that they could rank among the best if they wanted to.

Parents and teachers often argue that grades, comparisons with others, and teachers' judgments will spur students to do better. However, psychologists increasingly find that these strategies don't consistently motivate children in positive ways. Children accomplish more when judgments of their work don't distract them. Over the long term, classroom rewards and punishment often have the opposite of their intended effect, and they can actually decrease achievement-related behaviors. The psychologist Deborah Stipek concludes, "It is not the reinforcement per se that influences children's behavior in achievement settings. Rather, children's cognitions, beliefs, and values determine their behavior."

Summing up Ability

Grades quickly translate into global judgments about students. Even for such complex work as reports or essays, the single letter sums up its worth. If positive comments acknowledge strengths of the work, others rarely see them. Even the writer herself may remember the A or C long after she has forgotten the comments and perhaps the assignment itself.

A glance at the grades, points, and stars posted on the wall immediately tells who is the top student and who is not. In the world of these evaluative symbols, students increasingly sum up their own ability. We are less likely to hear a third grader say, "I know five stories" or "I choose books by myself" than "I got a C in reading." This makes sense to her because people use grades to form impressions of her ability. After she accumulates enough C's (it may not take many), a consensus develops. C becomes a rank and description of the student herself. Getting C's in the future makes as much sense as learning stories, making active choices, or even enjoying reading.

Hard Work—Why Bother?

When adults at school emphasize grades and other external judgments of learning (particularly in classrooms that feature single tasks), they contribute greatly to children's beliefs that their success or failure is caused by people or conditions beyond their control. They may say, "She is a hard grader" (The teacher is responsible) or "The rest of the class is too smart" (Bad luck. The smartest students have used up the limited number of top grades). We believe these attributions set the child on a downward rather than upward cycle of achievement. Feeling less control, the child exerts less effort, accomplishes less, gets a comparatively lower grade. He soon believes that he is less capable. All reinforce his lower status and lower self-esteem. At this sad juncture, who could bear to feel the awful responsibility for being less good or capable than one's peers? The worst of all self-fulfilling prophecies comes true: The child becomes incapable because nothing that he might do to succeed makes sense to him.

Children work harder when hard work makes sense. That happens in classrooms with obvious connections between effort and results. When that C reader learns that knowing stories, making choices, and enjoying reading are what matter the most, he will probably put forth quite a lot of effort to continue developing as a reader. If he learns instead that an *A* matters most, he may never accomplish what adults and peers all recognize as the most important goal. The importance of the *A* is a hard lesson to escape. Simply telling children "It's not the grade that matters most" rarely convinces anyone.

Perhaps if everyone who worked hard could get a "top" grade, grades might not be so counterproductive. Hard work could still pay off for everyone. However, grades are hierarchical. For top grades to have meaning, there must be lower grades. Children learn their usual grade and put forth the effort required to maintain that level of performance. Even the highest achievers may adopt a needlessly low estimate of what they can accomplish if they find it too easy to get a top grade.

Children increasingly move from specific to global self-judgments as they progress through school. Young children link their success more closely with their effort. The young child who does poorly on his addition problems may feel as smart as his more successful classmates. He will say, "I could have done better, I just didn't try." And young children attribute their performance to more specific, limited reasons, such as "I remembered the answers," "The teacher likes me," "Billy made me do it." On the other hand, older students more often attribute their success or failure to global, abstract, and probably permanent conditions: "I'm not good in math," "I'm not the type for college," "I'm smart."

Evaluations that Support Learning

We think children learn best when they participate in their own evaluation. Children participate when they check their own understanding and when they ask for and provide feedback to one another. Teachers who engage students in these activities don't give up their own evaluation responsibilities. However, they too must focus on the specific knowledge and skills that children learn. They must make assessments like "He understands division of fractions" and "She remembers details in reading but could benefit from discussion of themes." Such teachers shy away from global judgments (for example, "good in math," "B− in reading") because these judgments provide little guidance for deciding what specific teaching should follow. Moreover, they easily and often permanently transfer to children.

Evaluations that are fair and support learning can occur most easily when teachers design multiple tasks that offer children a variety of routes to success, and grades work best when teachers keep them as private as possible. Under these conditions, teachers exhibit a sensitivity to the ways even the most subtle, informal judgments stick like glue to the recipients. Multiple paths to success and private grades help prevent evaluation from becoming the raw material for classroom judgments about who is smart and who isn't.

Why, in spite of sound research evidence, do schools continue to evaluate in traditional ways? Beliefs that traditional practices help children learn, lack of familiarity with alternatives, and fear of changing the status quo all come into play. They are a central part of the school culture.

In this chapter we have identified five important characteristics of classrooms that shape the quality of teaching and learning in them. We have emphasized the power of teachers' beliefs about children's capability and the degree to which classrooms foster childrens' beliefs in their own competence and their willingness to work hard. We have stressed the importance of the knowledge teachers expect children to learn; the classroom's social organization; and the ways teachers evaluate.

These dimensions matter as much or more than any specific classroom design, curriculum, individual lesson, theories, materials, or elaborate school programs. How teachers act on them profoundly influences children's willingness and ability to apply their natural learning processes to formal school learning. Through these dimensions of classroom life children conclude that they can move smoothly toward success—actually creating their own options and paths—or that they must be tentative about taking risks and that they are not likely to succeed.

FOR FURTHER READING

Elliot Aaronson, *The Jigsaw Classroom.* Beverly Hills, CA: Sage Publications, 1978.

Albert Bandura, *Social Learning Theory.* Englewood Cliffs: Prentice-Hall, 1977.

Steven T. Bossert, *Tasks and Social Relationships in Classrooms: A Study of Classroom Organization and Its Consequences.* New York: Cambridge University Press, 1979.

Elizabeth Cohen, *Designing Groupwork: Strategies for the Heterogeneous Classroom.* New York: Teachers' College Press, 1987.

———, "On the Sociology of the Classroom." In J. Hannaway and M. E. Lockeed (eds.), *The Contributions of the Social Sciences to Educational Policy and Practice: 1965–1985.* Berkeley, CA: McCutchan, 1986.

Robert Glaser, "Teaching Expert Novices," *Educational Researcher* 16 (December 1987): 13–19.

David Johnson and Roger Johnson, *Learning Together and Alone.* Englewood Cliffs: Prentice-Hall, 1978.

Lauren Resnick, "Learning In School and Out," *Educational Researcher* 16 (December 1987): 13–19.

———, *Education and Learning to Think.* Washington, DC: National Academy Press, 1987.

Susan Rosenholtz and Elizabeth Cohen, "Status in the Eye of the Beholder." In

J. Berger and M. Zelditch, Jr. (eds.), *Status, Rewards, and Influence*. San Francisco: Jossey Bass, 1985.

Kenneth A. Sirotnik, "What You See Is What You Get: Consistency, Persistency, and Mediocrity in Classrooms," *Harvard Educational Review* 53 (1983): 16–31.

Robert Slavin, *Cooperative Learning in Student Teams: What Research Says to the Teacher*. Washington, DC: National Education Association. Rev. ed., 1985.

Robert Sternberg, "Teaching Critical Thinking," *Phi Delta Kappa* 67 (1985).

Deborah Stipek, "Children's Motivation to Learn." In Tommy M. Tomlinson and Herbert J. Walberg (eds.), *Academic Work and Educational Excellence*. Berkeley, CA: McCutchan, 1986.

Roland G. Tharp and Ronald G. Gallimore, *Rousing Minds to Life*. New York: Cambridge University Press, 1989.

Noreen Webb, "Interaction and Learning in Small Groups," *The Review of Educational Research* 52 (1982): 421–45.

CHAPTER FOUR

What Children Should Learn: The Academics

Sometimes schools act as if children are empty vessels. Fill them up with knowledge and let them store it until they need it. But learning requires using knowledge, not simply filing it away for some intellectual rainy day. Children do their best school learning when they use new knowledge to solve real problems. Few children care about or truly benefit from exercises like "What's 5 times 8?" Such abstract questions keep new learning disconnected from anything else children know or have experienced. And few children learn well from phony school assignments that place little value on the knowledge itself, such as "Answer questions 1–5 at the end of the story or you will have *problems* when you take the test." Such assignments emphasize avoiding trouble, not learning valuable knowledge. Yet empty-vessel theories, disconnected exercises, and misplaced motivation shape the form and content of much school curriculum. We think schools can do better.

COGNITIONS, CULTURE, AND CURRICULUM

Our convictions about schools, learning, and classrooms also apply to the school curriculum. First, a cognitive rather than a behavioral view of learning should guide the way schools organize and present knowledge. Schools and teachers should not exclusively view subject matter as an end in itself. Rather, subject matter can be the raw material for children's mental activity. Mental activity, rather than the aggregation of facts, enables children to turn their school experiences into knowledge they can remember and use.

We also prefer that teachers present knowledge in multidimensional classrooms. Multidimensional classrooms acknowledge that there are many legitimate ways for children to learn. We favor classrooms in which teachers connect children and knowledge cooperatively rather than in competition with one another. We prefer private, individualized evaluation over public, standardized assessments of children's learning. Finally, we prefer teachers who believe that all children, rather than just a few, can achieve the truly important knowledge that is taught. These conditions press schools to give all children access to highly valued knowledge. They discourage alternatives to high achievement.

We refer to a curriculum that helps all children make sense of their experiences as a *curriculum rich in meaning*. That is our shorthand expression for lessons that are concept- and theme-based and much more. This curriculum emphasizes knowledge worth taking time to probe and explore—perhaps a week, a month, or longer.

A curriculum rich in meaning encompasses the knowledge and skills that our society values the most. Most critics, philosophers, scholars, and parents agree on what to include: the books, ideas, events, and people who shape the diversity and commonalities of the world's cultures and our own. It is a curriculum of rigorous, high-level mathematics and science. It combines vocations and scholarship—the domains of the hands and the head. It helps keep children in charge with executive control over learning rather than simply following orders and grinding out the work.

As prior chapters make clear, the school and classroom features we prefer are not the norm. And neither is the curriculum we would like to see. How could it be? The conventional curriculum supports and reaffirms a behavioral view of learning. The typical curriculum conforms to school cultures firmly rooted in turn-of-the-century notions of social efficiency. It meshes with the widespread belief in large, unchangeable differences in learning ability.

So, most schools construct curriculum out of the facts and responses (both social and academic) we expect children to master. Brim-full of stock learning objectives, the curriculum tries to cover all the bits and pieces of information that supposedly add up to an education. To do so, curriculum designers arrange knowledge into tightly organized and sequential lessons. They emphasize knowledge that children can learn by working alone on simple tasks. And they stress knowledge that teachers and policymakers can measure by objective tests. Moreover, schools parcel out the curriculum according to children's age and adults' estimates of their ability. Schools distribute knowledge according to these widely held views about individual learning differences: Only a few children can handle the most complex ideas; many can master more watered-down versions; and others can learn only the simplest topics and skills. As a result, it is nearly impossible to find a curriculum aimed at producing a whole school of high achievers. Except for a few minor alterations, this concept of curriculum hasn't changed much during this century.

In this chapter we describe the typical curriculum in academic subjects. We then contrast it with the rich, meaningful curriculum we believe provides all children with access to the knowledge that educators, policymakers, and parents value most. In the next chapter we turn to school subjects that are not, in a traditional sense, academic: art, health, and physical and vocational education.

KNOWLEDGE THAT FITS TRADITION: THE TYPICAL SCHOOL CURRICULUM

The school curriculum includes the knowledge that society agrees children should learn at school. Parents and policymakers can find the details in course descriptions, curriculum guides, textbooks, and teachers' lesson plans. Rather than list them all here, we describe and critique the general curricular patterns found at most schools. As we do, we will note some essential elements of the academic subjects that schools often overlook. These elements form the core of a different, much less commonly offered curriculum.

The typical school curriculum coexists with (if not matches) the cultures of the community, school, and classroom. Think about those brightly painted dolls that come apart at the middle to reveal another nearly identical but slightly smaller doll inside. Inside that doll another is nested, and that one too opens to reveal another. In a way, schooling is like those dolls. The history of our civilization, our cultural definitions of an educated person, our national traditions provide the largest context for schools and curriculum. Within that is the similar, matching world of the school culture. Here policymakers, administrators, teachers, and parents reenact broad social values and habits through each child's school experience. Finally, the classroom appears at the very center, where we find teachers teaching and children learning the curriculum. What happens in classes must be compatible with the school and societal contexts. As we puzzle over the curriculum, we must be mindful of how these contexts compose the status quo that contains the curriculum and resists its change.

Traditional Curriculum Hallmarks: Behavioral Objectives, Prescribed Experiences, Observable Results

Adults don't usually view children as their own meaning-makers. More often, as we remarked earlier, they see children as something like sponges who should sop up knowledge quickly and efficiently. Consequently, schools keep the curriculum standardized and sequential. Usually schools express curriculum purposes through behavioral objectives. First, they state what children will be able to do. Next they design activities to bring about those behaviors. And then they observe or test the children. If children pass the test, schools infer that they have learned.

Much about this approach is satisfying. It explains learning by means of a tidy cause-and-effect equation. The effects are behaviors, which are, by definition, observable and measurable. This view of learning and treatment of knowledge fits the schools' and society's notion of how to educate large numbers of children efficiently. Aptitude, achievement, and classroom tests produce an abundance of numbers for educators and parents to use in ranking, sorting, and measuring children's learning. In the process they define learning as behaving correctly—getting the right answer.

For the sake of efficiency, typical curricula emphasize basic skills and facts—since these are the smallest possible teachable and testable units. Schools teach knowledge in prescribed sequences conforming to traditional subjects and grades. We see these elements of the school culture at work in the rigid adherence to phonics-based reading programs. We find them in geography lessons that teach map-reading and have children memorize terms and locate geographical features but fall short of helping children know why this information matters.

The desire for coverage also presses toward teaching small chunks of low-level information. Teachers, parents, and policymakers hate to leave anything out. In history, for example, new editions of textbooks often add recent events to an already crowded curriculum. Unable to teach it all, some schools still end American history at World War II. Even so, important concepts are strangled by details.

The typical school curriculum nearly always favors learning about over learning to do. Children learn *about* when they read a chapter in a history book without identifying themes that bridge the years and help children explain the conditions in their world or community. They learn *about* writing with prescribed paragraphs and grammar lessons instead of writing for the school paper, composing poems, or writing lab reports in science. Learning about something is quieter, seems more efficient, and is easier to test and measure than actually doing it. Learning about is also a throwback to earlier times, when education was an alternative to manual labor. Then, educated people were thought to work with their heads, not their hands. Today, our growing understanding of cognition and the changed nature of work challenges that separation of physical and mental work. Nonetheless, a classroom of children studying alone and silently is more seemly to many than one resembling a noisy, bustling workplace.

This separation between acquiring knowledge and using knowledge dictates that schools teach small facts and skills rather than large concepts. It causes children to be engaged in passive, low-level thinking rather than high-level thinking. The separation promotes superficial coverage of a wide array of topics and skills over a deep understanding of fewer, more central ideas. The typical curriculum bears little resemblance to the spontaneous, high-energy experience-gathering and problem-solving that children do so naturally. It is quite unlike the real, problem-solving worlds of managing households, succeeding in the workplace, and making democratic decisions.

Finally, children learn from the form as well as the content of this traditional curriculum. Often they learn lessons that adults do not intend or that are unrelated to what we usually associate with an education. In typical schools children learn that teachers and other authorities are in charge of knowledge. They learn that people are supposed to work and learn alone. Nearly every child learns that the most important knowledge comes in the form of right answers—the simpler the better. And they learn that even right answers don't mean much if they're not asked for on the test. Many learn that it sometimes pays to cheat. Some learn that working hard is not worth the effort. This is just a smattering of the unintended lessons children learn year after year from the structure of the curriculum.

Some Familiar Examples

Reading and Language Schools focus much of their energy on teaching children to read, write, and speak correctly. Reading skills, in particular, capture a giant share of the elementary curriculum. John Goodlad's study, for example, found that many first and second graders spend up to ninety minutes a day learning to read. A large portion of this time is spent learning to decode letters, combinations of letters, and whole words. Children work their way through progressively more difficult readers that teach them these discrete reading skills. Workbooks that match their texts give them extensive opportunities to practice each new skill.

Many basal-reader lessons focus on phonics. They use children's mastery of decoding skills as the basis for deciding when they are ready for the next lesson. Given this phonics emphasis, children learn the rules (and many exceptions) that govern how letters and combinations of letters translate into sounds. They move from recognizing beginning consonants, to consonant blends, to the many different vowel sounds, to practicing how to read inexplicable words like *cough* and *height*. They develop skill at sounding out words. Children who catch on quickly move into new books and higher reading groups. Children who learn to decode less easily continue to practice these skills in lower reading groups.

Phonics-based readers fit nicely with the cultural traditions of schooling. They offer a sequence of skills in standardized lessons for children to work on alone. They teach skills that are easy to measure. Graded basal readers work well for children who learn reading skills easily and at the teacher's or book publisher's chosen pace. However, they may be of little value to children who already have a skill or gain it quickly. Moreover, an inflexible reading curriculum may cause serious difficulties for children who don't learn prescribed sets of skills easily or on time. If teachers delay reading and *thinking* about stories until children master specific decoding skills, the reading method can become a reading barrier.

Perhaps as serious, far too many elementary children who master decoding skills still don't like to read. A look at the basal readers used by many schools (and especially at the workbooks that accompany them) can explain why. Some of the stories are imaginative, but most are devoid of meaning. Others use a litany of simple words (controlled vocabulary) that they substitute for the rich vocabulary found in the original versions of high-quality stories. Often reading selections don't begin to tap children's understanding of words, language structure, and experience. No wonder so many children think of reading as being tedious and don't associate it with excitement, knowledge, mystery, and escape from drudgery.

Recently, Claude Goldenberg, a researcher at the University of California, Los Angeles, studied a group of first-grade children as they learned to read in conventional ways. Many did fine, but some had experiences so distressing that their teachers predicted that they were unlikely ever to catch up with the others. For example, a few children had difficulty remembering and distinguishing among the consonants *d, p, b*. They spent nearly the entire school year studying, doing exercises on, and playing games with these few letters. As a result they missed real reading entirely—hearing and reading fewer stories than their classmates. They fell further and further behind their classmates, not only in decoding skills, but also in vocabulary development and comprehension. Perhaps most important, while other children were developing their self-concepts as readers, these children began to see themselves as nonreaders. By the end of the year, most were reading failures; some had to repeat first grade.

We don't blame phonics for this failure, since all children must learn to decode letters and words. Rather, we must look to the adults who slavishly adhered to a single method that didn't work for some children. When it was clear that the method wasn't working, what did the children get? More of the same.

Even a new generation of enlightened reading textbooks may do little to help children make sense of what they read. Many programs claim to go beyond decoding. They do a better job of teaching comprehension, critical thinking, and higher level skills. Nevertheless, not only do school textbooks hamper children's learning, many teachers' own thinking is bound by traditional reading approaches. Too many teachers, by their own design and even with quality texts, still ask children to look at isolated facts and to make only superficial inquiries into what their reading means.

The discovery of personal meanings in literature makes reading both pleasurable and educative. Yet many reading programs relegate children's personal involvement with their reading to enrichment rather than keep it at the very core of the lesson. Those children that schools encourage most to become personally involved with their reading are likely to be good readers already.

In later grades, children spend increasing school time on discrete language skills in addition to reading. They learn to spell, divide words into syllables, alphabetize, capitalize, punctuate, recognize synonyms, homonyms, and antonyms. And they try to master formal usage conventions (for example, saying "aren't" instead of "ain't" and "we were going" instead of "we was going"). Children learn to identify parts of speech. Sometimes they diagram sentences.

Elementary school children also write paragraphs, book reports, stories, and poems. However, these activities usually take a back seat to basic reading, grammar, and spelling skills. In middle school and junior high, the typical language-arts curriculum continues to emphasize spelling, vocabulary, capitalization, punctuation, usage, and grammar. Writing lessons focus on correct sentences and paragraphs and less often on reports.

In senior high the emphasis on language mechanics continues. Students in slow classes do many drills on decoding, spelling, capitalization, punctuation, conventional usage, writing simple paragraphs, and other basics. Learning kits, workbooks, and worksheets continue to be their learning tools. Few schools expect students who are not bound for college to read challenging, valued literature. Sometimes teachers justify the reading of popular magazines or comic books by saying, "At least they're reading."

College-bound students encounter increasingly long and difficult lists of vocabulary words. Their learning of the mechanics of paragraph writing leads to the mastering of conventional longer writing forms (the five-paragraph essay and the research paper). The stories, poems, and novels they read become increasingly complex. The literary devices they learn to identify (for example, irony, foreshadowing, metaphor) are more subtle. Most of these students get a taste of classic and modern writers: Shakespeare, Dickens, Ralph Waldo Emerson, Emily Dickinson, John Steinbeck, Ernest Hemingway. Teachers often consign works published since the 1960s to supplemental reading lists.

To learn to read and write well, children must, more than anything else, read and write. Ironically, some schools keep children busy filling out worksheets, circling the correct answers, looking up the answers to questions at the end of a story, and memorizing spelling and vocabulary lists. These children spend far too little time actually reading and writing.

A narrow focus on the mechanics of reading, writing, and speaking correctly may cause children to miss the essence of language—expressing and understanding ideas. Even the most skilled students often miss the central purpose of writing: to enable others to understand something important to the writer. Large numbers of high school graduates arrive at college knowing the parts of speech and how to write essays according to prescribed models but may have missed the opportunity to take themselves seriously as writers. Many write well-organized and correctly spelled, punctuated, and capitalized essays but at the same time view writing as a product to be judged rather than a process of developing and sharing ideas. Furthermore, this narrow focus is no guarantee that children will, as some apologists claim, organize, spell, and punctuate well. That so many children have poor mechanical skills is an indictment of the narrow focus, not a call for more of the same.

Mathematics Arithmetic places a close second in the essential knowledge and skills we expect children to learn. Next to reading and writing, math takes up the largest part of the elementary school day. Middle schools and junior and senior high schools require some math of everyone.

Like the teaching of reading and writing, math instruction in elementary school is heavily weighted with basic skills. The mathematics curriculum favors small units of seemingly unrelated knowledge. Typically, math classes emphasize memorizing and following formulas. They engage children in passive paper-and-pencil tasks. Activities and projects that bring to life the ideas and processes of mathematics are scarce. Schools teach children numbers and how to add, subtract, multiply, and divide. By the end of elementary school, they should also know how to compute fractions, decimals, and percentages. These skills *are* the elementary mathematics curriculum in most schools.

For most, junior high school math reviews these basic operations. Children placed in advanced junior high math classes may begin algebra in the seventh or eighth grade. Most don't encounter it until grade 9. Beginning in junior high and continuing into high school, mathematics learning diverges dramatically for different students. Those who catch on to basic math skills move into the sequence of algebra, geometry, and a second year of algebra. The best math students take courses in trigonometry and a very few, calculus. Those who don't catch on take general or consumer math classes. Here, students continue to review the basic math skills of elementary school. They may also study consumer skills such as writing checks and figuring interest rates.

The mathematics curriculum is nearly the same in most schools. Nearly everywhere, the textbook determines what children will learn and how they will learn it. Young and older children do math worksheets and problems from their books. Often slower children are made to repeat skills over and over in the hope that they will at last catch on. Too often that never happens.

Like the importance given the mechanics of learning to spell and sound out words, that given the computing of sums, remainders, products, quotients, decimals, percentages, and fractions goes without question. Even so, these basic skills are a part of—not a prerequisite to—learning essential mathematics concepts. Especially because of the availability of inexpensive calculators, poor paper-and-pencil facility with computations need not be a barrier to further math instruction.

Most mathematicians disagree with the way schools focus children exclusively on performing calculations, solving equations, and doing geometric proofs. They believe children need a steady emphasis on understanding the ideas that ground these computations. For example, Alan Schoenfeld at the University of California, Berkeley, laments that children come to see mathematics as little more than sets of rules. As a result, many children—even those whom the school judges to be successful—

doubt that they will ever master mathematics. They do not consider math a logical intellectual tool. And they have few opportunities to apply mathematical principles to real-life problems.

In one of his studies, Schoenfeld found that even bright geometry students in a well-respected school had little understanding of what they were learning. They performed well on tests only if the tests asked them to do isolated proofs. When they tried to apply proofs to constructing a circle, most of the students violated the very principles they had memorized. A narrow approach—remembering and following math rules—makes mathematics a pointless abstraction even for the quickest students.

Further, when children memorize math procedures without understanding what they mean, they often learn incorrect procedures. John Seely Brown and Richard Burton, researchers for the Xerox Corporation, call these errors bugs. Bugs are like faulty instructions in computer programs. Children who don't understand what mathematics procedures accomplish can't make sense of their mistakes, even when teachers point them out. The children keep repeating the same errors. Brown and Burton found that some children who memorize subtraction rules but never make real sense of them always subtract a smaller digit from a larger one, regardless of the problem. For example, on the problem "Subtract 9 from 11," the child may see a one and a nine and be able to come up with nothing other than 8. No other answer makes sense if he has not mastered the subtraction concept.

Viewing his own studies in the light of Brown and Burton's research, Schoenfeld claims that the conventional mathematics curriculum leads children to draw the following conclusions:

- Math procedures have little to do with solving real problems.
- If you know what you're doing, math problems can be solved in five minutes or less.
- Discovery, creativity, and understanding in mathematics are possible only for geniuses.

In the typical math curriculum, students may learn many essential math rules, they may cover all the traditional math topics, and they may perform well on mathematics tests but may not be able to making meaning of mathematics or apply mathematics principles outside their classrooms.

Science As in mathematics, textbooks drive the science curriculum in many schools. And, as with most academic subjects, textbooks are better suited for covering large numbers of topics and facts than for developing problem-solving skills. In science we find an ever-present curriculum battle between covering a wide range of topics and going into a few in depth. Scientists increasingly assert that less is more. That is, students learn more science principles from in-depth study of fewer topics. Yet, textbook publishers must compete for the approval of teachers and school boards who want all the familiar topics included along with the newest ones. Once topics are in the text, curriculum guides pressure teachers to cover them all. So most students get a taste of many science topics without stopping long enough to get a confident understanding of science principles.

For example, nearly all textbooks present the steps of the scientific method. Yet, few students have a chance to apply principles of scientific inquiry to real situations. As a result, few students understand that the scientific method is a *model* of what many scientists do—not a list of rules they must follow. No wonder so many real scientists shake their heads in dismay at school science.

Often science activities in the early grades focus more on making something fun happen than on having fun by making scientific observations and judgments. We know one teacher who likes to have science on Friday afternoons. He has a bag of science tricks that keeps children entertained at the end of the long week. One afternoon, for example, he had the children make soda pop in the classroom. The children loved it, but we worry that they learned little science. The teacher asked few questions and provoked little discussion of what had happened. We suspect the children saw the fizzy drink as something produced by magic without understanding what happened or why.

When older students do science experiments, they often follow prescribed routines and try to reproduce expected results. Their task is clear: get the results the teacher or lab manual is looking for. Sometimes children's dexterity in handling equipment, their reading skills, and their speed count more than understanding the idea behind the experiment. This cookbook approach to science bears little resemblance to the process scientists follow in the laboratory.

Perhaps the most serious problem with science is that schools don't teach enough of it. Recently, a National Science Foundation survey found that children in grades K–3 averaged only one and a half hours a week learning science. Children in grades 4–6 spent less than three hours a week. Part of the problem is that many elementary teachers have little more scientific knowledge than the general public, and they feel uncomfortable teaching science. Moreover, science rarely shows up on tests that

measure children's basic skills, which partly explains why it often receives much less attention than reading and math. Some elementary
teachers don't teach science at all. Some schools bring in science specialists for occasional science lessons. Specialists' lessons may be excellent, but even the best visiting lessons may give children the impression
that science is beyond the grasp of ordinary teachers and children. Also,
children's regular teachers are more likely to overlook unplanned opportunities for daily reinforcement of science principles if they do not participate in planning and teaching the science lessons.

Some secondary schools don't devote much time or resources to science either. In many junior highs, students can take science for only one
semester. Many senior highs require only one science class for those not
planning on attending college. Despite concern about our nation's increasing need for scientific workers, serious attention to science has not yet
made its way into schools.

Having little time and few resources, skilled science teachers cannot
fully develop their science programs. They, along with less skilled teachers, often resort to science shortcuts. Often they simply tell children
about science rather than let them do science. When this happens, science
often boils down to memorizing names and facts.

History and Social Studies Originally, schools taught social
studies so that children would be good citizens. As far back as the 1830s,
Americans thought social studies was particularly important for teaching
immigrants American ways. Today, too, we expect the study of history,
economics, and government to help students become responsible, law-
abiding, and knowledgeable political decision-makers.

Typically, elementary schools teach social studies units such as The
Founding Fathers or The Westward Movement. Junior high schoolers may
take classes in geography, American history, and government. Nearly all
senior high students take American history and government courses.
Many take elective courses in psychology, world history, economics, sociology, and law.

To some critics, the very term *social studies* implies a soft and relative
approach to knowledge. They would prefer students to focus on a body of
enduring historical facts—what they see as the building blocks of cultural
literacy. They prefer direct instruction of these facts in the traditional disciplines of history, geography, government (civics), and so on. And they
are critical of schools that focus on current values and issues while ne-

glecting historic events. They advocate a social studies curriculum that stresses how American leaders and heroes used solid values and courage to shape this country. Some, like the researchers Diane Ravitch and Chester Finn, voice concern that essential historical content is no longer preeminent in the curriculum. They suggest that emphasis on process, attention to the present rather than the past, and concern for teaching methods have overshadowed traditional history content.

Other, more progressive educators want children to study ideas about people and society that cut across the social science disciplines. For example, Ernest Boyer, president of the Carnegie Foundation for the Advancement of Teaching, recommends that "students go beyond a study of the disciplines to develop an understanding of human commonalities." Scholars like Boyer prefer a social studies curriculum that teaches about the diversity and similarities among the world's people—that helps students "place the human story in larger context." They also favor giving greater attention to the role of women and minorities and to a variety of interpretations and points of view about human events.

Advocates on both sides believe that their approach helps children develop the values and examples they need to be responsible adults. The first group can get very upset if they think social studies teachers unduly emphasize other cultures or values (for example, in units that present a global perspective). Some believe schools spend too much time discussing current issues. They worry that social studies education is morally flabby and prefer that teachers teach values as absolutes—not as issues for students to explore, discover, or clarify. The second group can get incensed if they think schools present American culture as superior or flawless. This group worries that facts of the past substitute for the issues of the day. They think that schools have an important activist role in challenging and improving society. Above all, they decry schools that are neutral or objective places, disconnected from the problems and passions of the real world.

Too often, however, schools serve the goals of both camps poorly. In most elementary and secondary schools the social studies curriculum includes a grab bag of ideas and subjects: history, economics, geography, government, anthropology, psychology, and sociology. And once again, bits and pieces, memorizing of facts and dates, and focus on the trivial characterize much instruction. Teachers and textbooks "tell about" rather than challenge children to use the knowledge they encounter. "Read the chapter and answer the questions at the end" is a common assignment to

fill students' learning time. Most social studies tests ask children to recognize true and false statements, select the right answer to multiple-
choice questions, match up the right names, dates, and places, and fill in
blanks with short answers.

   Foreign Language Of all the academic subjects, foreign languages occupy the smallest portion of the school curriculum. Few elementary schools offer any foreign language. The Goodlad study found
that only 4 percent of senior high teachers and 2 percent of those at junior
highs teach foreign language. Not surprisingly, many characteristics of
other subjects apply to the foreign language curriculum. Textbook exercises, worksheets, and tests emphasize recalling specific information, recognizing words and phrases, and taking dictation. Some foreign language
teachers, perhaps more than other teachers, engage students in doing their
subject. Students often carry on simple conversations in order to gain fluency. However, teachers and textbooks often tightly control these dia-
logues. The curriculum is often strictly paced with fixed sequences of
lessons and leaves little room for students to make their own meanings out
of their experiences with the language. In some ways, the foreign language curriculum is even less creative than other subjects. Students write
little original material and work on few projects of their own design.
   The substantial increase recently in students whose command of English is limited has not dented traditional approaches to foreign language
instruction. In fact, because schools consider foreign language as college-
preparatory coursework, few recent immigrants take these courses. This
is true even of those immigrants who speak Spanish, the most commonly
taught foreign language.
   Sadly, students' gains from studying a foreign language are often minimal. Students fulfill college-entrance requirements. They may gain a hint
of cross-cultural understanding. But most will have only a fragmented,
relatively useless knowledge of the language they studied. Many students
leave high school with a nagging sense that fluency in a foreign language
is an unattainable goal.

KNOWLEDGE RICH IN MEANING: A MORE
PROMISING CURRICULUM

   Very likely, you experienced a curriculum similar to that described above. And since you probably did at least "well enough," you
may wonder what else the curriculum might be. Haven't we described the

basic competencies required to become an educated adult? Our answer is yes and no. Certainly, we all need to be able to read, write, and compute. And we all need to know basic historical and scientific facts if we are to participate intelligently in adult society. Nevertheless, the commonplace curriculum may deny children opportunities to develop fully their ability to *make meaning* of these essential learnings even if they did learn all the facts—an unlikely event. In fact, most people do not feel that the school curriculum is good enough.

We believe that parents, policymakers, and schools need to look at how children learn naturally. The next step is to establish classroom conditions that support that learning. This view will lead to lessons built on knowledge that is important, challenging, complex, related to real life, and rich in meaning. Furthermore, curricula grounded in complex knowledge stand the best chance of stretching the intellectual sense making of all children. We cannot let rote learning, trivial assignments, and social concerns like deportment and neatness crowd out this complex knowledge.

We believe schools should offer a *common curriculum,* or the knowledge that all children should learn. Of course, this does not mean that all children eventually will know the same things (and they should not, given the many differences among them). But they all can understand much about the major ideas that lie at the core of the school curriculum. Students need to understand these ideas in order to succeed, whether in college or in the world of adult life and work.

A Good Lesson Is a Problem

Most real-life learning happens when we solve problems. Many curriculum reformers and cognitive psychologists now urge teachers to use real-world problem solving as a model for classroom activities. When teachers do so, they keep knowledge from drifting into the highly abstract world of "schooled" knowledge. The researcher Robert Glaser recently observed, "Faced with problems to solve where they are interested in the outcome and understand the goal, learners actively explore their environments, test beliefs and theories by their actions, and modify their approaches." Glaser says that the gradual refinement of problem-solving skills should be a major aim of schooling. Schools should pay more attention to developing "expert novices" who, "although they may not possess sufficient background knowledge in a new field, know how to go about gaining it."

Good lessons have children look for problems. The questions "Is there a problem?" "What is the problem?" and "How or why is the problem important?" are more than good attention-getting motivators. They are not *preparation* for lessons on reading, history, science, or calculus but are the real business of learning those subjects. When teachers ask these questions—or, better, when children ask them—they learn that problems are not simply obstacles. Rather, problems are important and interesting challenges.

Moreover, as the psychologist Robert Sternberg has emphasized, when schools present lessons as problems needing solutions, children learn to be problem-*finders*. This skill counts in a world in which many worthwhile challenges hide from all but the sharpest eyes. In real life, problems are hard to define and their importance is hard to determine. Taking this stance with regard to classroom knowledge may help children avoid a common consequence of schooling: After years of having problems presented to them, some children develop the attitude that if a problem exists, someone else (the teacher, the boss, the government) will let them know. Conversely, some learn that when they do notice a problem not already seen by others, they can get into trouble, become a bother, or worse.

Good Lessons Provide a Context

Good lessons don't present knowledge in isolated chunks. In a good lesson the essential ideas are inextricably connected to a context that explains each idea and why it matters. Lessons must place the knowledge to be learned in context because knowledge becomes meaningful (and memorable) only when we connect it to something else important. This helps to explain why Ravitch and Finn can point to a shamefully low percentage of teenagers who know in what half century Americans fought the Civil War. It isn't because no one ever told them. More likely, the students learned the dates outside of any meaningful context and promptly forgot them.

Language in Its Contexts "Natural" language development is a perfect example of complex and contextualized learning. Outside of school, children make little conscious distinction between listening and speaking. In the real world literate adults read, speak, listen, and write without self-consciously isolating these skills. We don't think, "Now I'm speaking so I will draw upon my file of speaking knowledge" and "Now I will switch my skill and knowledge base to begin writing." No, when we communicate, we focus on being understood in the context. We take in information for the purpose of understanding something that is important to us. That's what language instruction in schools could be.

In the multidimensional classrooms we described in chapter 3, literature, drama, public speaking, recreational reading, and research connect with each other and with children's prior experiences. When teachers construct larger, deeper, and longer-lasting assignments, they have more time to develop contexts and include more language dimensions. For example, instead of simply hearing a story, children might also write a similar one. They might act out a bit of the plot, look for and read another that is similar, or describe a personal experience the story reminds them of, and so on. This "whole language" approach helps children connect, not separate, knowledge. Literature—stories—is the key to a whole language emphasis. Stories are the glue to which all communication and language skills stick. Stories have meanings that attract other meanings. Rather than being the servants of skill-building, literature provides genuine reasons and opportunities for learning skills.

No child is too young or unskilled for such an approach. Before children are able to read or write they can tell stories to others. If someone writes the stories, children understand important connections among literature, storytelling, reading, and writing. Reading specialists have different preferences for how to capitalize on children's fascination with making up stories and then learning to read them. But most agree that the story itself ought to be central—not the errors children make or the skills they lack. For example, when children read aloud what they have written, it is probably best to pay little attention to all but the most reliable phonics rules. If a child knows and can speak the word, why not learn to read it? Reading level (as defined by basal readers) becomes irrelevant.

There is still another context for literature that goes beyond the stories and meanings themselves. This is the social context of storytellers and story makers. Asking children where ideas for writing come from, what published authors and children themselves hope to accomplish with their stories, or how writers struggle to put ideas together can be an invitation for children to join the community of storytellers and writers. As part of that community children will behave like writers and become the makers and users of stories.

The Context of Other People's Language Children who are lucky enough to learn a foreign language when they are young find easiest access to other cultural communities. These are powerful social contexts that support children's effort and persistence as language learners. And if they speak, read, listen, and make stories in other languages, these entwined communicating skills reinforce one another.

The Context of Mathematics In the mathematics curriculum we look for opportunities to apply math skills and ideas to real problems. *Doing* mathematics means far more than working paper-and-pencil math problems. Children learn mathematics best when they can manipulate objects and actually see and feel the relationships among the things that mathematics describes.

Embedded in a real-world context, math knowledge can go far beyond the traditional addition, subtraction, division, equations. Even very young children can learn mathematical ideas such as congruence and symmetry. Young children can learn sophisticated concepts of measurement, statistics, and probability. Students of all ages can estimate and make approximations. They can judge the reasonableness of the solutions they use mathematics to find.

Mathematical ideas are too central to understanding the world for schools to confine them to math classes. The real world does not limit math ideas to special professions or activities. Certainly in science, definitely on the playground, absolutely in art, without doubt in social studies, even in language arts, schools should make mathematics concepts important. If schools stressed the ubiquitous nature of mathematics, we're convinced that strong math students could use their mathematical understandings to support them in other classes. We also are sure that those who struggle with math would have far less trouble if math concepts turned up throughout the school day.

Studying Society in Contexts In social studies classes, we would like to see children act like historians, political scientists, geographers, anthropologists, sociologists, and economists. We'd like to see them use history and social commentaries to help observe and make sense of their own lives. We'd like to see them do original research and reenact society's decision making and problem solving around critical social issues.

The central curriculum issue is not which of the countless social concerns a class of young social scientists should investigate. Any of the matters that are crucial to adults—raising children, avoiding drugs, earning a living, feeding the hungry, organizing a community, pursuing freedom—are worthy of investigation. A vast intellectual context—the funded knowledge of the world that fills the world's libraries and consciousness—should support these investigations. Here the histories, names, dates, locations on the map, habits, values, art, and so forth of the world's people past and present wait for children. Children will remember details and chronologies once they have a reason to seek them out and a context in which they can place them. We don't believe there is a conflict between gaining the knowledge that constitutes cultural literacy and learning enduring human themes that cross traditional disciplinary lines. Both are important, and we don't have to make a choice. Current values and long-standing issues provide the social and intellectual contexts for knowledge that our society has always found important.

Good Lessons Use Knowledge from Life as Well as from Books

In the real world, we don't go running to a textbook or a teacher every time we have a problem to solve. Usually, we or someone nearby already has most of the information we need to solve most problems. Children bring to classrooms a store of informal knowledge that they act on but can't always describe. Instruction often neglects this informal knowledge and by doing so loses a valuable learning resource. Informal knowledge is often the personal context children use to get started making sense of new ideas. Unrecognized, informal knowledge can also obstruct children's understanding. In the examples that follow we stress younger children's informal knowledge. As children get older they have even more extensive stores of experiences that both enrich and obstruct new learning.

Social studies lessons can build on the world children already know—the family, the neighborhood, the city. Young children may go on local field trips that focus on the special qualities and complexity of what is already familiar. Local businesses, service providers, and parks that are part of children's lives contain fascinating information that often escapes children's notice. The school and classroom themselves, along with the cafeteria worker, nurse, and custodian, are also valuable sources of knowledge. Through such study children can learn the value of discovering more about what they already think they know.

Learning to use language forms the very center of children's earliest attempt to make sense of the world. Young children want to know what words mean, and they want to make meanings with words. They play with words, say them, sing them, and invent them. Children love words that are big and important sounding. They love short words that they play with as if they were toys. Just from sopping up their environment, preschoolers expand their vocabularies enormously. The child psychoanalyst Bruno Bettelheim reports that by the time they enter school most children know and use four thousand words. Most children of five have mastered our sophisticated grammatical system; they make few mistakes when they form words into quite complex sentences. Children whose speech is rich in colloquial or foreign expressions understand and use sophisticated language constructions. Children don't have a conscious awareness of grammatical structures. They use their informal knowledge of language patterns to make sense of what they read and communicate with others.

Children also notice and do many essentials of science long before they enter school. If we watch how they put curiosity into action, we can see the rudiments of the scientific method. From their earliest months children explore the world and develop theories about how things work. They test their theories over and over, watching carefully to see what will happen. Like scientists, they use information to confirm theories and come up with new ones. Think about a one-year-old sitting in a high chair, dropping toys or cookies over the side. The child watches carefully to see what will happen. While his theorizing is not conscious, this young Newton is constructing theories about what happens when objects fall through space. The curious one-year-old is quick to put new observations to use: When Mom is in the room, she will pick up the dropped item and place it back on the tray. The child tests this new hypothesis again and again: Object tossed; Mom picks it up. Object tossed; Mom picks it up. . . . The child squeals with delight. He has confirmed a theory.

We'd like to see school science help children develop their natural curiosity and theory-making inclinations. This most basic curiosity is what drives science. At the core of the most distinguished scientist we find the same basic human impulse to "find out" that we saw in our one-year-old. As children get older their original experimentation gets elaborated with a powerful question, Why? Sometimes the why becomes an invitation for others to join in experimentation.

Informal knowledge and theories children develop on their own do not always aid school learning, however. In subtle, often hidden ways informal knowledge can cause children to miss or misinterpret new knowledge. Adults need to correct the considerable wrong information children store up. For example, children do not necessarily discover accurate scientific principles through their own experimentation. Considerable recent research has uncovered a great many naive conceptions of science that hinder children's learning scientific principles. Children's theories about the world are usually not foolish; rather, they represent what their common sense tells them (for example, the sun comes up and goes down).

In all subjects, teachers can make children's informal knowledge an explicit part of problem solving. Curricula in science and other subjects should sometimes allow as much time for undoing misconceptions as for teaching correct ones. Often, adults fail to recognize that children have elaborate rationales to support their wrong conceptions. Children and adults alike hold tenaciously to facts that they have always believed and reasoned to be true. Perhaps these are beliefs their parents held. Simply telling a child he has the wrong answer and proceeding with instruction will not replace incorrect with correct knowledge.

Many children identified as less able can make important contributions and enhance their sense of competence when the teacher values their informal knowledge. Often these children are as clever at bringing useful informal knowledge to a problem as their classmates who are quicker to learn the formal knowledge.

Is the Answer Right or Right?

In everyday life there is seldom one right solution to most real problems or one right approach to solving them. But most school problems usually have right procedures to follow and right answers to find. Of course, spelling a word does require a single solution; the word is correct or incorrect, and the world has little patience for creative alternative spellings. Most real-life problems, though, lack definitive sources like dictionaries to give an indisputable answer. Real-life solutions have to be compatible with so many ideas, fit so many contexts, and suit the knowledge and opinions of so many people that two people rarely come up with the same ones. Furthermore, the same person often will not select the same solution twice if given the chance to change her mind or learn from her experience.

Many teachers face tremendous pressure to favor problems that have best solutions and to teach the best way to solve these problems. Accountability tests pressure schools to emphasize right answers. And that, in turn, fosters lessons built on easily measurable bits and pieces rather than on complex ideas. Children soon learn an informal but powerful rule: Unless an endeavor leads to a best solution—one that will show up on the test—it isn't worth the effort.

Even worse, when children's reasonable answers don't match the teacher's right answers, they may come to distrust their own thinking and reasoning. Recently, we came across a small book called *The First Grade Takes a Test*. In the book the "test lady" gave the children sheets on which they were to mark the right answers to her multiple-choice questions. The first question gave the children two wrong and one right choice about what rabbits eat. One boy knew that rabbits need to eat carrots to keep their teeth from growing too long—a sophisticated bit of knowledge that few other children had. Not finding carrots as one of the choices, he drew a carrot next to the boxes on the answer sheet. He wanted to be sure that the test lady knew what rabbits needed. Of course, the point of this story is that the boy's perfectly correct answer would certainly be wrong. Another point is that the answers expected by teachers and test makers are rarely completely and exclusively correct.

Single right answers have their place. Even so, in classrooms where knowledge is challenging and complex, attention to narrow, single-answer tasks will not displace opportunities for multiple right answers. For example, children should be able to select among several mathematical approaches to solving problems. It can be as valid for a child to discover a less effective approach as to memorize the correct one. Teachers need to value such discovery as much as they value memorization. In the real world people compute mentally. They use trial-and-error processes and rarely expect to get things right the first time. They *expect* to come up with some useless answers, some imperfect solutions that will get by, and, finally, with something that works quite well—until they can do better.

In Good Lessons Everybody Helps

One test for the richness of classroom knowledge is whether children can learn as well or better when they work with others.

People outside of school solve problems together, but in schools we usually hear "Do your own work!" Of course, we have all been plagued by coworkers who let us down. Nearly everyone has wound up doing all the work or letting someone else do all the work because it was the easy way out. We have also experienced groups in which power struggles, disagreements, and confusion allowed no work at all to be produced. And yet, working in groups often produces the best and most satisfying solutions. Knowledge learned together is very often different, better, richer, more elaborated, and more useful than knowledge learned alone.

For example, although many consider mathematics to be a solitary activity, children can teach and learn from one another. They can ask questions, explain ideas and strategies, and try out solutions with one another. The explaining they do serves them days or years later when they have to recreate both the answers and the reasoning that went into those solutions. To become experts, novice problem solvers need to understand and explain to themselves the logic, the reasons, and the process they use. Well-structured group work promotes this necessary explanation and understanding.

Typically, schools allow students to work together in social studies more than in most other subjects. Much of this group work is quite ordinary. For example, students work together to answer the chapter questions. However, some exciting possibilities ought to inspire teachers in all subjects. We have watched five- and six-year-olds working together with wood, saws, and hammers to construct a replica of their city's transportation system. They built a harbor, freeways, a railroad station—all places they were studying and had visited. And we have seen nine- and ten-year-olds working in small groups to make adobe bricks and construct buildings for their study of California history. These city-dwelling children learned firsthand about building houses (rather than simply buying them). They learned how native Americans used free natural resources (mud) and how people historically coped with scarcity (timber). They learned about the practical concept of insulation and about the insulating properties of different materials. They learned a long list of relevant social studies ideas from these lessons. Just as important, the children in these classrooms *experienced* how people work together to solve problems.

Many high school social studies teachers involve students in simulations that recreate historic events, legal processes, and economic systems. Students may participate in a mock legislature or United Nations meeting. These lessons require students both to learn the facts and then to apply them to lifelike problems and circumstances. The interactions among students promote learning of both facts and principles as students apply their knowledge and make it useful to the group's common purpose. Increasingly, computers, videotape, and other technologies will make social studies simulations more realistic. Groups of students will be able to make sense of concepts and events that many schools now present as dry and far-removed from the experiences of real people.

The Three Causes of War Are . . .

Good lessons emphasize the complicated nature of important problems. They also teach that important problems don't go away easily.

Consider the hypothetical case of two students writing on nuclear waste. Chris began her essay, "There are no easy solutions to the problem of disposing of nuclear waste." Julie began, "There are three important steps to disposing of nuclear waste." Chris has as much data about the problem as Julie does. Nonetheless, Chris may receive the poorer grade if she reveals some of her struggle over her ideas in the paper itself. Julie may have an easier time since her essay lends itself to a certain tidiness of structure and organization.

Having read thousands of such beginnings, we predict that of the two

Chris will be more likely to make sense of the problem as an environmental, human, and personal issue. Chris will correctly, realistically approach the problem as one that is not about to go away soon. She is more likely to go home full of passion regarding this real-life concern. In years to come she will probably follow this issue and be receptive to new developments. On the other hand, Julie may be more likely to set this topic aside once she has done the assignment. She may see her entire involvement with it as a school problem or a writing problem—not a social or personal one.

We prefer curricula that acknowledge that real problems persist and defy easy solutions. They don't present knowledge in a succession of self-contained packages. Instead, they ask children to connect the vital concerns of earlier lessons to current ones. Such lessons counter the all-too-frequent, if implicit, school message, "Once you've thought about the problem or learned a skill, you're free to forget it."

Two Lessons Contrasted

Children will study botany—whether as a course in its own right, a unit in a biology class, or part of general science—several times during their school years. The usual approach to lessons in plant biology teaches specific facts. Instruction occurs in a sequence that makes sense to publishers and teachers. Children, on the other hand, may hardly notice the themes or larger ideas. They focus on defining scientific terms (for example, photosynthesis, osmosis, deciduous) and memorizing the most important principles (for example, plants are green because they contain chlorophyl; plants produce oxygen). Short-term lessons often last as little as one class period. The teacher has a specific learning objective in mind, but the class moves on regardless of whether children master the objective. This cycle repeats throughout the year until the teacher has covered all the objectives.

Contrast this conventional approach with a semester- or year-long assignment in which children observe and make sense of the processes by which plants grow. An actual garden anchors this lesson. The garden provides children a place to cultivate and observe a variety of plants. Children have a chance to experiment with the plants by altering light, water, nutrition, and other growing conditions. Each child participates in hands-on work and works with others while observing, recording, and forming and testing hypotheses. Each shares prior experiences and offers growth predictions based upon articulated reasons. Many different experiments occur simultaneously, and children follow the progress of those that relate to their own hypotheses.

Each child explores and articulates observations about the plants' progress, his student-group's productivity, and his personal sense of accomplishment. Each child considers and shares the aesthetic values and contribution to the quality of life that plants afford. The teacher encourages all the students to write creatively, to listen to music, to draw, read, and talk about themes having to do with plant growth and the science of plants. When children ask what activities typically found in English, art, and music classes have to do with science, the teacher encourages the vigorous class discussion that follows.

Each child investigates real-life consequences of plant growth. He considers consequences to farmers, to the public, to the environment, to businesses and government. Each child looks at the careers and life styles of those whose work centers on plants: growers, wholesalers, retailers, experimental botanists, chemists, conservationists, rangers, teachers, florists, and so on. Each student presents a formal oral report. Each presents a written account of his observations and work and participates in a group effort to present conclusions. The teacher holds each child accountable for concepts he can reasonably master (photosynthesis, osmosis, the nature of cells, plant reproduction, and so on).

For what grade is such a lesson appropriate? What should be the ability level of the students? Must students speak English very fluently in order to learn and make a contribution to their student groups? None of these concerns about age, skills, or language fluency need prevent children from working and making sense together. In fact, in a lesson with such diverse tasks, diversity among students can encourage and enrich the learning opportunities. If the teacher believes that all children are capable, each child, regardless of prior experiences, age, reading or writing skill, or tested ability, can learn very well from such a lesson.

Worthy Objectives

We don't present the above as a model science lesson. However, it does highlight differences between classrooms that present rich and meaningful knowledge and those that emphasize "skill-and-drill" lessons. Not all lessons have to be parts of semester-long projects. And not every effort to keep students actively engaged in concept-based, problem-solving lessons will succeed. There are bound to be mistakes, a lack of experience or resources, and plain old human fallibility. Teachers who attempt such lessons warrant support. Parents and policymakers should prefer a worthwhile lesson that falls short to a well-executed lesson founded on trivial knowledge.

Are we concerned that some children may become capable conceptual thinkers yet acquire no knowledge? Will children learn broadly, become proficient at identifying important concepts, be able to work together, and become excellent problem solvers, and not learn how to read, multiply, spell? Will they answer enough multiple-choice questions on the reading test or know the names of the presidents? Such fears are seldom borne out. Most children lucky enough to be in classrooms that provide rich learning opportunities end up doing remarkably well on conventional measures of school learning.

SOME CURRICULAR RULES OF THUMB

A good clue to the richness of the curriculum can come from teachers' and administrators' attitudes. Do they speak with understanding and enthusiasm for the content of the classes? Do you sense that the elementary teacher is captivated by the opportunity to teach math concepts to the youngest children? Or does he apologize for not being very good at math himself? Are the teachers politically aware? Do they read and write? Would they rather talk to you about their subject than complain about how little students know about it? Do they speak with conviction about why mastery of their curriculum is essential to be an educated citizen? Or do they justify the content by noting that the school board requires it, or that children need it to succeed next year or to pass a test? Does the principal praise her teachers and speak knowledgeably about what children are learning in classes? Does the principal point out the creative and thoughtful ways that individual teachers at his school push the art of teaching beyond the commonplace?

Some rules of thumb can help you recognize classes that let children learn knowledge and skills in meaningful contexts. First, most meaningful lessons last a while. Some take a few days, others a week or, if they encompass key ideas and themes, a semester or more. Second, lessons will typically require active learning tasks rather than passive ones, and they often have children working together rather than alone. And, third, the content should appeal to any curious learner of whatever age and skill. So try it out on yourself. Are you fascinated? Would you want to keep on reading and listening? Can you think of lots of interesting questions? Do you wish you could join in with the teacher and students? If so, it sounds like a good class for everyone.

FOR FURTHER READING

Francie Alexander and Charlotte Crabtree, "California's New History – Social Studies Curriculum Promises Richness and Depth," *Educational Leadership* 46, no. 1 (1988): 10–13.

American Association for the Advancement of Science, *Project 2061: Science for All Americans.* Washington, DC: American Association for the Advancement of Science, 1989.

James A. Banks and Ambrose A. Clegg, *Teaching Strategies for the Social Studies: Inquiry, Valuing, and Decision Making.* New York: Longman, 1985.

J. S. Brown and R. K. Burton, "Diagnostic Models for Procedural Bugs in Basic Mathematical Skills," *Cognitive Science* 2, (1978): 155–92.

Audrey Champagne and Leslie Hornig (eds.), *This Year in School Science, 1986: The Curriculum.* Washington, DC: American Association for the Advancement of Science, 1987.

Lynn V. Cheney, *American Memory.* Washington, DC: National Endowment for the Humanities, 1987.

Michael Cole, *Thinking: The Importance of Context.* Madison, WI: Center for Effective Secondary Schools, 1987.

The College Board, *Academic Preparation for College: What Students Need to Know and be Able to Do.* New York: The College Board, 1983.

Elliot W. Eisner, *Cognition and Curriculum: A Basis for Deciding What to Teach.* New York: Longman, 1982.

Peter Elbow, *Writing without Teachers.* London: Oxford University Press, 1973.

Robert Glaser, "Teaching Expert Novices," *Educational Researcher* 16 (December 1987): 13–19.

Alan Glatthorn, *A Guide for Developing an English Curriculum for the Eighties.* Urbana, IL: National Council for Teachers of English, 1980.

Claude Goldenberg, "Making Success a More Common Occurrence for Children at Risk for Failure: Lessons from Hispanic First Graders Learning to Read." In J. Allen and J. Mason (eds.), *Reducing the Risks for Young Learners: Literacy Practices and Policies.* New York: Heinemann, 1988.

Bob Gowin and Joseph Novak, *Learning How to Learn.* New York: Cambridge University Press, 1984.

Mathematical Sciences Education Board, *Everybody Counts: A Report to the Nation on the Future of Mathematics Education.* Washington, DC: National Academy Press, 1989.

National Science Board, *Educating Americans for the 21st Century.* Washington, DC: 1983.

Diane Ravitch and Chester Finn, *What Do Our 17-Year-Olds Know: A Report on the First National Assessment of History and Literature.* New York: Harper and Row, 1987.

Lauren B. Resnick, *Education and Learning to Think*. Washington, DC: National Academy Press, 1987.

Alan Schoenfeld (ed.), *Cognitive Science and Mathematics Education*. Hillsdale, NJ: Erlbaum, 1987.

Alan Schoenfeld, *Mathematical Problem Solving*. New York: Academic Press, 1985.

Sylvia Scribner and Michael Cole, *The Psychology of Literacy*. Cambridge: Harvard University Press, 1981.

Theodore Sizer, *Horace's Compromise*. Boston: Houghton Mifflin, 1984.

James Squire (ed.), *The Dynamics of Language Learning*. Urbana, IL: National Conference for Research in English, 1987.

Robert Sternberg, "Teaching Critical Thinking," *Phi Delta Kappan* 67 (1985).

CHAPTER FIVE

The Other Basics

Classes in the arts, personal and social well-being (health, skills for adolescents, drug education, sex education), and work-related skills bear little resemblance to the real things. Like freeze-dried coffee, they are convenient imitations. The classes may capture some of the flavor of real art and music and genuine life-enhancing skills, but connoisseurs would never mistake these school imitations for the genuine articles.

In the shadows of the "solid" subjects, these subjects warrant parents' and policymakers' concern. We are convinced that the core of learning, experience, and knowledge in art and music, health and physical education, business and work has merit in its own right. And we are certain that the usual school distinction between academic and nonacademic classes does not serve children or society well. These other basics are essential to our children and to our culture. Knowing about them is an integral part of a well-rounded, liberal education.

Elective courses periodically suffer as a result of an intensified emphasis on academics. It is a cycle that most adults have been influenced by or watched since the Russians launched Sputnik in 1957. In the wake of frantic post-Sputnik efforts to upgrade students' math and science performance, so-called nonbasics were squeezed into small corners of the curriculum or cut out entirely. Many critics today complain that another shift in the late sixties and early seventies interrupted the trend to increase academic rigor in schools. They believe that a backlash that called for more relevance diluted the academics. Many still blame students' and schools' present deficiencies on the educational changes of the late 1960s. Then as now, schools treat relevance and academic rigor as mutually exclusive. Perhaps a more accurate criticism of certain late-1960s excesses would be to note that when schools implemented reforms they often tossed out the academic baby with the irrelevant bathwater.

Certainly, concern about academics is warranted. Some teenagers actually graduate from high school lacking basic literacy and computation skills. In many academic subjects, even the top U.S. students fall short of their counterparts in other nations. But we have little evidence that periodic *shifting* of priorities from an attempt to achieve a balanced curriculum to a concentration on academic basics has produced gains in student achievement. What schools have yet to attempt on a large scale is a combining of the two into a single priority. Schools have yet to assume that important knowledge is spread uniformly throughout the curriculum and not confined to classes called English, math, and science.

And once again, the narrow perspectives of the past hamper reforms that can address the problem. Today, analysts increasingly link the United States' loss of dominance in technology and international trade to flaws in schools. They cite flagging school achievement as a factor in our seeming inability to outdistance the Soviets in the space and arms races. They point to our steady humbling, if not drubbing, at the hands of the Japanese in the international marketplace. These national worries generate loud calls for more and tougher math, science, and language instruction.

Once again, schools have responded to these concerns by boosting their emphasis on language, mathematics, and science and increasing the time students study them. It is not clear how or whether these reforms have paid off. Test scores in basic mathematics and reading skills may have inched up in the past few years, but even this scanty progress cannot clearly be attributed to toughened standards. One sure effect is that increases in school time spent on academic subjects have further eroded the time available for other subjects. Such policies have closed off additional avenues to high-level thinking and alternate ways of making sense out of the environment. Most schools spend little time on the arts. Physical education has gone from a daily requirement to an elective subject in many states. Vocational and career education has been steadily relegated to the lowest-achieving students. Many schools now offer an increasingly lopsided curriculum—one that largely ignores the arts, physical education, health, and vocational subjects.

Traditionally, nonacademic subjects are central to a broad general education. They offer students unique ways of knowing, creating, and making sense of the world. As we noted in chapter 2, our growing understanding of intelligence places great importance on analysis, critical thinking, creativity, and adaptability. Visual–spacial abilities, musical proclivities, bodily–kinesthetic adeptness, and personal skills are assuming importance alongside of language and logical-mathematical aptitudes. Art, music, health, physical education, and a whole array of subjects related to work easily engage students in active, real-world problem solving. These subjects can quite naturally require students to discover and define problems and view them in sense-making contexts. They can encourage students to appreciate the complexity of problems and to work together to solve them.

THE ARTS

Most people think that the arts are good for children. But few think the arts as important as reading, math, science, and social studies. If not exactly frills, the arts are usually considered expendable if resources get tight. Parents and policymakers rarely express outrage when children don't do well in the arts. And though students report that they enjoy art in school more than many subjects, even they don't think art is very important. Why should they? Except for rock and roll, television and movies, and advertising art, most adults don't spend much time, attention, or money on the arts.

Our culture treats genuine artistic expression and appreciation as beyond the reach of ordinary people. Real art belongs to those few very unusual individuals who are thought to have special inborn gifts or who are wealthy or effete. Few expect children to develop artistic knowledge or competence in classrooms. This is one reason why many school districts concentrate the arts, particularly the performing arts, in special magnet schools. These schools usually screen their applicants for talent the children developed elsewhere. Other school-sponsored arts opportunities such as field trips or workshops are used mainly to provide enrichment for gifted or high-achieving children. Special programs and magnet schools often do an exemplary job. However, they also reinforce specialized rather than universal arts education.

Most elementary schools use the arts to provide ordinary children with some variety in their school day. Art, music, dance, and drama bring children a little fun and diversion from their paper-pencil-and-book routines.

Only exceptional schools expect any but the most gifted to develop real knowledge or skills in the arts. For the others, the value of drawing, singing, dancing, and acting lies in the opportunities they provide for self-expression. Of course it frustrates most trained art teachers that schools expect the arts only to provide a quasi-therapeutic creative outlet and that children may receive little sound or rigorous arts instruction.

A common belief is that the arts can bring out special talents in students who are not skilled in academics. Sometimes this happens, and it can be wonderful for those students. Another belief is that everyone's attempts at art are of equally high quality—independent of standards within the discipline. This belief is subtly different from the belief that every child can succeed in art. Just as we don't accept a child's first multiplication efforts if further instruction can help him improve upon them, schools need to follow up children's early, if less successful, art attempts with more coaching and instruction. The school's lack of emphasis on the gaining of skills and understanding in art, compared with that given other subjects, sends the clear signal that art isn't very important. When children realize that art isn't very important at school, they don't gain much self-esteem even if they are among the few who find success. Being praised in a second-class subject doesn't count for much.

By junior high many art and music classes serve special purposes of one sort or another, and these purposes don't always include a high-quality experience for all children. Instrumental music classes may enroll only those who began playing instruments in elementary school or who have had private lessons. Sometimes these classes require that students have the personal resources to rent or buy instruments. The visual arts or drama often catch the low-achieving students who don't qualify for more academic electives like journalism or foreign language. On the other hand, college-bound students are often too busy with academic requirements to fit art into their schedules. Even if they could, they would have to surmount the low status these classes often have.

Some schools rely on their arts programs for promoting good community relations. Poster contests stimulate the involvement of business and volunteer groups. Parents coming to school take pride when their children's art decorates the walls. Choral music concerts enliven PTA meetings and back-to-school nights. The school band fuels both school and community pride by marching in city parades and providing half-time music at football games.

Perhaps these uses of art and music education accomplish something of value. However, they barely tap the potential contribution of the arts to children's education. Many cheapen the arts and mirror the low status of the arts in our culture. Doubters need only consider the following unlikely event: Some athletic activity—perhaps a football demonstration—takes place during the "half-time" of a well-attended music festival while the crowd gets their hot dogs and goes to the restrooms.

Neil Postman in his book *Amusing Ourselves to Death* criticizes the push to make academic classes entertaining. He worries that classroom lessons increasingly mimic the structure and form of television and so make education less intellectually demanding. Art Powell and his co-authors of *The Shopping Mall High School* compare high school classes to boutiques. Students simply browse and sample or try on subjects without getting intensely involved. They also describe negotiations between students and teachers that help keep classes easy. Art classes are particularly susceptible to such pressure, given their low status. Many art teachers feel forced to respond to the unmistakable message: If you make your classes serious and demanding, you risk losing the best students, who want to reserve their efforts for their academic classes. Furthermore, demanding classes may drive away the poorest students, whose enrollment is essential to the maintaining of any art program at all.

"Back to Basics" Means "Back to Art"

Despite these common patterns, art is an education basic. The College Board's report *Academic Preparation for College: What Students Need to Know and Be Able to Do* asserts that the arts contribute to students' flexible thinking, disciplined effort, and self-confidence. The arts embody complex forms and techniques of expression. They often communicate subtle meanings.

Good art education goes far beyond the show-and-tell coursework that many students experience. It goes beyond matching a painting to its painter or listing Doric, Ionic, and Corinthian columns in the chronological order of their development. Art asks us to know what a painter, a sculptor, a composer, or a performer was trying to communicate. It demands that we understand how forms, techniques, and special properties of different media contribute the meaning of our experience. Understanding both the forms and the meanings of art requires careful study, critical thinking, and hands-on experience with the media themselves. The arts introduce children to the delicate balance between craft and the expression of meaning—between knowing the ideas and skills of art and doing artful work.

The College Board booklet describes what is essential for college success as well as for college entry. It lists five essential areas of ability in and knowledge of the arts. It claims that all students entering college (not just those intending to major in art) should have the following competencies:

- The ability to understand and appreciate the unique qualities of each of the arts.
- The ability to appreciate how people of various cultures have used the arts to express themselves.
- The ability to understand and appreciate different artistic styles and works from representative historical periods and cultures.
- Some knowledge of the social and intellectual influences affecting artistic form.
- The ability to use the skills, media, tools, and processes in one or more of the arts.

Education experts such as those who prepared the College Board's *Academic Preparation for College* consider the arts essential. However, colleges and universities can be downright discouraging to schools that want to offer a strong precollegiate arts program or to students who want to take art courses instead of the traditional academics. Some colleges look carefully at children's background in the arts when they consider applications, but most do not. The College Board's own Scholastic Aptitude Test (the most powerful and influential of all entrance exams) does not measure the abilities the College Board itself recommends.

The same school and classroom conditions important to learning academic subjects also apply to the arts. First, art teachers must believe that all children are capable of learning art. This is a particularly difficult requirement for elementary school teachers who did not major in art. Often they don't believe in their own knowledge about or ability to do art.

Second, the school culture must place a high value on art. Art, as a subject in itself, must command teachers' and students' time and attention. For example, children can learn the value and seriousness of the arts when teachers incorporate art and music history and appreciation into history lessons. Children can learn the unique capacity of different art media to demonstrate math and science principles. Students can learn both the aesthetic and the functional merits of the arts as they do projects in other subjects.

Some schools do make art important. The National Endowment for the Arts supports "artists-in-residence" programs in a number of schools across the country. Its funding allows practicing artists, dancers, and musicians to share their art-making processes and their self-discipline with students. Artists-in-residence quickly communicate that art is not easy. A few high schools teach music theory, history, and composition and develop orchestras in addition to the more conventional marching bands. A few integrate the arts with the study of other subjects. For example, some high schools are now energetically developing core programs in the humanities. These few schools try to soften the rigid divisions among traditional disciplines. Students receive substantial exposure to history, criticism, and technique in the arts within their integrated study of literature and social studies.

A GRAB BAG OF WELL-BEING

Over time, personal and social concerns have become part of the curriculum. The public expects schools to teach children about good health and nutrition. It expects schools to keep children physically fit, teach them safety rules (at home, with strangers, on bicycles, in automobiles, and so on), and counsel them about careers, interpersonal problems, college, drugs, and so forth. These topics and services consume schools' resources and children's time. They also consume the time and energy of adults, who debate how to teach them and even whether it is the school's job to teach them at all.

Here is a merest hint of the questions raised in countless schools year after year: Should schools teach children how to drive safely? Why not families or the Department of Motor Vehicles? Do children need instruction in organized games, or do they just need time to play? Should there be standards for physical fitness—suggested numbers of pushups, speed around the track, meters jumped. Should children learn about the effects of drugs on respiration, mental alertness, and sexual potency? Should teachers relay information to children about the causes and prevention of AIDS? If so, at what age and under what circumstances? Should schools encourage children to explore their own values regarding these topics? Should they teach values, even if they conflict with the children's or their parents' values?

Here are a few conditions that should inform a discussion of these questions. In September 1988, *Education Week* reported that according to a survey funded by the U.S. Department of Health and Human Services approximately half of the eleven thousand teenagers questioned "said that the AIDS virus can be transmitted when donating blood and that washing after sex can reduce the chances of being infected." "About 40 percent of the girls and 25 percent of the boys polled said they had 'seriously thought' about committing suicide. Nearly 20 percent of the girls and 10 percent of the boys said they had attempted suicide. Most students said they do not use seatbelts or bicycle helmets, and many reported that they had driven with an intoxicated driver." About a quarter "said they had had more than five drinks on one occasion during the previous two weeks. Many reported having diets high in fat and sugar, and more than half were unable to understand the nutritional information on a cereal box."

Reaching into this grab bag of personal and social issues is sure to generate controversy. Some people think these topics are essential to children's and society's well-being, and others think they are useless or destructive. Impassioned differences of opinion surround the content and teaching methods of commonly accepted academic subjects—so it is not surprising to find dramatically differing views about the value of less traditional subjects. We should expect it in areas that relate to private religious beliefs or political agendas. However, if treated academically and seriously, any topic or issue of interest or concern to the community is legitimate school knowledge. Deciding when and how students ought to examine community worries or interests is the job of curriculum and learning specialists.

Our interest in serious academic approaches to personal and social concerns is not a plea to wring the fun out of school. To the contrary, the immediacy and relevance of children's personal and social lives can enliven school.

Health

Most students find the abstract health topics taught at school boring. Having the invulnerability of youth, they simply can't relate. Yet, nearly all children and teenagers find their own and their friends' physical development fascinating. They relish stories about people with interesting diseases or weird abnormalities.

Even so, schools usually teach human physiology in the absence of real health, fitness, or social issues. In health or biology classes, teachers often present human circulation, digestion, even sexuality as just so much plumbing—pumps, pipes, valves, tubes. Children chart, color (red crayon for the arteries, blue for the veins), and memorize. Then they take a test to see whether they've learned the facts. Moving right along, the next lesson explains the skeleton as if it were an erector set with so many sticks, joints, and levers. Next week, they will take on another topic.

Little of this typical approach has much to do with students' own health, fitness, or well-being. Neither does it greatly affect sense making and behavior regarding drug and alcohol abuse, eating disorders, sexuality, AIDS, pollution, suicide, abortion, gangs, cheating, or exercise. Often schools carefully filter out the concerns of real life instead of teaching children how to address them.

Chemistry, physiology, psychology, sociology, physics, history, and geography should enrich children's understanding of their own and society's health and well-being. But these classes may conspicuously avoid mentioning controversial, untraditional topics. Ironically, the greater the consequence a health issue has for children's lives, the more some people fight to keep it out of schools. Only recently have schools been able to discuss, explore values, and offer information about drug abuse and cigarette smoking. Only after the country's belated recognition of the AIDS crisis have schools found it possible to mention such topics as homosexuality and "safe sex." Some still see concerns like loneliness and friendships as being too sensitive or outside the school's purpose.

Drug abuse, nutrition, alcoholism, responsible sexual behavior, AIDS, homosexuality, pollution, suicide, abortion, gangs, cheating, and physical exercise are topics that, if appropriately presented, can offer real-life contexts to students. They can also provide examples of how real-world problems relate to school subjects that may otherwise be abstract, dry, and classroom-bound. These topics, after all, are the real-life concerns of practicing physical and social scientists, who hardly consider them expendable parts of their of their own disciplines.

Of course schools must exercise sensible cautions. First, much foolishness can go on in school in the name of relevance. For example, some classes engage children in poorly designed discussions of drug abuse in which the children learn very little about the science of drugs and their effects on the brain. Second, teaching personal and social topics across the curriculum (in all classes to which the topics are related) requires elaborate planning, which is something teachers have little time for. Finally, controversial matters are not all best taught to all children in the same ways. Schools must consider the developmental appropriateness of topics concerning children's sexuality, and so on. Schools need to tackle controversial topics with caution. But when schools avoid controversy and relevance and keep health-related topics carefully compartmentalized, they consign health and well-being to trivial corners of the curriculum.

You Are What You Learn to Eat

We want children to understand health and fitness as twenty-four-hour-a-day matters. Covering a few lists of health-related do's and don't's won't suffice. Consider the narrow approach schools often take to nutrition. Not so many years ago, an emphasis on simple facts led to having children memorize the now-discredited seven basic food groups. These lessons stressed the importance of eating lots of dairy products and red meat. An entire generation gained rather little understanding about nutrition. Even if today's facts are more accurate, they will undoubtedly be superseded by new knowledge. Just as in other subjects, schools cannot hope to teach children all the nutrition facts they should know. Certainly, schools can't make such facts stick in ways that influence children's behaviors. (After all, information about the seven basic food groups didn't forestall the junk-food revolution.)

Schools are more likely to influence good health and nutrition if children learn basic principles. That health is affected by what we eat and breathe and by an environment that extends far beyond our dinner table, school, and immediate community is one such principle. The ultimate goal is to help children become skilled health and nutrition problem solvers. That is most likely to happen when schools embed nutrition facts in many different contexts. These contexts can occur across a broad spectrum of the curriculum and can be reinforced across disciplines year after year.

Children should examine, for example, how advertising interacts with their food choices. Likewise, they need to account for fads, peer pressure, and family preferences. Study of history, geography, and ethnic differences can easily include nutrition. In fact, children won't learn all the essential concepts of these other subjects without considering foods and nutrition.

Play, Sports, and Fitness

Observers as far back as Plato have commented (not always seriously) that the young ought to go to work, not to school. Only in midlife, they argue, do people have the experience and temperament to become serious students. We don't know any societies that have adopted that educational strategy. We can't even imagine what one would look like. However, it's very easy to picture a different reversal: a society in which it is the fashion for the young to be sedentary and the middle-aged to be serious, energetic exercisers. Actually, it doesn't take much imagination to conjure up a picture of Dad out jogging, Mom at the gym, and the kids at their desks or in front of the television set. We see examples every day.

Most adults are not avid exercisers (though, clearly, more are now than ever before). And we probably don't need to worry much that most children will stop being physically active—though American children have a widely documented lack of fitness. Even so, this is one more irony—a sad one—that points out gaps between what we know and say we value and what we actually provide to children in schools. Many children have too little opportunity for vigorous exercise. Many are overscheduled with highly organized, nonactive pursuits. Others lack safe facilities for free play or team games. Still others participate only in overcoached, adult-dominated competitive sports.

Many children are wonderfully active and fit, and they owe much of their fun and health to exercise at school. But many others' physical education is limited to lining up, taking roll, choosing teams, waiting for turns, and hanging around in right field or on the bench. Some schools are dropping requirements for physical education entirely. Many high schools that retain it do so in part for the wrong reasons. In some cases, very large physical education classes (often sixty or more students) siphon off students from overly large academic classes. Children in these large classes may get little supervision and less exercise. Other funding-related problems include the costs of providing and maintaining playing areas, gymnasiums and equipment, lockers and showers, and so forth.

If money and the commitment to exercise were not obstacles, most schools would still need to revamp their physical education programs to make them appropriate for all the children. Such a revamping should probably begin by considering children's self-concepts first rather than their bodies. Social interactions are crucial to self-concept in the classroom and are especially important on the playground. Children's views of themselves as healthy, fit (or at least potentially fit) persons depend heavily on the consensus developed on the playground. Typical approaches to team and sports activities require public performance and assure comparisons (others are watching, choosing sides, and so on) and single standards for evaluation (winning, scoring, and so forth). Children adjust their views of themselves and others in subtle increments. It doesn't take long until everyone knows how valued a child is on a team or in a race. Children proclaim global judgments more loudly on the playground than they would ever be allowed to do in the classroom ("He's good." "She stinks!" "Do we have to take him?").

Schools don't have to maintain practices that needlessly cause discomfort or lowered self-concepts or diminished enthusiasm for physical activity. Schools can organize even traditional team sports such as baseball and football in ways that minimize the painful effects of comparisons. But we might hasten to add, Why bother to do that when there are so many noncompetitive, individual activities that are even more physically engaging? After some adjustment, students can come to accept activities like running, swimming, aerobic dance, and gymnastics as being as much or more fun than traditional team sports. Besides, these are activities that people stick with long after they leave school.

Enlisting the Children

It's easy to present convincing evidence in classrooms that many current health and fitness fashions are unhealthy. The ideal body is not the dangerously thin one. Deep, frequent suntans increase the likelihood of wrinkles and cancer. Junk food affects moods and school performance. Reckless driving and recklessness on skateboards and bikes cause injury. Irresponsible sexual behavior can bring unwanted pregnancy and deadly disease. Drug abuse ruins lives. Teachers can also marshal proof that frequent, rigorous exercise, good nutrition, and sound health habits make people feel good. Most children will dutifully learn these facts and repeat them back on tests. But once they step out of the classroom children experience a powerful and relentless bombardment of contrary messages. Everywhere they look, the culture tells them to get thin and tan, eat junk, take foolish risks, experiment with sex and drugs, and live sedentary lives.

Parents and schools can't protect children from all the dangers and enticements of a world that can be cruel and deceptive. If children are going to manage sensibly, they will have to be able to do much of their coping on their own. But schools do far too little to lead children to safely appreciate the struggles and tensions that are inevitably a part of making sensible health and fitness decisions.

The school curriculum should help children confront the social appeals that entice them to practice destructive behavior. Children should examine products and advertising. Engaging in a critical scrutiny of the media's messages and methods will serve children's health and fitness needs long after the fads and interests of the moment are forgotten.

To make such lessons effective, the school culture should practice what it teaches. Cafeteria food and snacks are often of little nutritional value. Some schools routinely sell and serve junk food from machines. We know of one school in which a teacher's unit on dental care was interrupted for a pep assembly intended to promote a schoolwide, competitive chocolate-candy sale. One high school newspaper we are familiar with regularly runs advertisements for a tanning salon.

It may not be the school's role to censor such ads. But it is certainly the school's responsibility to have students probe the social and health implications of the products being sold. The fact that schools send children out to sell what is bad for them may be less a nutritional issue than one of morality and credibility. In either case teachers and children should examine these common practices.

PREPARING FOR WORK

Language, mathematics, science, social studies, and the arts form the heart of the school curriculum. They are the intellectual basics. Physical education and health programs aim to prepare students for healthy, vigorous lives. Vocational education tries to get students ready to be working adults.

In elementary school most children touch on vocational education as part of the social studies curriculum. As students learn about their communities, they spend some time learning about the work people do. In junior and senior high schools, vocational education becomes a separate subject area. Most vocational classes at these levels try to provide students with specific knowledge about jobs, actual skills, and good work attitudes. Teachers hope these experiences will help prepare students for business, industry, or farmwork. Because the home has traditionally been most women's workplace, home economics (cooking, sewing, and childcare) has also been part of the work-related curriculum. In many schools, typical work-experience programs provide senior high school students with school credits for their part-time jobs—sometimes in a business or industry they have been studying. They also acknowledge that students can learn important habits and values from working at paying jobs.

Vocational education became part of the American school curriculum for a number of reasons. The community expects that preparing students for work will bring economic benefits both to the community and to the students themselves. Vocational education is expected to provide knowhow that enables students to get good jobs. The community benefits by having a pool of skilled workers prepared to maximize production, profits, and consumer purchasing power. Vocational education also tries to accomplish social goals (as distinct from economic benefits). It has sought to provide a place in schools and the work force for students who might otherwise fail, drop out, and join the unemployed. Increasingly, work-related education has attempted to provide and equalize access to education and jobs for poor and minority youth. In the past and present alike many educators and policymakers see these students as being less likely to benefit from the intellectual side of school.

Also behind vocational education is the idea that "manual training" can complement academic studies. Thus by including work-related skills, schools can provide a balanced education for all students. Developing skill with the hands can simultaneously present challenging and worthwhile problems for the mind. If students work with wood, metal, and soil, they can achieve alternate and important "ways of knowing." They would miss these learning experiences if their education concentrated exclusively on books and words.

Disappointing Results

Unfortunately, vocational education has been pretty unsuccessful. Typically, students complete a required junior high school course or two in homemaking or industrial arts. Perhaps they have a semester of consumer education or career awareness in senior high. But many college-bound students take no more than a single work-related course. Students identified as slow learners or seen as ill-suited for college are the ones who typically end up in vocational classes. Many educators believe that they are "better with their hands than their heads." (So much for the ideal of giving all students opportunities to think with both their heads and their hands.)

Despite its past popularity, work-related education in senior high schools has a poor record when it comes to helping students get jobs related to their training. It hasn't seemed to help students command better salaries or to lessen their chances of unemployment. Suffering under limited budgets, many programs end up using obsolete equipment, and students learn obsolete skills. Many teachers have a hard time keeping up with changing labor-market needs and up-to-date training methods. Worse, many school programs concentrate on training students for very specific, low-skilled, entry-level jobs. Factory sewing, dry cleaning, building maintenance, retail sales, and planting and picking in agricultural fields are some examples. Programs like these are common in schools with many poor and minority students. Work-related training in these schools focuses on getting students ready for the low-level jobs that are available to them now rather than preparing them for future work opportunities.

The problems with skill training in high schools are not likely to go away. As the rate of technological change accelerates, skill obsolescence will become more and more of a problem. And the increasing number of very low-skill jobs (fast food, labor, data-entry, and so forth) hardly warrants school programs. Moreover, specific job-related skills appear less and less frequently on the list of attributes employers say they want. Employers don't seem to value schooling for the specific skills that students gain. Rather, success in school may show that students can be trained for specific jobs by employers. Increasingly, business and industry leaders cite literacy, flexibility, problem-solving skills, and general knowledge as the most appropriate preparation for the complex and changing demands of the workplace. And analyses of how jobs change in response to advanced technologies suggest that more and more workers will need these characteristics in the future. Typical vocational education does not help students acquire these competencies. An important question is whether low-level training is what parents, educators, and employers actually want schools to provide students.

Preparing for the Future

How might schools provide students with the knowledge, skills, and attitudes to function intelligently in an uncertain technology- and information-based work world? One thing is certain: Jobs will increasingly require workers to apply basic knowledge and well-developed problem-solving strategies to the unpredictable and nonroutine problems and circumstances the future holds.

Schools can probably best help students develop these fundamental skills when they organize work-related education around *meaningful* knowledge. For example, concepts from philosophy and economics explain how society works. Their application results in the economic structures and principles we follow in the production, management, and consumption of goods and services. These processes are at the heart of adults' work. Social principles and processes are clearly vocational. There's no reason why vocational programs can't make them the central organizing concepts that students learn. Philosophical concepts help explain how adults organize and govern societies. Economic principles explain how societies coordinate, distribute, exchange, and consume materials, work, and property. Historical perspectives on how these principles develop and change provide a foundation for future-oriented classes in business, consumer education, and work experience.

Economics classes? Philosophy? History? Isn't this awfully heady stuff for vocational education? You bet it is. But to assume that job and career preparation should be less demanding than preparation for college is a disservice and an insult. Is this too tough on those students who may not read and write as well as their college-bound peers? Not at all. That some define real-world relevance as quick preparation for a low-level job does not mean that schools should compromise their primary mission. That mission is to have all children leave school prepared to enter the mainstream of the American work force. Preparing for a specific entry-level job won't do it.

Fundamental concepts of physics, chemistry, geology, biology, and mathematics underlie nearly all industrial and agricultural activity. These principles explain the properties of materials used in production, and they determine the methods used to transform materials into goods and services. In the most forward-looking schools, broad technology concepts from the sciences and mathematics are beginning to replace industrial trade education. In some of these schools, technology, including computers, is clearly the purview of vocational education.

We can offer only a glimpse of the kinds of vocational activities that all parents—including those who want their children to go to college—value. But we will sketch two examples of vocational lessons that in no way compromise intellectual rigor for the sake of hands-on activities.

Young children can learn concepts of production, distribution, and consumption. They can consider how all products must grow or be manufactured. They can learn that products have points of origin and must get to the people who can use them. They can understand that all people have needs and wants that make products necessary. These concepts come alive when children participate in lessons in which they produce a product, transport it, and sell or barter it for something else of value. The concepts can be reinforced by visits to shops, industries, stores, farms, and air freight and rail terminals. Young children can construct vehicles, ports, cities, and stores using blocks, wood, and simple tools.

Senior high schoolers can revisit these blended vocational and academic concepts with classroom study of theory and historical development (genetics and the development of hybrid crops, for example). They can conduct controlled in-school laboratory and shop experiments that require inventing, growing, constructing, and programming. They can go out into the real world and work alongside adults who actually do the jobs the students are studying.

In addition to engaging students in complex and challenging knowledge, work-related instruction can emphasize the social skills that make the difference between those who succeed in the working world and those who do not. The world of careers requires adults who work cooperatively, honestly, and energetically. Students can learn to appreciate and respect the talents of the diverse array of others with whom they will work. They can gain the skills to find, communicate, and solve problems as team members. They can learn to make decisions, risk commitment, and have confidence in their ability. Vocational courses, just like academic ones, and perhaps more easily, can present learning activities as real-life problems. Work-related problems are full of ambiguity and have important consequences. They are bound to specific constraints. Their solutions depend on formal knowledge *and* creative "figuring-out." Depth, rigor, and intensity can guide such lessons. Certainly these count heavily in the real world of careers.

So whatever happened to just providing some shop classes for students who aren't very smart and like to tinker? These classes might have kept students busy until they could graduate and go to work in the factory. Well, many of the factories aren't there any more. Those that are don't want students who have been "trained" with a few shop classes but lack the advantages of a general high-quality education. They want workers with the same attributes and background knowledge as those students who go to college.

The time has come to rethink what vocational education should be and how it can best be delivered. Vocational education must be revitalized so it can give all students the skills they need for successful long-term employment. To accomplish this, educators must reintegrate vocational education into the mainstream of the school curriculum. Together educators and policymakers must find ways to make vocational programs sensitive to rapid changes in the economy and in educational needs, and anticipate future changes. Such vocational education is vital for all students, not just those in traditional vocational education programs. Schools must reject the notion of an implicit "occupational ceiling" for those who study in vocational programs. Learning about work is important for all children. Future doctors, attorneys, and professors all need the knowledge and skills to become successful working adults. Indeed, all students and all employers will be better served by an integrated view that combines work with the head and the hands, the academic and the vocational. The major challenge currently facing schools may be to make this new conception of vocational education a reality.

FOR FURTHER READING

American Alliance for Health, Physical Education, Recreation, and Dance, "National Adolescent Student Health Survey." Washington, DC: 1988.

Elliot W. Eisner, *Cognition and Curriculum: A Basis for Deciding What to Teach,* New York: Longman, 1982.

Arthur D. Efland, "The Arts and Physical Education in General Education: A Canonical Interpretation." In Ian Westbury and Allan C. Purvis (eds.), *Cultural Literacy and the Idea of General Education.* NSSE, Chicago: University of Chicago Press, 1988.

Howard Gardner, *Frames of Mind: The Theory of Multiple Intelligences.* New York: Basic Books, 1983.

Jeannie Oakes, "Beyond Tinkering: The Reconstruction of Vocational Education." In George Copa and Jane Plihal (eds.), *Revisioning Vocational Education.* St. Paul, MN: University of Minnesota Center on Technical and Vocational Education, 1986.

Neil Postman, *Amusing Ourselves to Death.* New York: Viking, 1985.

CHAPTER SIX

Making the Grade: Evaluation, Testing, and Grading

"Mr. Horton is a hard grader!"

"I got a happy face on my paper, and Derrick got a sad one."

"First they put me in the dumb class, but then Mrs. Armbruster said they made a mistake."

"I'm only six points from an A!"

"We have to take the CTBS test on Friday, but it doesn't really count."

"Mrs. Conrad told me that I had good ideas in my essay, but I need more concrete examples."

"I wish Stephanie could be in prealgebra with me, but she has to stay in basic math because she's bad in fractions."

"The whole class did terrible on the geography test, but it's O.K. She grades on the curve."

"It's not fair. The only reason Jeff got an A was because he did so much extra credit!"

"He said the arithmetic test showed I don't know how to regroup, but he's going to show me how at lunch."

"I read like a fifth grader. We took a test."

"I can't take the 'science and society' class. It doesn't count for college."

"Hah! Kevin's little brother failed kindergarten. He didn't pass the test, so he can't go to first grade. How stupid can you get to flunk kindergarten?"

These snippets of conversation reveal school and classroom evaluation practices that have enduring consequences for what and how well children learn. They signal loudly whether children will succeed at school.

Such statements should sound familiar. Except for an increasing reliance on standardized testing, schools' evaluation methods haven't changed much in decades. Most adults remember teachers who graded easy, and some who graded hard. Some teachers graded "on the curve," and others used mysterious, unpredictable schemes for awarding points, percents, A's and F's. Sometimes extra credit could boost a grade; late homework often meant points off. And there were always tests. A test could be a two-question "pop" quiz designed to reward the children who got back from recess on time and punish those who were tardy. It could be a test on the Constitution that all eighth graders took to determine whether they would graduate from middle school. Whatever the form, most students saw testing as the very meaning and essence of school. Then as now, what would be on the test told students what and how hard to study.

If your schooling was typical, there were times when you could tell by the second or third week of school who would get good grades for the entire year. Sometimes you could tell who wouldn't last the semester. There were classes in which nearly everyone got a good grade, felt smart, and prepared for college. In other classes few students did. Tests, grades, promotion to the next grade, and the fear of not passing touched every aspect of school life. Even friendships were influenced—keeping together those who had similar test scores, grades, and classes.

Perhaps even more today than in the past children's sense of worth and life chances are entwined with school evaluations. Even so, parents and the public rarely think critically about how evaluations fit into the overall scheme of schooling. Like other school regularities, the real effects of test scores, grades, and teacher recommendations lie buried under layers of unchallenged assumptions. When these assumptions are scrutinized, evaluation turns out to be far more complex and far more at odds with sound learning practices than most educators know or can admit.

Evaluation of student learning is necessary, and it can serve children and schools very well. Evaluation can reveal the informal knowledge children bring to school, and it can show teachers what children need to learn next. It can help teachers and policymakers judge how well children have learned what was taught and point to needed school and classroom reforms. However, schools, parents, and policymakers need to use evaluation with a sophisticated understanding of its effects—intended and unintended. Classroom quizzes, nationally normed tests, grades, and other evaluation tools are not by definition destructive. However, evaluation is potent. Even when responsibly used, it translates easily to global judgments about children. When used irresponsibly, it has enormous potential for unfairness and abuse.

An Overview

To help parents and policymakers be sensitive users of evaluations we will try to explain some of their technical underpinnings without going into unnecessary detail about test construction and analysis. Too much attention to technical matters can make us lose sight of the powerful political and social effects evaluation and testing have on children and schools. In order to pay attention to these effects parents and policymakers need to be aware of rather subtle distinctions among the purposes of evaluation. Evaluations do more than assess what children have learned and inform teachers about what lessons should come next. Schools' evaluations sort children for future schooling opportunities, assess school and teacher quality, and help schools run efficiently. We will frame our discussion of evaluation to keep these political and social purposes in mind, and as we do we will ask three practical questions close to the hearts of parents and policymakers:

What did she learn?

How is he doing?

What will become of her?

Answering the What did she learn? question requires educators' professional skills in determining children's achievements. In the best cases, children and teachers answer this question together by probing, fact by fact and concept by concept, what children know. We can't separate the artful use of this type of evaluation from the five dimensions of classrooms that we advocated in chapter 3. Evaluation is most productive in classrooms where the teacher believes that all children can learn, and the child believes that he can work hard to cause his own success. Evaluation is more likely to lead to appropriate future instruction in classrooms in which the teacher presents knowledge as rich, complex, and full of meaning; in which children participate actively and work with others; and in which evaluation and grading systems are personalized.

The second question, How is he doing? occupies most of our attention in this chapter, as it does in schools. The answer to this question does not usually reveal the details of what children actually know. Rather, it produces an estimate or summary of what they have learned—often expressed in grades, grade-level test scores, percents, rankings, and so on. Schools and parents typically use these estimates to compare and judge children's performance. Here, we will consider three kinds of comparisons:

- Criterion-referenced—comparing the child's knowledge to what the school expected him to learn
- Norm-referenced—comparing the child's knowledge to that of other children
- Child-referenced—comparing the child's knowledge after instruction to what he knew before.

Each comparison relies heavily, although not entirely, on testing. Each generates evaluation information that has both merits and potential for misuse. Both criterion- and norm-referenced evaluation can be used to measure and judge children's proficiency in basic skills, mastery of subject-matter knowledge, and teacher and school quality. However, both types of tests can lead schools to stress low-level learning rather than the complex conceptual understanding and problem-solving skills that are critical for children's development as learners. Norm-referenced evaluations (tests and grades) have statistical underpinnings that contribute to misunderstandings about differences among children and their prospects for school success. Both can pressure schools to overemphasize topics and skills that turn up on tests. In contrast, child-referenced evaluation reflects an attitude toward learning as much as a way of assessing it. This attitude, consistent with much of the rest of this book, begins and ends with an understanding of each child's skills, knowledge, and needs. However, child-referenced evaluation can also be misused. For example, some inner-city schools claim that children's improvement represents great success even when their absolute level of learning remains very low.

The last question, What will become of her? asks how the school will use evaluation to rank, sort, and certify a child. Evaluation results help the school determine whether a child passes or fails an assignment. They show up as report-card grades. They help determine whether to promote her or have her repeat a grade or class. If the decision is to promote, schools use evaluation results to *select* children for particular programs or classes. In these ways, schools tie future educational and postschooling opportunities to the results of evaluation. Because of the serious consequences of these decisions, the type, quality, and fairness of evaluation not only affect students' school experiences, but also play a role in determining students' life chances.

As schools move from the most individual and specific question, What did she learn? to the more global and social ones, How is he doing? and What will become of her? the child, parent, and teacher feel less and less in charge. With each question schools move from specific, descriptive information about a child's learning toward symbolic representations. These global assessments serve management needs and social functions more than they serve children's learning. Evaluations range from guiding a child's learning to determining what the child will be.

Because of their serious consequences, schools try to use evaluation results fairly and professionally. They nearly always attempt to keep them as uncontaminated as possible by arbitrary factors that might be inaccurate or biased. Nevertheless, in the end these judgments are always subjective, and schools' good intentions may not protect children from abuses of the evaluation system.

HOW EVALUATION WORKS

What Did She Learn?

The most difficult and important job of evaluation is answering the question What did she learn? The answer assigns no overall values and makes no comparisons between children. This is the safest and most helpful question parents and teachers ask. What did she learn? focuses on an individual child, not on the class or a national average.

Teacher-led Evaluations The most common tools for answering the question include the familiar classroom assessments. Tests, including essay, short-answer, oral-recitation, true/false, multiple-choice, and other types of question, can help determine what a child has learned. The mainstays of classroom evaluations, they are essentially one-shot, single-direction evaluations. That is, the teacher asks a question and the child has one opportunity to demonstrate his knowledge.

Evaluation serves children well when capable teachers get *specific* information about children's learning. These teachers analyze children's responses to test items. They look at the knowledge and skills children display when they participate in class. They observe how children interact and how they solve problems. They follow closely the nature and appropriateness of children's reasoning as well as the correctness of their answers. With this information, teachers can assess what their students learned. They can also judge the success of their teaching. Gary Natriello, a researcher at Teachers College, Columbia University, has called this the *certification* purpose of evaluation. The teacher uses information to establish whether the child has achieved a certain level of mastery of the curriculum. Parents also need this feedback about what children have learned, and so do children.

When evaluation provides information about what children have learned, it also helps teachers decide what to stress in future lessons. For example, careful analysis of math and science tests can pinpoint gaps and errors in children's knowledge and help teachers design lessons to overcome specific problems. As a general rule, the more descriptive the evaluation, the better use teachers can make of it. Nevertheless, many teachers do little of this type of testing and have few opportunities to modify their instruction on the basis of evaluations.

Interactive Evaluations Interactive evaluations are good alternatives to traditional one-way, teacher-led evaluations. When teacher and student go back and forth, there are more ways for the teacher to help the child express what he knows. Interactions can be open-ended. When teachers ask children probing questions like, "What do you think of that?" "What will you do next?" "Why did you do it that way?" and "How did you figure that out?" they get as close as they can to the heart of the child's learning. The child's responses will reveal his sense-making—not just his conclusions.

Interactive evaluations generate responses that guide teachers as they help, explain, and provide feedback. Both teachers and children can make "course corrections" when the child gets stuck. These exchanges can help children become more comfortable with evaluation and increase their efforts to do better. Children can begin to see evaluation as a process by which a friendly person helps them identify and overcome roadblocks to learning.

What did you learn? should form the core of classroom evaluation. The more often this question is asked, the easier it is for students to identify and receive the help they need. It is a question children can learn to ask themselves. What did you learn? is likely to generate a narrative—a story that requires children to put some of their thinking into language, to sort their knowledge into sequences, and form whole impressions and conclusions. As children construct logical answers that include descriptions, facts, experiences, and problems, they *use* their knowledge. This gives them access to richer and more complex knowledge than they could gain by repeating facts they heard or recognizing and choosing the correct answer on a test.

The feedback children receive in the form of new questions and subtle encouragement prompts them to push beyond their first hunches. Under the pressure of conventional testing a common first inclination is to give up—to say, "I don't know" or select any answer just to get over the discomfort. As the child explains what she has learned, she raises her own questions. She elaborates and clarifies. Both child and teacher might discover that the multiplication the child thought she knew (and passed a test on) last week has been forgotten. A question might uncover that transcendentalism—a confusing blur in yesterday's literature class—now makes more sense. The next steps in learning become more clearly focused and continue from where these answers end.

Nothing can be more essential to learning than for children to be their very own test makers and question askers. We want children to internalize *seeking* knowledge—not give that responsibility to others. We want them to see knowledge as embedded in the creative question asking that is at the center of inquiry, wonder, curiosity, and even the scientific method. If we want to understand what children know, we must listen to their questions.

Self-evaluation is rooted in evaluations that are interactive and social. When children explore both their own and one another's understanding, they become valued partners in learning cooperatively. When they ask themselves, "What do I know?" "How do I know it?" and "How can I find out more?" they are on the way to becoming independent thinkers who can use others as resources. Many fewer of these interactions are possible when schools confine evaluation to one-way assessments.

Teachers can keep interactive evaluation nonthreatening and nonjudgmental, in part, because it can be negotiable. By negotiable, we mean that teachers don't need to ask questions in the same way of all children. Furthermore, they can accept many answers, depending on the question and on children's prior knowledge. For example, children often seem to know very little when their teachers or classmates first ask a question. If the teacher (or the test) accepts the first response as the final answer, this may confirm that the child knows very little. Given the chance to think about the question and receive some clarification, however, the child might reveal more knowledge than anyone thought he had, including himself. Such interaction invites follow-up questions and additional elaborations.

Not only do teachers gain more insight into the child's knowledge, they elicit important misinformation that can create obstacles if not corrected.

Interactive evaluations keep children working. Nobody gets off the hook by giving perfunctory, even if correct, answers. Children can less easily excuse themselves by quietly accepting a bad grade before the exam even takes place. Moreover, reasoning and figuring out take place *as a part of* the evaluation process, not just before it. Ongoing evaluations push children far beyond the usual classroom study habits of skimming the chapters, doing problems, and studying before a test, and never again bothering with the material.

Careful, confidential recording and reporting of what teachers observe during interactive evaluations can help next year's teacher know what a child has learned. It can serve to direct future lessons. Such information can help parents support their child's studies. They know what he has learned and where he needs more help.

Reporting Answers to What Did He Learn? Elementary schools usually give parents specific information about what children learn. Teachers regularly send home samples of children's work. Often they write letters to parents explaining the goals of classroom activities. Many schools schedule conferences so that teachers and parents can discuss the child's learning. Many send home narrative reports about the child instead of report-card grades. Some develop extensive check sheets so that teachers can report exactly what skills children have gained. Parents should expect their child's elementary school to keep them informed. However, they may have to go to school and ask, "What did she learn?"

In upper grades teachers are responsible for large numbers of children. Consequently, they find it harder to initiate personal conversations or write reports about what any one child is learning, and they rely almost exclusively on test scores, points earned, and grades to communicate to parents and other teachers. These scores, points, and averages provide only abstract information. They sum up past learning and represent it with a symbol—usually a number or a letter. This type of information is neither specific nor descriptive. It tells little about what children have actually learned and gives few clues to what they need to learn next. Scores, points, and grades don't describe specific strengths or weaknesses. They give only global information: He is a B student. She is below average. He is in the top 10 percent.

Because they are so quantifiable, simple, comparable, and public, scores carry with them value-laden judgments of good or bad, better or worse, sufficient or inadequate. Such evaluation results are irresistibly suited to making global judgments about children. In contrast, personalized and interactive evaluations invite fewer public comparisons, with their inevitable impact on children's self-esteem ("I'm average," "Will people still think I'm smart if I don't get an A?").

Parents have an important role in this more constructive kind of evaluation. Parents need to ask their children what they learned and then allow the children plenty of time to work through, figure out, and get frustrated as they answer. Obviously, this works best if parents and children have established a relationship that makes questions and wondering seem like fun instead of like checking up. Additionally, parents should not hesitate to contact a child's teacher. Most teachers welcome parents' asking, "What is she learning?"

How Is He Doing?

Would reports that convey only what children learned satisfy parents? Probably not. Doing well or poorly in school carries such important consequences that even skillfully drawn summaries of *what* children learned would leave parents wanting to know more. Parents inevitably want to know *how* their children are doing—that is, whether their children's learning measures up to an expected standard. Similarly, a list of what children learned would be unlikely to satisfy teachers in higher grades, universities, the business world, the military. All along the education path nearly everyone who might teach, employ, or even provide auto insurance for a young person wants to make a quick judgment about how well he does in school.

To determine how a child is doing, teachers and schools need a point of reference. They have to ask, "Compared to what?" or "Compared to whom?" Schools regularly make these two kinds of comparisons. They compare what a child actually learned with what the school expected him to learn. And they compare what one child learned to what other children of the same age learned. These comparisons provide reference points. Unlike discussions or reports of what children are learning, comparisons with a particular standard convert easily to grades, points, or ratings. Information that tells whether a child is above or below grade level, in the top 30 percent, or got an 88 on the test compares the child's performance with a standard.

Parents, teachers, and children want to know how well the child is doing compared to the formal curriculum, and teachers often compare children's learning with the knowledge and skills they are being taught.

These comparisons are criterion-referenced since they compare the child's performance to a criterion—what children were supposed to learn.

In this way what was taught serves as a standard for judging what was learned. By talking with students, observing, reading their work, and/or giving tests and quizzes, teachers continuously ask, "How much of what I taught did this child learn?" Teachers have to identify specific information for the questions or test items that help them estimate how much was learned. This is a complex, difficult process. One central dilemma is that rich conceptual knowledge and problem-solving skills are not easily broken up into small bits that can be tested. When the teacher tries, knowledge and skills can lose the essential qualities and relationships we hope children will learn.

Next, the teacher must have a way to judge and record the results of the child's answers. Most teachers frame their evaluations according to a standard, even if the standard is very informal. "He solved 90 percent of the problems correctly." "She learned only five of the twenty spelling words this week." "He was able to explain why so many early towns developed near major waterways."

Such evaluation lets students know what the teacher considers most important. It communicates the level of accomplishment required for success. It directs students' attention to what they need to know and whether they learned it well enough. Gary Natriello calls this the *direction* purpose of evaluation. Specific knowledge of what children need to learn, presented in a nonjudgmental way, provides guidance for their future learning.

Natriello also suggests that such evaluation can motivate children. School assignments often involve learning that students often would not undertake on their own. By knowing what the teacher expects, children are more likely to feel that they can meet the expectations. They are more eager to make the effort necessary to learn, even if they are not motivated by an intrinsic desire to know.

However, criterion-based evaluation often goes beyond instructional and motivational purposes. Criterion-based standards also determine what grades children receive, who passes and who fails, and which children the school will promote to the next grade. For example, a teacher might establish before a test that 90 percent correct will be an A. Even if everyone in the class or no one does that well, that standard determines how she will assign the grades. Some states and school districts establish standards they call promotional gates. These are tests that children have to pass before they go on to the next subject or grade. All these methods respond to How is he doing? by comparing what a child knows to what he was taught.

Tests—The Most Common Way to Measure How Well Children Learn the Curriculum Testing is full of paradoxes, but the biggest paradox of all is this: The more accurate, scientific, and reliable a test is, the less the questions may measure what we really want to know about what children have learned. Smaller, more specific bits of knowledge are easier to test objectively than larger ideas that require explanation and interpretation. Knowledge and skills that are predictable and unambiguous make better test items than problems that require interpretation and novel approaches. For example, it can be most difficult to use a paper-and-pencil test to assess how well a child can hypothesize and try out solutions to a problem. Few teachers have the time or expertise to design such tests.

Questions that have simple answers (true or false or multiple choice) give reliable results since they have right answers that all test scorers agree upon. However, reliable results are not necessarily better results. Passing a multiple-choice drivers' test says little about one's driving skill. Similarly, simple tests tell little about a child's thinking about the concepts at the heart of good lessons.

Of course, some tests are better than others. Even so, no single test or type of test will tell the whole story of what children know. A child who correctly multiplies may not understand that the numbers can actually represent real-life items and ideas. Likewise, a child may be able to distinguish separated sounds (*ch* and *sh*) on a test, but she may not know how to use them when they occur in unfamiliar words. Knowing the year the Constitution was ratified tells nothing of child's knowledge about or appreciation for the Constitution itself. Most science teachers, for example, want their students to acquire the complex attitudes and knowledge of science. They value most having their students think and act like scientists. However, many feel limited to paper-and-pencil tests that involve calculations based upon memorized formulas.

It is not easy to test for *all* of what children learn. Neither is it easy to keep untaught ideas out of tests. Both teacher-made and commercial tests are flawed by these problems.

Teacher-made tests are usually better matched to the actual curriculum than those produced by commercial test publishers, the school district office, or the school department. Nonetheless, a recent study at UCLA confirms that there are plenty of problems with teacher-made tests. Teachers have little training in how to construct test items. They often write questions that demand only low-level responses. Most tests measure only a narrow range of what children could have learned. They often lack good directions for how to take the test.

Many tests assess more than what a child has learned in the current year. To answer many test items, some children will need information they did not have a chance to learn. Children who at the beginning of a class already have some of the knowledge and skills the class will teach have an obvious advantage. Because they know more, they often appear to have learned more. For example, a fourth grader's reading ability or prior knowledge of history may improve his score on a test covering the current history lesson. As a result, the child who starts out knowing more often gets better grades and more praise and attention. Another child, who may have worked harder and actually gained more new knowledge and skill, may get a poorer grade. That's not particularly good for either child, yet it is one pitfall of conventional testing practices.

Once tested, children rarely have a chance to examine, challenge, or learn further from the test. The press to cover the curriculum makes it difficult for teachers to spend time going back. And few children have the motivation to go back and dwell on their errors. After all, errors provide painful evidence that they studied too little, guessed wrong, or aren't smart. Besides, tests are frequently terminal—that is, they end a unit of study. Knowing what was missed often doesn't matter since the class is going on to something new. Few teachers expect a child who scores 75 percent to master the missed 25 percent and then take still another test to confirm the learning.

Basic Skills Tests Nearly all states and school districts require children to take standardized basic-skills tests to assess their knowledge of the basic curriculum. The California Achievement Test (CAT), the Iowa Test of Basic Skills (ITBS), and the Comprehensive Test of Basic Skills (CTBS) are tests they frequently use. Increasingly, many states and school districts use results on these tests to make schools and teachers more *accountable* for achievement. Accountability, in a very loose sense, involves comparing children's achievement with what policymakers think they should achieve.

Educators and policymakers usually intend these basic skills tests to raise schools' standards and, thereby, increase children's levels of achievement. However, many observers note serious problems with such testing. For example, George Madaus, a testing expert, has documented several ways such tests may backfire. In many cases, teachers spend too much time and energy getting children ready to do well on the low-level skills that are on the test. As a result they neglect important concepts and skills that are not on the test. Often children devote less time to reading books, discussing ideas, writing, and projects. Many teachers "teach the test." That is, they have children practice the actual test questions ahead of time. Some teachers take their cues from the widespread faith in testing and believe that teaching the test is the best way for children to learn. Others spend lots of time showing students how to be "test-wise"—to do intelligent guessing based on cues built into the questions. All these responses erode the validity of the test as a measure of learning.

Another major testing problem is that, on average, poor and minority students score significantly lower than middle-class and white students on standardized tests of basic skills. Researchers don't fully understand why. However, considerable evidence suggests that these children (along with many white, middle-class children) know far more than their test scores show. They demonstrate far greater competence when the tester asks them to talk about ideas or perform skills in a real-world situations.

Testing for Grade-to-Grade Promotion Many states and school districts use readiness, proficiency, or competency on basic skills tests to determine whether they will promote children to the next grade. If a child scores below an established cutoff point, the school may keep her in the same grade. For example, in a recent year Minneapolis schools held back 10 percent of their kindergarteners because they scored too low on the readiness test for first grade. In other schools, students may be put in a special class with others who have serious academic difficulty. Many states require high school students to pass minimum competency tests before they can graduate from senior high school.

Certain presumptions underlie the criterion-referenced tests used for these purposes. One is that the test actually represents the body of knowledge or skills children had the opportunity to learn. Another is that success in the next grade actually requires a particular percentage of the knowledge that the test measures, and that schools can determine what that percentage is. In fact, few tests are so precise.

While most proficiency tests use multiple-choice formats, another trend is to test with more complex tasks. To do this schools try to objectify assessments most people think of as subjective and difficult to standardize. There has been some progress in assessing children's writing abilities, for example. Such tests often ask students to write an essay or business letter as part of their proficiency or entrance testing. Increasingly, the judgments of two or more scorers replace a single reader's assessment. These readers compare each student's work to a sometimes elaborate standardized scoresheet or rubric. Using this guide, trained scorers assign points according to how students employ composition elements. Grammar mechanics, vivid use of language, and subordination of ideas are just a few examples. Sometimes the lists contain ten or twenty items or more.

Using multiple scorers who are trained for the particular essay-type test is a costly but necessary alternative if the scoring is to be reliable and valid. The procedure is particularly crucial if the school insists on using a single test to qualify or disqualify students for promotion or for a special program. However, the scores that result from even the best tests can't be treated as scientific findings. The performance of both tester and tested can vary from day to day. A score on any test is never more than an approximation of what the child knows or can really accomplish.

One of the biggest problems with this type of accountability is determining whether the consequences are productive and fair. Do children learn more if schools hold them back a grade? Do they learn more if they score a few points higher to meet the standard? Are the consequences fairly assigned?

For example, there is no evidence that rigid promotion policies and graduation standards improve student achievement. Common sense tells many to hold back slower-achieving children. Especially in the earliest grades, why not give children who fall behind a chance to catch up with more academically adept peers? But Lorrie Shephard and Mary Lee Glass report persuasively in *Flunking Grades* that stringent grade-to-grade promotion requirements may actually retard academic progress. Moreover, repeating early grades increases the chances that, as teenagers, children will drop out of school. *Comparably skilled* children in earlier grades who stayed with their classes stood a better chance of not dropping out.

Proficiency tests disproportionately retain poor and minority students, as a consequence of their typically lower test scores. This adds serious social consequences to retention policies. Finally, proficiency tests can easily undermine teachers' sense of professionalism. Stripped of their primary role in children's assessment, teachers can wind up feeling less in charge of children's progress. When policymakers try to link higher standards to tests that only roughly measure those standards they often fail to consider these consequences.

For these reasons, proficiency tests have generated controversy and even court challenges. Recently, Georgia rescinded its ninety-minute paper-and-pencil test for promoting kindergarteners as a result of the protests of educators and many policymakers.

Testing to Measure Teacher and School Quality When schools, administrators, policymakers, or the public use test scores to judge teacher or school quality, the schools marshal substantial effort to make sure children do well on the tests. Sometimes this works out well for children. Sometimes it doesn't. The pressure is particularly great in states in which newspapers publish children's scores, school-by-school. Some states publish lists of the very best- and worst-scoring schools. "The good, the bad, and the ugly," is how one state testing director we know refers to his state's rankings. Bad press on these simplistic measures of learning can have profound consequences. Schools know that many parents will use the scores to judge whether a school is worth attending. They know that business people and real estate agents will advertise whether the school raises or lowers property values. In some states low-scoring schools must develop extensive improvement plans. Some states withhold special funding from low scorers; some give cash awards to those schools that do well.

Under these "high stakes" conditions, minimum competency or basic skills tests can have an enormous impact on teaching and learning. They bear directly on children's opportunities to learn the rich and complex knowledge that does not translate easily into test scores. When teachers divert attention from the subject to the test, they may limit opportunities for thinking and problem solving. Often, the very children who need the most time to figure out larger concepts, read longer books, and write thoughtful compositions suffer the most: they receive extensive drill on smaller tasks in preparation for basic skills tests. Tests also affect the curriculum for highest-achieving students. It is not uncommon for university-bound seniors to end their regular instruction months early to start coaching for tests. Increasingly some teachers feel coerced into teaching to the test because their own evaluations rest on how well their students perform. Occasionally some teachers and school administrators simply cheat. They have children rehearse actual test items, coach children during the test, or change answer sheets after the test is over.

The Objectivity of Testing Educators often refer to standardized testing as being objective. They contrast these tests with subjective tests, including essays, short written responses, oral explanations, demonstrations, and so on. Calling a test objective usually means that the teacher's understanding of and sympathies for an individual student won't influence the grade. Neither will subjective interpretations of facts or procedures influence the correctness of the answers. Such tests can undervalue students who master important concepts, and they can overvalue skills such as rote memorization.

Parents and policymakers often insist on hard, scientific, and objective evaluation results. Having such results, they think they will know exactly where their own and other children stand. Many also like factual evidence about how good the school, its teachers, and its administrators are. If such data were possible, they believe they could rest easy when results showed that all is going well and they could act when the evidence indicated trouble.

In truth, the technology of educational testing never offers more than a starting point for further inquiry about what children know and how good students are. All testing, even the fill-in-the-bubble, matching, true-false, and multiple-choice kind, is far more subjective than most people realize. What's more, the familiar subjective assessments can often be fairer and more useful ways of evaluating a child's knowledge and progress. Evaluations of essays, contributions to discussions, use of knowledge in novel ways (in projects, for example), and so on are all subjective, and yet they can reveal a great deal about learning. In fact, the Stanford psychologist Robert Calfee argues convincingly that the best and most professional evaluation may be a compendium of subjective, informal, and only loosely scientific assessments made by teachers.

However, others remain concerned about the potential inaccuracy of informal assessments. They criticize may teachers' inability to keep their overall impression of the child's behavior and intelligence separate from tasks they evaluate. Most teachers agree that much professional skill and discipline are required to remain objective about a child in the face of the many irrelevant factors that may creep into subjective assessments. For example, a child with faint and shaky handwriting challenges the fairness and objectivity of any teacher reading his composition. Misbehavior and grating personality traits are difficult to disengage from a child's skills or progress.

Whether objective or subjective, all methods for assessing how well students have learned the expected curriculum are subject to serious questions. Nearly all these testing problems have two dimensions. One is the difficulty of measuring by conventional methods what children actually know. The second is the global effect of assessing specific learnings—that is, the confusion that arises between measuring what the child learned and judging the overall worth of the learner, the teacher, or the school. This confusion often leads schools to make decisions based on test scores that can have detrimental effects.

How Is He Doing?—Norm-Referenced Tests and Comparisons with Other Children

The humorist Garrison Keillor gently characterized his mythical town of Lake Wobegon as a place where "all the children are above average." Clearly, he meant in the hearts of the adults who love them. If Keillor based his assessment on the children's standardized test scores, he would have to invent another mythical town where all the children were *below* average. That's the statistical law.

Certainly, the citizens of Lake Wobegon are too decent ever to wish ill to others' children. Even so, if they were intent on their children's getting into the best colleges, it would be in their interest to have children in other towns do poorly on tests. Mark Twain wrote bitterly that every prayer for victory implies a prayer for another's defeat. Likewise, wishing for a high score on a norm-referenced test, in a sense, is like wishing for others to get a low score. Of course, Mark Twain was not writing about education. He was writing about war.

The question How is he doing? often means Whom [or how many] is he doing better than? Schools could answer the question by comparing the child's performance with the knowledge he could have learned. Instead, they compare it with how other children did on the same assignment or test. Most educators, parents, and policymakers, too, are decent and wish only the best for all children. Nevertheless, it is difficult for them to avoid acting on their wish for their own children or the children in their class, school, or state to beat the others. And it is not surprising, given these wishes and schools' evaluation practices, that the casualties of schooling are as senseless as the casualties of war.

Standardized, Norm-Referenced Tests Standardized, norm-referenced tests provide the most technically sophisticated comparisons among children. These are commercially published tests like the Scholastic Aptitude Test (SAT) and the basic skills tests we referred to above. Scores and evaluations based on these tests are *norm-referenced*. This means that raw scores (the number of right answers) are converted to standardized scores that permit easy comparisons of a child's score to those of others who took the test. These scores often convert to percentile ranks ("He scored in the top 10 percent nationally") or grade-level equivalents ("She's reading at the seventh-grade level").

Most schools give standardized, norm-referenced tests of reading and math. They often test yearly to chart children's progress in comparison with other children. Keeping track of children's grade levels and percentile standings makes some educators feel more professionally secure. Test data reassure many parents, especially if their child scores well above average. Test makers package and market their products in ways that emphasize them as technological advancements. In the very inexact practice of educating, test scores are one seemingly scientific tool to which educators turn.

Norm-referenced tests *can* inform parents, educators, and policymakers, but only in a very general way. They can highlight special populations of children who do very well or very poorly—by geographic area, by gender, by parent income, and so on. They can quickly screen for some children who have considerable skills and for others who may have learning problems.

Because the purpose of norm-referenced tests is to compare and rank children, the tests are constructed deliberately so that as many children will score above the statistical average for their grade as below. In statistical language, this result is a *normal* distribution (when this distribution is graphed, it becomes the familiar bell-shaped curve.) When test makers "norm" their tests, they try out the questions on a large group of children and select those items that best discriminate among them. In other words, they eliminate items that most children can answer correctly as well as items that most children miss. This process is required since a test can't reveal differences if all or most children answer the same questions in the same way. The norming process allows test manufacturers to set particular scores as indicative of superior, average, or below-average performance. Because they use a large reference group of children, one child's score can be compared to those of other children of the same age or grade who have taken the test.

This strategy depends on testing a sample of knowledge and skills on which children vary widely. By definition, it must ignore the learning that most children have in common. These tests can be misleading if test items do not represent the knowledge that we want children to know. Standardized tests are usually written with little responsiveness to what a particular community teaches—let alone a particular class. Single test items, even groups of items on a topic, only hint at the depth and richness of the understanding that is possible. Most important, these tests cannot reveal the way children think about the facts they know. Finally, many test items are badly written, and some "correct" answers are in fact just plain wrong. All we can be certain of is that the tests tell how well one child does on a series of test items on which children's answers vary. Unless carefully interpreted, such results present a distorted picture of what children know and are able to do.

Another misleading feature of norm-referenced tests is the possibility that a small difference in the number of right answers can make a large difference in how a child compares with others. On some tests a difference of two or three answers can move a child up or down a whole grade level. This is especially true for children whose scores fall in the highest and lowest ranges. These, of course, are the ranges that often serve as barriers or opportunities for promotion or special programs.

Finally, comparisons based on norm-referenced test results are rarely neutral. Scores are not seen merely as being higher or lower than a percentage of other scores. Inevitably they are judged as good or bad. Consequently, they are ripe for translation into the global labels we discussed in chapter 3. Norm-referenced tests affect admissions to colleges, state and local pride, concerns for national prestige and security, the profits of large corporate test makers, individual careers of educators and policymakers, property values, and so on. Because of these powerful and crucial effects, they are open to abuses that go beyond simple misunderstandings.

In 1988 John Cannell, a West Virginia physician, raised serious ethical concerns over norm-referenced tests. Posing as a school superintendent shopping for a new test for his district, Cannell telephoned test publishers. He reports that when he expressed concern that his students might do poorly, the test companies assured him that his students would indeed score above average: the teachers simply needed to prepare the students for the tests. Cannell investigated further and found that in nearly every state, most children were scoring "above average" on norm-referenced tests—a statistical impossibility. Apparently, most tests had not been renormed for many years. (This is a costly process that establishes new averages by a readministering of the test to another large group of children.) So, test makers were comparing children in the mid-1980s to children who had taken the test years earlier. Not only had curricula shifted to match the tests better, but schools had been coaching for the tests for years. Perhaps Cannell has discovered Lake Wobegon's secret.

Some have questioned John Cannell's methods and facts. Nevertheless, he has brought a serious problem under public scrutiny. Test scores have high stakes attached to them, and the selling of tests is a big business. Such conditions make both schools and test makers ripe for corruption as they keep testing away from what ought to be its primary mission: enhancing teaching and learning.

Grades that Compare When teachers grade they rarely use standardized, norm-referenced tests. But they do typically assign grades at least partly by comparing students' performance on tests. Further, their assumptions about grades seem quite influenced by the formal, norm-referenced testing described above. In a technical sense, grading on the curve could mean that the classroom teacher goes through all the steps a major test publisher might. He would consider his class as representative of the whole population of students who received the same teaching and test. He could then treat the scores according to the statistical and probability conventions associated with a normal distribution.

Of course, these conventions help predict the distribution of *chance* events. For example, if we rolled a pair of dice hundreds of times and graphed the results, two and twelve, having the minimal possibilities of occurring, would be represented at the lowest, extreme ends of a bell-shaped curve. Seven would be in the middle, highest part of the curve because it turned up most often. Assuming a representative group of children whose learning is, like rolling dice, predictably random, the teacher could then give an equal, small number of children at the top and the bottom of the distribution A's and F's, respectively. A larger number near the top and bottom would get B's and D's. The largest group in the middle would get C's.

In actual practice, very few teachers have the statistical knowledge or the poor judgment to attempt these formal procedures. What teachers usually mean when they say they grade on the curve is that they use the performance of the whole class to establish a distribution of grades that roughly matches a bell-shaped curve. Typically, the teacher may simply have in mind that a few children should get A's, a few more B's, most C's, and a few D's and F's. The actual distribution of grades may vary widely from class to class and teacher to teacher. Some teachers further adjust grades on the basis of whether they feel they have a low-or high-ability class, whether they feel positive about a class that worked hard, and whether they think the instructional time was sufficient. Some teachers consider themselves hard graders with high standards and are stingy with A's. Others use top grades to motivate low-performing children to improve. But in spite of these modifications, the tradition for a normal distribution is so strong that teachers whose grading strays too far from this average are viewed with some suspicion.

Grading on the curve shifts attention from actual learning to comparing students. Assignment of grades on the basis of test scores highlights the problem. A low-scoring student may learn more as a result of class instruction. A high-scoring student may learn practically nothing if he already knew the material. In this case a child who learns less can get the higher grade. Moreover, if a teacher grades on the curve, and the whole class doesn't catch on, some students with minimal understanding will still get high grades. Even worse, when everyone in the class has a high level of understanding, grading on the curve may mean that some children who learn a lot can nevertheless earn poor grades. It is not uncommon for very high-scoring students to be treated like rate-busters in the workplace— shunned because their performance makes everyone else look bad.

We came across a bizarre case of grading on the curve a few years ago. A high school physics class enrolled the six highest-achieving seniors in the school (to the envy of teachers of other classes). The teacher set out to make the class "like a college course." He announced that he would grade on a modified curve. One student would get an A, two would get B's, and the other three, C's. Obviously, all these students had strong records of success in science classes. All were likely to learn a great deal about physics. This procedure was not only obviously silly but jeopardized the college admission chances of all but one of these superior students.

It takes an extreme case like this for most parents or policymakers to notice grading practices. While few teachers make such ridiculous use of grading on the curve, most do compare children when they assign grades. Few teachers feel comfortable giving either all high grades or all low ones, and few school administrators would allow it. The belief that children will inevitably differ in the degree to which they master classroom knowledge (regardless of the quality of instruction) supports comparative grading. The extreme example of the physics teacher clarifies three problems often overlooked when teachers base grades on comparisons. First, such grades are anything but objective. Second, they may bear little relationship to how much students actually learn. Third, they may ensure that success will be a scarce commodity that can't be had by every child.

Experienced teachers carry with them certain standards from past years. Scores and grades are often subtly adjusted to this "memory-reference." Such teachers talk with colleagues at their own and other schools, and these contacts inform their evaluation decisions. This is certainly a professional and reliable way of raising and maintaining high standards. It probably keeps grading close to the spirit of criterion-referenced (grades based on what they taught the children) evaluation. Secondary teachers in particular who don't have frequent professional contact with colleagues at their own and other schools may base their standards on their school experiences when they were students—often an unreliable criterion.

Teachers also manipulate grades in many ways. They use and combine numbers, letters, and symbols to arrive at grades that report, essentially, the teacher's judgment of a child's work. Sometimes teachers attribute scientific accuracy to the sophistication of the formulas and numbers used. However, one teacher we know actually speaks of "laundering" his grades. He scores assignments and test results in points and then converts them to percentages. He translates the percentages to letter grades (90% for an A, 80% for a B, and so on), then averages his grades by giving them a numerical equivalent (4 points for an A, 3 for a B, and so on). He believes this mystification wards off objections by students and parents. Another teacher reports that she has had far fewer complaints and challenges since she got a grade book program for her personal computer. She thinks her numbers seem more authoritative and fair when printed out in faded dot matrix.

Probably, children with very good grades have learned more than those with very poor grades. However, that is about the extent of the confidence we can muster when it comes to grades. Letters and numbers often don't report or even claim to report an accurate account of a child's specific knowledge. A child's grade or score may be the same as that of another child even though both have very different knowledge or have made dramatically different progress.

Many grades also reflect effort as well as learning. For example, no matter how much a child learns, he may not get a good grade unless he turns in the assigned homework. Grades can also reflect classroom behavior. A child who constantly causes trouble at school is likely to receive a lower grade because of it. Likewise, well-behaved, cooperative children may receive misleadingly high grades that don't reflect their performance or improvement. Obviously, social and behavioral considerations are important. Parents need to know about them. However, they further confuse what grades mean. Again, although reliable information is elusive under the best circumstances, parents can nearly always enhance their understanding of what grades mean simply by talking with the teacher who gave them.

How Is He Doing?—Comparing Children's Learning with Their Own Prior Knowledge

Finally, schools use what we call child-referenced evaluation. In this least common approach to evaluation, the teacher uses pretests and initial informal assessments before, during, and after instruction to guide lessons and judge progress. The comparison here is between what children know after instruction and what they knew before. The teacher bases grades or points (if she uses them at all) on improvement.

Few teachers use child-referenced comparisons as the *primary* way of assessing learning and providing feedback to the child. However, many allow this method of evaluation to at least influence their instruction and grading. Some teachers set individual learning goals and give high grades to all children who reach them. They might individualize grading standards. For example, if a pretest indicates that a child already knows 50 percent of the vocabulary words, the teacher might require a score of 95 percent for that child to get an A. Another child with a pretest score of 20 percent might only need to get an 80 for an A. After all, to achieve 80 percent the second child would have learned more new words than the first child.

However, teachers, parents, and children often complain that this method is unfair. They protest that the smartest (highest-scoring) children should get the best grades—regardless of individual goals or improvement. Such protests are not surprising. Grading on learning rather than on level of performance runs counter to long-standing school traditions. It wreaks havoc with comparisons among children. Nonetheless, we're convinced that, of all possible comparisons, those that judge children by how much they have actually learned or improved help the most.

Even evaluations based on gains and improvement have their potential for abuse. It is important to check that adjustments of instruction and standards for individual children do not result in a watered-down curriculum. Any adjustments must be held up to the standard of a curriculum that is full of rich and valued knowledge. That is the only protection that low absolute levels of learning won't be justified because the children improved so much. The improvement standard can also have its pitfalls when extended to an entire school. For example, a school where nearly all children are low achievers may be heralded for raising test scores from an abysmal eleventh percentile to a merely dreadful sixteenth percentile. Finally, it is indeed possible to gain useful information by comparing one child to others. We simply disagree with schools' and parents' preoccupation and lack of caution with these comparisons.

So, How Is He Doing? It is hard to escape the pervasiveness of grade or test winners and losers. Low test scores and poor grades, even the threat of them, can alter lives in unproductive ways. In schools, tests and grades often become the tail that wags the dog. Testing is useful when it gives information that helps teachers select appropriate learning activities. Tests can help measure a child's progress or improvement. Tests can show what a child who has had the opportunity to learn actually learned. Test information can be put to good use by those who understand what the test measures and what the results mean.

Sometimes tests provide useful clues as to why a child has difficulty at school. Some standardized measures detect particular learning disabilities, and others may provide clues to a child's effort or motivation. However, for reasons we will explain in chapter 8, only trained psychologists should administer these types of tests, and only to individual children. And schools should always consult parents before and after they administer such tests. These tests, along with general intelligence tests, are not appropriate for classroom use.

Finally, standardized tests are sometimes legitimately used to determine the performance and abilities of *groups* of children rather than individual children with regard to curricular goals. Some of these tests ask each child to complete only a few questions. Then analysts combine individual responses to assess the entire group (the reading proficiency of all third graders in the school district, the writing performance of eleventh graders in the state who attend schools with a high level of poverty, and so forth). As long as policymakers and educators form conclusions only about the specifics measured, these tests can help assess the effectiveness of the learning opportunities schools provide. In the best cases, state education departments and school districts use these testing programs because they provide a uniform method of assessing instruction. Combined with other indicators of resources, teacher quality, and instruction, they help determine whether the educational system is effective.

That initially simple question, How is he doing? turns out to be not so simple after all. A child's entire school year can be summarized in a test score, a collection of A's or D's, or a single GPA (grade point average). Parents, policymakers, and educators themselves have a hard time uncovering the actual learning that lies behind these condensations. In spite of the problems known to accompany tests and grades, these measures of children and their performance can still overwhelm the real business of schooling—attention to learning.

As children get older the uses made of their test scores and grades gradually change in character, from reporting how well a child has done to determining future opportunities for learning. The emphasis shifts from the individual purposes of helping a child learn to the social purpose of deciding which children will receive the best education.

What Will Become of Her?

The most socially relevant evaluation question—and the most worrisome—is What will become of her? The judgments embedded in test scores and grades influence teachers' and parents' expectations of what children will accomplish in school and adult life. And they further influence what children expect of themselves. Schools use grades to decide which students should receive academic awards and which students are eligible to participate in extracurricular activities. Grades and scores help teacher's decide which students will be promoted or retained. Grades help children decide what classes they will take. By the end of high school, grades and tests determine whether or not a child will go to college, and, if he goes to college, which colleges will admit him.

We can predict with considerable accuracy that children whose early grades and test scores are interpreted to mean they are smarter will continue to do better. As their years of schooling add up, the differences between them and those who do less well early on steadily increase. At high school and college graduation ceremonies, when awards and advanced degrees are being presented, we can note the immense pleasure and enormous relief of proud family members. However, these achievements rarely shock anyone. Nothing is guaranteed, but most successes were anticipated early in the schooling process. Likewise, few of those parents whose children did not "make the grade" at graduation feel surprised. Long ago there were grades, tests, and judgments that prophesied this lack of success. And the prophecy was fulfilled.

In chapter 1 we briefly described how schools develop structures that help make early predictions come true. Ability grouping and tracking help turn early judgments into self-fulfilling action. Group and track enrollments signal most clearly what the school thinks of children and what they think they are likely to become. In the following chapter, we explain what parents and policymakers need to know about these structures that schools use to sort and eventually certify children for different future opportunities.

EVALUATION SERVES SOCIAL AS WELL AS EDUCATIONAL PURPOSES

Schools rely on evaluation for reasons that go beyond helping children learn or determining their futures. Here again, we confront the familiar theme that schools, like industry, want to be efficient. Schools adopt complex standardized evaluation systems to keep records, make decisions, and report to parents. These systems require the shorthand conveyances of grades, percent scores, and so on. Most teachers have too many students and too little time to hold discussions with each child's parents or write narratives of each child's learning, either to send home or to use as school records. Most schools and parents settle for shorthand symbols that communicate quickly, "Everything's fine" or "Be concerned."

Schools use standardized shorthand methods for keeping track of children's progress because the larger society requires it. Colleges and employers depend on test scores, grades, and class placements to tell them which students meet their standards. Additionally, most state legislatures have accountability systems that let the public know how well schools in the state are performing. These systems rely primarily on students' test scores to judge the quality of schools. Many states reward, punish, or provide assistance to schools based on this information.

Increasingly, evaluation takes on the aspect of an educational sweepstakes. The prizes for students are entry into a gifted class, selection as school valedictorian, admission to a prestigious prep school or university, a discount on car insurance, and so on. Schools gain rewards and recognition or garner humiliation, censure, and state intervention. With the stakes so high, schools are under mounting pressure. They must document their decisions about students in ways that will stand up to parents' inquiries and sometimes to parents' lawyers. High stakes also pressure schools to make sure students score well on state tests. Sometimes the pressure leads to a distortion of the curriculum, coaching, and outright cheating. All these pressures can prompt evaluation misuse.

FOR FURTHER READING

Ann E. Boehm, *The Parents' Handbook on School Testing.* New York: Teachers' College Press, 1982.

John Cannell, Friends of Education, 1987.

James Crouse and Dale Trusheim, *The Case against the SAT.* Chicago: University of Chicago Press, 1988.

Morton Deutsch, "Education and Distributive Justice: Some Reflections on Grading Systems," *American Psychologist* 34, 391–401.

FairTest, a quarterly publication of the National Center for Fair and Open Testing, Cambridge, Massachusetts.

Norman Fredrickson, "The Real Test Bias: Influences of Testing on Teaching and Learning," *American Psychologist* 39, 193–202.

Edward Haertel, *Student Achievement Tests as Tools of Educational Policy: Practices and Consequences.* Berkeley, CA: University of California Commission on Testing and Public Policy, 1988.

Walter Hathaway (ed.), *New Directions for Testing and Measurement: Testing in the Schools*. San Francisco: Jossey-Bass, 1983.

Joan Herman and Don Dorr-Bremme, *Testing and Assessment Practices in American Public Schools: Current Practices and Directions for Improvement*. Los Angeles: Center for the Study of Evaluation, University of California, Los Angeles, 1984.

Thomas Kellaghan, George F. Madaus, Peter W. Airasian, *The Effects of Standardized Testing*. Boston: Kluwer-Nijhoff, 1985.

Gary Natriello, *Evaluation Processes in Schools and Classrooms,* Report No. 12. Baltimore: Center for Research on Elementary and Middle Schools, Johns Hopkins University, 1987.

Jeannie Oakes, *Educational Indicators: A Guide for Policymakers*. Santa Monica: The RAND Corporation, 1986.

Office of Educational Research and Improvement Task Force on State Accountability, *Creating Responsible and Responsive State Accountability Systems*. Washington, DC: U.S. Department of Education, 1988.

David Owen, *None of the Above: The Myth of Scholastic Aptitude*. Boston: Houghton Mifflin, 1986.

Lorrie Shephard and Mary Lee Smith, *Flunking Grades*. New York: Falmer Press, 1988.

CHAPTER SEVEN

Tracking: An Old Solution Creates New Problems

For years, schools have assigned children to groups and classes on the basis of their estimate of the children's ability. Many elementary schools provide separate classes at each grade for high, average, and low achievers. In addition, high schools prescribe different sequences of classes, called tracks. Students heading for college and those expecting to take jobs right after high school will be in different tracks. Nearly all schools divide academic subjects (typically English, mathematics, science, and social studies) into separate classes for different ability levels. The vocational or general (noncollege) track usually coincides with the lower academic levels. College-bound students enroll in the high-ability tracks. Despite these commonalities, not all schools have the same tracking systems. Rather, schools vary in the number of tracked subjects, the number of track levels, and how they decide where to place students.

Schools also assign students to tracked classes for reasons other than ability. Often, schools place capable but bothersome, poorly behaved children in low tracks. Sometimes a student's hard work or insistent parent gains him admission to a high track. Particularly in secondary schools, the arranging of class schedules for hundreds of students also affects grouping practices. The mere act of developing the master schedule generates more tracking than most schools intend.

The regularities of keeping school running also affect tracking systems.

Administrators must make sure that each student has a class every hour. Each class must have approximately the same number of students. Additionally, each student must be placed in the correct class for his or her ability level. With all these constraints, even large schools can wind up with little flexibility for placing children. For example, instead of being able to place a student in any of five English classes, the school may have only one class in which to place a low-ability student. An average student may be able to take only one of two classes. Students identified as gifted, honors, remedial, English as a second language, and so on may have very limited choices.

Sometimes a class like health education also becomes tracked when students' other tracked classes keep them together for part of the day. For example, suppose students in the third-hour remedial-reading class move en masse to the fourth-hour social-studies class. Social studies thus becomes a low-track class despite the fact that the school does not have a tracking policy in social studies. We know of one drivers' education class that filled with gifted students in this way and became known as the advanced drivers' education class! Additionally, subjects like art and home economics often become low-track classes because students in the college-preparatory curriculum rarely have time to take them.

Assumptions about Tracking

Most people assume that children learn better if they learn with others who have similar capabilities. This assumption rests on the largely outmoded views of human ability that we described in chapters 2 and 3. The traditional view holds that children have dramatically different abilities that require different and separate schooling. The extreme position is that many students lack the intelligence to learn high-quality knowledge.

A second assumption is that less capable children suffer emotional and educational damage if they must learn with brighter classmates. Many expect that slower children in mixed-ability classrooms will develop poor self-concepts and attitudes toward learning.

Third, most schools, parents, and policymakers assume that tracking placements are accurate and fair. They assume that schools can and do make good judgments about which classes will most help children succeed.

Finally, most teachers and administrators contend that tracking makes teaching easier. Some believe that it is the *only* way to manage student differences.

ANSWERING THE ASSUMPTIONS

Children, of course, do differ in their backgrounds, developmental levels, interests, and learning styles. They also differ in the ease with which they succeed at typical school lessons. Not surprisingly, these differences influence what they learn at school. By the time students enter high school, differences in school achievement are considerable. However, the common practice of putting children from their earliest school years into separate classes to accommodate these differences is neither necessary nor very effective. In fact, serious social and educational consequences can result. A wealth of research has yet to find evidence to support any of the above assumptions.

The most serious obstacle to understanding tracking is that it is hard to imagine schools without it. Tracking is part of the school's culture. People take it for granted just like the school's other structural arrangements. For example, few question the organizing of instruction according to traditional subjects like history, English, and so on. Only rarely does anyone ask why schools group children in *grades* according to their *ages*. It is difficult to imagine schools without these structures. And it is just so with ability-grouped classes and tracking.

So, when we ask parents, educators, and policymakers to reconsider tracking, many jump to what we call *the worst possible case*. First, they anticipate that absolutely all differentiation among children will stop. They express concern that schools will teach all children in the exact same way and at the same time. We'd like to put some of these fears to rest. Sometimes children who are having particular difficulties (say, learning how to do long division) need to be grouped for a short time to receive special help. Sometimes those with similar interests should be grouped for a special activity or lesson. Moreover, we wouldn't recommend that schools teach calculus to all children regardless of their prior math experiences. We do not think that some children should wait to study calculus until all children are ready. And we do not suggest that the band director give every child who wants one a place in the school's jazz ensemble. And we would never suggest that children who need extra or special help should not receive it. In short, our arguments for more common school experiences do not deny that children are different and that they should have opportunities to learn differently in school.

Tracking Does Not Promote Achievement for Average and Lower-ability Children. And It May Not Benefit the Smartest Ones

Tracking doesn't work well for children in the low and middle groups. Benefits to children in the highest groups—when they occur—are often at the expense of students in the other tracks. Most children are not in top classes. So, most researchers conclude, most students do not benefit from tracking. For example, in the early 1980s about 62 percent of senior high school students were in average or below-average classes. As a group, these children experienced clear and consistent disadvantages from tracking. What's more, some studies suggest that students in high school vocational tracks don't even get better jobs as a result of their training. Shocking as it is, high school graduates who say they have taken vocational-preparation programs may actually be less employable than if they had not taken them. When they do find jobs, they are likely to earn lower wages than other, similar high school graduates. Some graduates of vocational programs do only about as well on the job market as high school dropouts.

Over the years of schooling, ability-grouped classes can exaggerate children's earlier developmental and motivational differences. Younger children who are initially fairly similar in background and skills become *increasingly* different in achievement when they are separated into classes for students with different abilities. Their hopes for the future also change in ways that are consistent with their track placement. This effect accumulates until high school, when wide differences among students are most obvious. One reason for this long-term effect is that track placements rarely change. Most students placed in low-ability groups in elementary school will continue in these tracks in middle school and junior high. Senior high schools usually place these students in non-college-prep tracks. In English and math, low-ability classes are often remedial. Remedial classes typically drill students on low-level skills while the achievement gap between them and their classmates continues to widen. Astonishingly, schools consistently and sincerely present this near-guarantee that children will fall farther behind as an opportunity for them to catch up.

Certainly, there are notable exceptions. Many teachers know of children who get inspired and catch on despite their labels and classroom placements. Some children, by sheer grit, pull themselves out of low-ability classes and succeed in higher classes. However, these cases are exceptions. Furthermore, they may occur in spite of track placement, not because of it.

What's most surprising is that tracking does not necessarily promote achievement for high-ability children. That tracking *can* work well for the top students should be obvious. Certainly, it is possible to create excellent classes in the midst of mediocre ones. Start by providing better teachers, the most successful students, and, often, smaller class sizes. Add special resources, a sense of superior academic mission, perhaps a parent support group. With these advantages it is no wonder that these top students will get the best education in town.

What *if* the special advantages for the top 10–30% *resulted* in a poorer education for all the rest? Might tracking still be worth it? After all, these top students, some claim, need special grooming to be our future scientists, business executives, and government leaders. Evidence exists that top students do not necessarily learn less in mixed-ability classes. Many studies show that highly capable students do as well in mixed classes as in homogeneous groupings. Research on the cooperative learning strategies that we described in chapter 3 is adding to this evidence.

Ironically, being at the high end of the tracking scale is no longer a guarantee of most favored treatment. Often, senior high schools have two or even three tracks, marking some students for the better colleges and other students for the rest. A student may be in classes called college-prep (regular), accelerated, honors, or advanced placement. Each of these classes has its individual status. They are not equal in reputation, teacher quality, class size, resources, or expectations for excellence. Where these multiple classes exist, many colleges give preference to applicants from the higher classes. In many states, for example, an A grade earned in certain classes is worth more grade points for college than an A in a regular college-bound class.

Students who are already highly motivated can become quite competitive among a very small population of highest-achieving children. Those who are not in the *very* top sometimes feel like failures when they compare their status with that of the better students. Very few educators see this competition as helpful to the most capable students.

Tracking Does Not Help Slower Children Feel Better about Themselves

Slower children do not need to suffer emotional strains when enrolled in mixed-ability classes. Of course, some classrooms are rife with the destructive public comparisons we described in chapter 3. In those classes all children who are not the highest achievers—and perhaps even they—risk humiliation. Children can also suffer emotionally from placement in classes for slow students. Being in a low track can foster poor self-concepts, lowered aspirations, and negative attitudes toward school. Some studies conclude that tracking leads low-track children to misbehave in school and eventually to drop out altogether.

Tracking May Not Be Fair and Accurate

Not all students will benefit equally from lessons. There is nothing particularly unfair about that. However, tracking *prejudges* how much children will benefit. The result is that some children do not have access to classes in which academically and socially valued subjects are taught. Nearly all children can learn from good literature. Nearly all can learn a second language. Nearly all can benefit from studying algebra. Some will learn more, some less. Tracking excludes many children from ever being in some classes. Furthermore, when schools err in their judgment, they are more likely to underestimate than to overestimate what children can accomplish.

Fairness is also an issue when we consider the well-established links between track placements and students' background characteristics. Poor and minority youngsters (principally black and Hispanic) are disproportionately placed in tracks for low-ability or non-college-bound students. Schools consistently overlook minority students for admission to programs for the gifted and talented. Blacks and Hispanics are more frequently enrolled in vocational programs that train for the lowest level occupations. Their vocational training is more likely to include building maintenance, commercial sewing, and institutional care. On the other hand, children from wealthier families enroll in higher-status vocational courses like accounting, computers, and business law. The political scientist Kenneth Meier and his colleagues have recently discovered that this track-based segregation is found especially in urban school districts that have desegregated their schools. Students in such schools are often resegregated by their enrollment in tracked classes.

Defenders of tracking claim that it is based on merit—that a child's school achievement, not his race and social class, directly determines his track placement. Some claim that students' own choices, will, character, and motivation determine track placements. In fact, low motivation, poor effort, and the like are at least partly the *result* of school experiences and tracking. The claim that a child has *earned* an inferior educational experience is unfair if his prior experiences place him at a disadvantage. Finally, if being in the low track prepared disadvantaged children for success in higher tracks, perhaps that initial placement might be fair. If the low track opened up future career or school opportunities, then we could justify it. In fact, neither happens.

Standardized test scores usually play a very important role in children's track placements. As we suggested in the previous chapter, schools that use these measures risk enormous unfairness. Individual differences in children—especially in young children—are subtle. Those differences that are easily determined through testing may not be the most important. But other influences also affect early and even senior high school track placements. Social indicators such as maturity and cooperativeness can influence track decisions. Physical development can affect personal appearance, height, and handwriting, and these in turn may influence teachers' judgments about a child's suitability for a particular track. A parent's interest or clout can also affect track placement. Illness, family trauma, or moving to a new school can throw children out of sync with the school's test.

However, while differences among children are sometimes subtle, differences among tracked classes are not. Sometimes slight and irrelevant student differences at the time of placement can have large consequences in the quality of education children receive.

Does Tracking Make Teaching Easier?

The assumption that tracking makes teaching easier pales in importance when we look at the abundant evidence of its general ineffectiveness. That its harm is greater for poor and minority students further weakens the ease-of-teaching argument. Even if we could ignore ethical concerns, tracking would make sense only if it gave teachers truly homogeneous (unmixed) groups. In fact, it doesn't.

Within tracks, children always display considerable differences in learning speed, learning style, interest, effort, and aptitude for various tasks. Often, tracking simply masks the essential problem of teaching any group of twenty to thirty-five people. Such instruction always requires, and should require, a wide variety of teaching strategies. Not all children will benefit from the same tasks, materials, and procedures, even if the school grouped them because of their similarities. Multiple criteria for success and rewards—the conditions we described in chapter 3—benefit all children, regardless of grouping practices. Unfortunately, tracking deflects attention from these instructional realities. When instruction fails, the problem is too often attributed to the child or perhaps to a wrong placement.

Tracking may make teaching easier for some teachers who prefer to teach as if their students were all alike. This does not mean that any group of children—high, average, or low—will benefit most from that instruction.

THE DIFFERENT CURRICULA IN DIFFERENT TRACKS

Access to Knowledge

Students in ability-grouped classes have access to very different types of knowledge. Track levels form boundaries around their opportunities to develop intellectual skills. We identified many of these differences in our earlier research on tracking and reported them in *Keeping Track: How Schools Structure Inequality*. We found that children in high-ability classes in secondary schools are more likely to study the topics and skills that colleges require. In junior and senior high school English classes, for example, high-ability students will probably study both classical and modern fiction. They will learn the characteristics of literary genres and analyze good narrative writing. They will write essays and reports based on library research. They will study vocabulary designed to boost their scores on college entrance exams. The high quality of their course content promotes critical thinking and problem-solving skills.

Low-ability children, on the other hand, rarely if ever get these types of knowledge. Their teachers do not expect them to learn the same skills. Prominent in low-ability English classes, for example, are xeroxed exercises, workbooks, and commercially produced basic skills kits. Students' reading may be limited to easy-to-read stories that do not require more than basic skills. Their learning tasks most often include memorizing or copying answers and taking quizzes. Critical thinking and problem solving, if they are emphasized at all, are presented in packaged programs; they do not emerge from a course full of valued knowledge. Low-ability classes are far from being "relevant" and practical, as they are often claimed to be. Because teachers usually teach basic topics and skills out of context, learning tasks are often more abstract and removed from the real world than in high-ability classes. Since low-ability classes omit so much important knowledge, students who spend even a brief time in such classes can miss the experiences they need to reenter and succeed in higher classes.

We can see similar patterns in secondary math, science, and social studies and in ability-grouped elementary classes. A far more restricted range of topics and less depth characterize remedial and average classes. Some of the most dramatic evidence comes from the highly publicized

Second International Math Study. The study found that American eighth and twelfth graders lag behind not only Japanese students but also students in most industrialized countries. In contrast to students in other countries, only those American students in top classes had access to many important math topics and skills. The limited exposure to math concepts set limits on the achievement of many more American children. In their book *The Underachieving Curriculum* Curtis McKnight and his colleagues reported that the American tracking system does not provide appropriate learning opportunities to students of different abilities. Rather, tracking restricts what students can achieve.

Opportunities to Learn

Two critical opportunities for learning are the time children spend in class and the teaching strategies. In both respects children in higher classes have better opportunities. They spend more time on learning activities and less time on discipline, socializing, and class routines. Teachers expect children in high classes to spend more time doing homework. They usually teach more enthusiastically, and they make their instruction clearer. They use strong criticism and ridicule less frequently than teachers of low-ability classes. Often they organize tasks better and give children a greater variety of learning activities. We're convinced that these differences in learning opportunities embody fundamental schooling inequities. Those children who need more time to learn appear to get less. Those who have the most difficulty learning have fewer of the best teachers.

Classroom Climate

Feeling comfortable and liked in class is more than just a nice addition to learning. When teachers and students feel successful and trust one another, they free up class time and energy for teaching and learning. In the absence of a friendly, trusting climate, students spend energy interfering with the teacher's agenda. The teachers spend time and energy trying to maintain control. Teachers of high-ability classes more often encourage children to become independent, questioning, and critical thinkers. In low-ability classes children perceive the teachers as less concerned and more punitive. Their teachers emphasize discipline, following directions, arriving on time, and sitting quietly.

Likewise, children in low-tracked classes often feel excluded from social activities and find their classmates unfriendly. Problems and arguing interrupt class more frequently. While students in higher classes are much more involved in their classwork, students in low-ability classes seem apathetic. Being more likely to fail, it is much riskier for them to try hard and give the appearance that they care.

The quality of classes for average students usually falls somewhere between the high- and low-class extremes. *The Shopping Mall High School*, a revealing look at American high schools, reports on the experiences of average students. The authors, Powell, Ferrar, and Cohen, found a proliferation of classes and special programs for high-ability students and those with handicaps. By contrast, schools treated most students in the middle as unspecial and taught them in quite unspecial ways. In average classes, many teachers expected far less from students. They established set routines of lecture and worksheets. They held time and workload demands (both class and homework) to a minimum. Teachers accepted and sometimes even encouraged distractions. They rarely asked students to think deeply or critically.

These classroom differences suggest why students who are not in the top tracks may suffer because of their placements. We can't attribute the differences to mean-spirited or discriminatory teachers or to anyone else. Obviously, what teachers believe is possible influences what and how they teach. Average and low-ability students miss high-quality school opportunities because they and their teachers believe less is possible in average and low-ability classes.

Different tracks have characteristic classroom cultures. Like offices, factories, and other workplaces, classes develop a powerful consensus that sets standards for production. The highest tracks are most business-like. The lowest tracks can actually discourage anyone from being serious. In all classes, those who are out of step are in for a hard time. An office staff might shun a rate-buster, and a production team might apply pressure to a laggard. So children exert pressure on their classmates (and even on the teacher!) to conform to class norms. The track level may be the most significant information that children and teachers use to form their notions of how long and how hard students should work. This consensus is largely informal and builds over time. However, actors outside the classroom also support the consensus. The formal, written curriculum expects less. Expectations of parents and supervisors are lower. Children in other classes share the common meanings given to low ability, honors, and other tracks.

Of course, high-quality experiences are possible in classes at all track levels. Exemplary methods, skilled, dedicated, and even charismatic teachers, abundant resources, and a slew of other intangibles can combine to make a silk purse out of the unlikeliest low-ability, sow's ear class. However, only the most extraordinary low-ability class matches in standards, learning opportunities, and class climate even ordinary high-track classes.

Magnet Schools

While not usually identified as tracking, magnet schools and programs may be the latest form of tracking. Magnet programs typically focus either on special interests or on special abilities, and they try to attract children from the entire district. Most magnets either occupy a separate building on a school campus or have their own campus. Some have their own teachers and materials and keep students for the entire day. Others share buildings and teachers with the regular program. Some students attend regular as well as magnet classes.

Most magnets select a particular subject-matter emphasis, but some combine subject matter with a style or value orientation. For example, a fundamental magnet program might focus heavily on teaching children basic skills and traditional curricula. It would teach American history rather than theme-based social studies. Fundamental programs typically avoid certain less traditional subjects like health or drama. They may have strict codes for dress and other behavior. Some magnets focus on the arts; the Performing Arts High School in New York is a famous example. Some emphasize science and mathematics, humanities, or a particular vocational area. New York's Aviation High is a well-known example of a vocational magnet school. Still other magnet programs provide alternative instructional methods such as "open schools," where children can participate in setting learning goals. Finally, some magnets are for students perceived to have superior intellect or talent: gifted, gifted and talented, highly gifted, and so on. Others are designed for low-achieving or alienated students. For example, the Peninsula Academies in the San Francisco Bay Area seek to keep potential dropouts in high school.

When magnet programs are selective—whether they target their programs for high achievers or for potential dropouts—they become another form of tracking. Like high-track classes and gifted programs, selective magnets for high achievers often offer extra resources, exceptional teachers, and highly motivated peers. Parents who choose these programs for their children usually express satisfaction with the quality of their education. Our major concerns rest with the children who are left behind. They may attend very ordinary schools with teachers and peers who are without a special status or mission. These ordinary schools make do with normal funding, and in the end, they are places where most children receive their education. A contrasting concern arises when magnets limit their enrollment to potential dropouts or students identified as being "at risk." These schools may have all the problems associated with low tracks—they separate, stigmatize, and offer little access to high-status knowledge and skills.

THE HISTORY OF DIFFERENCES

A rich, intriguing history sheds light on why tracked schools make sense to nearly everyone. This history incorporates many of the features we looked at in previous chapters. Beliefs that form the social context for schools, testing practices, and the factory model of efficiency all support tracking premises. Also compatible with tracking are conventional grading practices and specialization of subjects. Finally, the nagging fear that there isn't enough really good education to go around fuels tracking. Most of all, this history clarifies the dominant belief that has guided schooling during this century. That belief is that we understand most about children when we look at their differences. Tracking is the primary way schools act on that belief to organize children and opportunities.

Turn-of-the-Century Problems

Conditions at the turn of the century continue to shape schools today. Immigration sharply increased and cities were in a shocking state of decline. Sharp social disruptions related to factory-based industry triggered social crises of major proportions. Then, as now, society turned to schools for salvation.

Parents, policymakers, and educators alike saw in schools a way to solve a whole array of problems. New immigrants needed to learn American ways. Schools were an avenue for upward mobility. Factories needed trained workers. Footloose urban youth required supervision. And schools needed to continue their traditional role of providing high-status knowledge to prepare some students for the professions.

After a long debate about how to educate children for such diverse purposes, educators settled on a newly coined view of democracy. They defined *opportunity* as the chance to prepare for largely predetermined and certainly different adult lives. Facing overwhelming challenges, schools chose solutions that were compatible with social beliefs about racial and ethnic differences. In time the solutions themselves perpetuated the problems their creators intended to solve.

Elwood Cubberly, a prominent educational scholar of the time, wrote, "Our city schools will soon be forced to give up the exceedingly democratic idea that all are equal, and our society devoid of classes . . . and to begin a specialization of educational effort along many lines in an attempt to adapt the school to the needs of these many classes." [1] The superintendent of Boston schools tried hanging onto a few more democratic sentiments. In 1908 he expressed a view close to Cubberly's but not so different from what may be heard today: "Until very recently [the schools] have offered equal opportunity for all to receive *one kind* of education, but what will make them democratic is to provide opportunity for all to receive education as will fit them *equally well* for their particular life work." [2]

The Influence of Testing

Concurrently, two phenomena supported different schooling for different children. One, standardized tests, provided a seemingly scientific and meritocratic basis for the sorting process in schools. Standardized psychological testing, founded on principles of individual differences, helped to institutionalize beliefs about race and class differences in intellectual abilities. In some instances schools used testing to offer scientific confirmation that some children had clear learning limits. These children were largely poor, minority, and non-English-speaking. Early testing supported the view that some children's intellectual, moral, and even biological differences were vast and immutable. Many held a misguided view of social Darwinism—that era's "scientific" version of racial differences. They suggested that the darker-skinned, recently arrived immigrants from southern Europe were on a lower rung of the evolutionary ladder. Children of the native-born, northern European stock had evolved much further.

Intelligence-test pioneer Lewis Terman wrote, "Their dullness seems to be racial. . . . Children of this group should be segregated in special classes. . . . They cannot master abstractions, but they can often be made efficient workers." While these views did not go uncontested, school tracking practices eventually corresponded to them. Schools adopted the

---

1. Elwood P. Cubberly, *Changing Conceptualizations of Education* (Boston: Houghton Mifflin, 1909), 15–16.
2. Boston Schools, *School Documents*, no. 7 (1908).
3. Lewis Terman, *Intelligence Tests and School Reorganization* (New York: World Book, 1923), 28.

prevailing belief that inherent group differences explained the enormous variation in students' potential for school learning.

Scientific Management

The other development that seemed to make sense of treating children differently was the philosophy of "scientific management." As we described in Chapter 1, educators quickly embraced the methods of the expanding manufacturing sector of the economy. They used scientific management principles to devise well-rationalized methods for separating students. In the spirit of the age, this approach made wonderful sense to school managers and to boards of education. Valuing children's diversity for the contributions it could make to society made little sense.

As a result, educational managers brought into schools time-and-motion studies, centralization, authority concentrated at the top, rules for best methods, and so on. They touted these as the only ways to bring order and efficiency to schools' disarray. Following the model of the efficient factory, schools increasingly saw children as "raw materials" out of which they would fashion their "product"—productive adults. The apex of scientific management was manifest in the assembly line. One line might turn out Fords—to be sure, all running well and doing what Fords should do. Another line would turn out Lincolns—clearly a superior product. Managers did not value individual differences along the assembly line. Differences were defects in the product. So it has been with the school's scientific management ever since: individual differences within tracks often get labeled as flaws.

Today's Legacy

Today, too, many educators, parents, and policymakers link intellectual aptitude and prospects for success to race and class. They believe that these differences are profound and unchangeable. Fewer people blame biological differences than once did. However, many still look for racial/genetic differences to explain differences in children's performance. Today environment and culture are more popular and socially acceptable explanations. We must not deny the powerful effects of environment. Family, neighborhood, and school matter a lot when it comes to influencing which children are well equipped to start school. The question schools face is not whether children are different but how schools should respond to differences.

Schools' response, past and present, produces lower-track and vocational programs that are often detrimental to children. The lower the track, the greater the disadvantage. Placement in low tracks begins a cycle of restricted opportunities, lower achievement, and greater differences between children in low and high tracks. These placements neither overcome academic deficiencies nor provide access to high-quality learning opportunities. Furthermore, the tradition is so strong that even in the suburbs, schools with largely homogeneous populations of white, middle-class children also subject children to needless differences in education quality.

In many schools, tracking poses a major impediment to improving the educational experiences of all children. Tracking can be a self-fulfilling prophecy that prevents schools from expecting success of everyone. It teaches children that if the school does not identify them as capable in earlier grades, they will not do well later. Few students or teachers can defy those expectations.

Tracking is the school's way of organizing children, and it reflects social beliefs, traditions, and values. As such it is too complex and entrenched to be abolished overnight. Individual teachers, schools, or even school districts are not empowered to change tracking without considerable effort, time, and disruption. Tracking will always seem to some people a necessary practice for sorting children. As we marshal data that discredits the *academic* consequences of tracking, we must remember that tracking developed for *social* considerations. The final arguments must be both academic and social. We must decide whether tracking suits children's learning needs, whether it conforms to our democratic values, and whether reasonable alternatives exist.

RESPONDING TO TRACKING

Recognize the Complexity

Tracking is changing from a hardly noticed to a deeply controversial schooling practice. Parents, educators, and policymakers are just starting to express dissatisfaction with tracking systems. Inevitably, they discover that changing the tracked nature of schools is no simple matter, regardless of how gradual a change they advocate. When someone raises the question, it quickly becomes political. There are few professionals or parents without strong opinions about it. Often, those interested in maintaining advantages for the children on top voice the most powerful opinions in support of tracking. Typically, advocates for minorities and the poor voice the strongest opposition. Parents of average students are less expressive. They may resent the school's seeing their children as having almost-but-not-quite top potential. On the other hand, many such parents worry about what might happen if children in the lower tracks were placed with their own.

The same fears that desegregation raises complicate proposals for changing tracking in multiracial schools. Because race, class, assessed ability, and track placements are interrelated, heterogeneous (mixed) ability grouping may mean racial integration in classes where none existed before.

A serious consideration of "de-tracking" schools requires dramatically altered assumptions about nearly everything at school: students, learning, and the purposes of schooling. Tracking assumes that some students can't or won't learn. Successful mixed classes require the belief that all students can and will. Parents, educators, and policymakers rely on tracked classes to identify, label, sort, and certify children for roles in larger society. To create successful mixed-ability classes schools need to deemphasize sorting for the future and concentrate on giving the best education to all children.

The creation of constructive alternatives to tracking presents technical as well as political problems. Success for all students in some mixed classrooms should not lead parents, educators, or policymakers to believe that simply mixing up students and leaving everything else the same is the answer. Effective alternatives require fundamental changes in school organization and classroom practices. To do away with tracking, schools will require curriculum and teaching strategies quite different from typical school practice. There are no ready-made staff development packages or teaching formulas to help schools and teachers move smoothly toward less tracking.

However, we do have some clues. For example, Japanese schools appear to give children a better start toward high achievement than American schools. The Japanese, who are certainly no more egalitarian or fair-minded than Americans, do not routinely track students until late in their education. It is clear to them that separating children according to ability is not necessary for children to excel. Japanese children manage to do very well without gifted classes. They spend time in their early schooling learning the skills of working together in groups. The Japanese commonly divide children into small groups, each with its own student leadership. These groups have some responsibility to be sure that each child learns. Schoolwork is assigned to the group. And it is the success of the group, not the individual, that is most important.

Japanese schools have their problems too. In Japan, enormous pressure is exerted on children to succeed in exams. Children with special needs or those whose skills bloom early or late can, as in our own country, fall through the cracks. And cultural conditions are very different from those in the United States. Fewer Japanese mothers work. Many make a career of serving their children's education. Our point is not that we should do schooling the Japanese way, but that the Japanese system illustrates a particular strength and possibility. In a highly competitive society that pressures children to excel, children with different abilities benefit from working and learning together.

Americans should look at how Japan and other nations use mixed-ability classes without sacrificing the most highly skilled children. However, they need to look even more carefully at the full picture of American schools and culture. Right now, tracked classes make sense because they reflect prevailing beliefs, values, and interpretations of experience. Genuinely successful approaches to untracking schools will be American ones. Local schools will embrace them and build their programs on a different set of beliefs, values, and assumptions.

Alternatives will be most effective if they begin early. Junior high may be too late, and first grade is not too early. Although difficult, such changes are compatible with current elementary schooling methods. Many elementary schools actively pursue the schooling principles we outlined in chapters 3, 4, and 5. However, those principles that are necessary to guide mixed classes clash head-on with the standard practices of high schools. There, grouping, teaching, and evaluation policies firmly adhere to the notions of sorting, standardization, and competition. Additionally, secondary educators are constrained by what students experience in earlier grades. Typically, low-track high school students have been in low-ability groups and remedial programs since elementary school. The gap between them and their more successful peers has grown wider each year. Not only does achievement differ dramatically, so do students' attitudes toward school and toward their own ability to succeed. By junior high track-related achievement and attitude limit tracking alternatives.

Nevertheless, that secondary schools face special problems does not imply there is nothing they can do about tracking. They can start gradual changes, even if they retain some tracking. For example, instead of being dead ends, low-track classes can become preparatory for higher-status classes. Schools can offer some college-prep courses over a two-year period for students who lack the necessary background. Instead of being used to repeat classes, summer school can give extra time to children who didn't grasp all the important concepts. Schools can reduce the number of tracks in certain subjects. They could cut out tracks altogether in a few subjects or grades. Social studies class or the entire seventh grade is often a relatively easy place to begin. With a little more effort, other subjects and grades can be mixed.

Combined classes composed of students with more than one level of ability can be team-taught or multigraded to permit flexible subgroupings around specific skills. Counselors can recruit students for academic programs rather than use strict placement criteria for keeping them out. Slower students can be mainstreamed into regular or more advanced classes. After-school peer or adult tutoring can help children keep up with their classmates. School policymakers can establish criteria for racial and ethnic balance in classes at all levels. They can include special programs such as those for the gifted in their balancing requirements. Schools can blur the distinction between vocational and academic programs by infusing vocational curriculum with academic concepts and enriching academic classes with real-life, hands-on learning experiences.

Can school districts take advantage of some of the merits of magnet schools and the feature of allowing parents choices of schools without creating more tracking? One way of avoiding at least some of the problems would be for school districts to allow each child the choice of a school with a special focus and a special mission. Fortunately, many magnets do have open enrollment policies and select students by lottery or on a first-come, first-served basis. These schools, especially those that have attracted a diverse student body, can be very successful. Part of their success is explained by studies showing that children benefit when schools pursue their own local mission unhampered by rigid ties to the central office. Most magnets are given this latitude by their districts. Furthermore, theme-oriented, nonselective magnets may have the greatest chance to pursue a special mission without departing from the principles of a common education.

Obviously, the changes likely to promote high-quality learning for all students in heterogeneous classrooms go beyond fine-tuning current practice. They require fundamental changes in the structure of schooling and teachers' work. Finally, as with most major reform initiatives, teacher professionalism is central to successful tracking alternatives. Working with their communities, school staffs can design changes that are compatible with school goals and politically manageable. However, unless teachers can develop and experiment with fundamental changes in school organization and classroom practices, little will change. Teachers will need a measure of professional autonomy before alternatives to tracking can be intelligently conceived or enthusiastically endorsed.

What's Best for Your Child and All Children?

Tracking is a problem for parents who are trying to negotiate the best education for their own children. Once informed about tracking's effects, most parents, like most educators, lament the consequences. Most understand the frustration of trying to offer high-quality lessons to children the school labels "low ability" or "slow." On the other hand, it surprises many to learn that average children are also at a disadvantage in a tracked school.

Parents and teachers worry about protecting the education of top students. Many find it hard to believe the research evidence that academically able students can continue to do well in mixed classes. Besides, the top tracks *do* offer educational and social advantages to students. Parents find it difficult to surrender these clear advantages for promises that their children would do "no worse" in mixed classes. Yet there is little comfort in such a system for most parents. After all, most children are not in the top track. Even white, suburban, high-achieving schools assign a large percentage of students to mediocre experiences in lower-ability classes.

Getting one's own child into a higher track or a highly selective magnet school is a far from adequate solution. High-track classes are no likelier to be multidimensional than low ones—although some magnet programs might be. Moreover, the competition may be intense and the opportunities for public comparisons great. With those cautions, our advice to parents is first to look for a nonselective magnet or heterogeneous program that features multidimensional classrooms and engages children in rich and complex knowledge. If those options are not available, you probably need to lobby the school to have your children placed in as high a track as they can handle. The high track is no guarantee of quality, but the odds are that it will be a better educational experience than a lower track.

What's best for your child in the long run? What's best for all the other children? We would hope that parents would engage their school boards, district administrators, principal, counselors, and teachers in discussions of tracking issues. Information-gathering questions are good for starters. How schools track is a matter of public policy and deep concern. Rules, procedures, and consequences should be explicit. How does the school make tracking decisions? How are teachers assigned? How many classes are tracked? How many children assigned to low tracks move into higher ones? What is the distribution of track enrollments according to children's (and teachers') race and gender?

Whether and how these questions are answered will reveal much about a school's commitment to all its children. Even more telling is whether the school can follow these questions with a careful, open, and tolerant probing of assumptions and values. Such an inquiry is an arduous, courageous, and rarely attempted undertaking in education. However, we should expect to do no less if we intend to make schools humane, equitable, and truly educational places.

FOR FURTHER READING

Elizabeth Cohen. *Designing Groupwork: Strategies for the Heterogeneous Classroom.* New York: Teachers' College Press, 1987.

Curtis McKnight and others, *The Underachieving Curriculum.* Champaign, IL: Stipes, 1987.

Kenneth Meier, Joseph Stewart, and Robert England, *Race, Class, and Education: The Politics of Second Generation Segregation.* In press.

Jeannie Oakes, *Keeping Track: How Schools Structure Inequality.* New Haven: Yale University Press, 1985.

Carolyn J. Persell, *Education and Inequality: The Roots and Results of Stratification in America's Schools.* New York: Free Press, 1977.

Arthur Powell, Eleanor Farrar, and David Cohen, *The Shopping Mall High School: Winners and Losers in the Educational Marketplace.* Boston: Houghton Mifflin, 1985.

James E. Rosenbaum, *Making Inequality: The Hidden Curriculum of High School Tracking.* New York: Wiley, 1979.

Robert E. Slavin, *Ability Grouping and Student Achievement in Elementary schools: A Best Evidence Synthesis.* Report of the National Center for Effective Elementary Schools. Baltimore: Johns Hopkins University, 1986.

David Stern and others, *One Million Hours a Day: Vocational Education in California Public Secondary Schools.* Report to the California Policy Seminar. Berkeley, Ca: University of California School of Education, 1985.

CHAPTER EIGHT

Children with Special Needs: Different and Not Always Equal

Some success stories:

- A child who could understand ideas very well had difficulty memorizing small bits of information. She learned as much as other children but scored low on tests and got very discouraging grades. She attended regular classes, but each day she also spent one class period being tutored by a teacher with special knowledge of learning disabilities. Her special teacher mediated when crises arose and helped her regular teachers adopt some alternate ways to help this child learn. She graduated with her peers and went to college.
- A blind teenager attended junior high with his sighted peers. He spent about half of the school day in regular academic classes, excelled on tests, and got good grades. He toted his braille-writer with him from class to class to take notes and work on assignments. During the other half of the day, a teacher who specialized in educating the visually handicapped tutored and encouraged him. The teacher's instructional aide searched for a supply of "talking books." She translated assignments and worksheets into braille and typed his finished homework.
- A sixth grader who was quite average in most respects demonstrated some remarkable skills in and a passion for mathematics. Her principal arranged for her to begin advanced courses at a nearby high school

while she continued elementary school. Pleased with this plan, the school then enrolled two very capable elementary children in the high school orchestra.

- A child from a family that speaks only English learned Spanish in elementary school. The school's goal was that all children should become proficient in a second language. Many children from Spanish-speaking families also attended this school. Nearly all of them were as successful with English.

These success stories happened in ordinary public schools. Unfortunately, such stories, if not rare, are not the rule either. Yet schools must give every child, regardless of disability, social status, gender, or race, the best education possible. Children with physical, learning, or emotional disabilities must not be handicapped by barriers that schools can help them avoid. Schools must help children whose native language is not English so they can learn with their English-speaking peers. And schools must help children who come from families that are not white or middle class be as successful as their schoolmates who do. Most schools act on these goals, propelled both by principle and by law. Nevertheless, most schools themselves are handicapped by bureaucratic requirements and by their own inability to conceive of creative ways to help children with special needs.

As a general rule, the best way to teach all children is in a regular classroom. Even though it's a controversial topic among educators who specialize in "special needs," most research evidence suggests that if children need special help, schools should let them receive it among their "normal" peers. Increasingly, experts in special and compensatory education conclude that educating all children together creates the fewest barriers. That happens most naturally when the regular school classroom accommodates the unique abilities and styles of all children. When specialists and regular teachers work together, children with special problems can often succeed in a regular classroom. This is nearly always more productive than trying to create different classrooms for special groups of children.

The multidimensional classes we described earlier can come close to meeting every child's needs. A variety of paths to success, a belief that all children can learn, and private and individual evaluations benefit all children—not just those with disabilities. However, even in such classrooms, some children may require attention, technology, or skills above and beyond those provided routinely to all children. The thrust of research and experience is clear: Help those who need it, but don't isolate and stigmatize them. In the success stories above, a *combination* of regular classroom experiences and special interventions worked on behalf of these children.

Regular classes are frequently inhospitable to children with special needs. Most educators and policymakers do not feel able to accommodate children with special needs in regular classrooms. Their first inclination has been to provide special help outside regular classes. Some see disabled students as so fragile that they need protection from regular classroom pressures. Another, usually unstated motive for separation may be to protect regular students and teachers from children who are different. Those who are not accustomed to being around the disabled may become embarrassed, distracted, and afraid.

In actual practice schools often neglect children's needs in separate programs. In the worst cases, special alternatives simply become the lowest track in the school. Schools then saddle disabled children with all the pernicious effects of tracking as well—lower educational opportunities, lower aspirations, lower self-concept. Some schools see gifted children as having a handicap of sorts—or, at least, as being very special. For these children separate programs often turn into the highest track.

SPECIAL NEEDS

In less enlightened times society hid the disabled. Families often closeted away children with serious physical and mental problems. Frequently, they were an embarrassment to families and the object of strangers' curiosity, fear, and ridicule. Parents who could afford schooling for seriously disabled children sent them to special schools—often boarding schools. Many children, especially poor ones, received no education at all. Milder problems simply went unrecognized. Adults chalked up children's unexplained difficulties at school to their being slow, having behavior problems, or just being odd.

Today, compulsory education and the increased value of a high school diploma make it imperative that schools educate nearly every child. A more generous sense of fair play may push schools to be more inclusive. Also, people recognize that the disabled can perform at higher levels than we used to think. Especially if they have some special understanding and help, many with disabilities do as well as others. In the past when children had trouble fitting in at school, they quit. Most of them found jobs and led productive lives. Families assumed responsibility for children with more debilitating problems. Sometimes private organizations and charities helped. Only recently has public policy tried to compensate for obstacles associated with poverty, disability, neglect, or being a non-English-speaker.

Today, both physically and mentally disabled children attend school. Increased knowledge about what disabled children can accomplish and more accepting attitudes combine to open up opportunities. Federal laws requiring a free and appropriate education for handicapped children are both a cause and an effect of these attitude changes. Many private schools that previously excluded disabled students now admit them as well.

The variety of children's handicaps and special needs is large, but no larger than the variety of names we invent to label them. Our look at tracking shows how schools have adapted the concept of individual differences among nonhandicapped children. Over the years schools have also identified special educational, physical, and psychosocial problems thought to be outside the normal range. New categories surface and old ones disappear as educators, psychologists, and physicians refine their definitions of disabling conditions. Then, as federal and state policymakers fund programs to meet these special needs, the categories make their ways into schools. For example, over the years schools considered some children feebleminded, dull, or simply not suited for schoolwork. Trainable, or educable mentally retarded, learning disabled, and special are more recent labels. Schools and government agencies have described poor children and those from families that speak little English in terms ranging from uneducable to culturally deprived. Today we say they are disadvantaged or at risk.

Juvenile delinquents formerly went to reform schools or dropped out of school altogether. Now many states label them socio-emotionally disturbed and often assign them to special classes within regular schools. Others are enrolled in continuation, alternative, or opportunity schools, separate from but closely aligned with the community's regular schools. In the past, exceptionally precocious children skipped grades if they outdistanced their peers academically. States now respond to the belief that very high IQ scores show a need for a different sort of education altogether. Most states fund special treatments for these gifted and talented children.

Along with special funding have come elaborate accounting and defining procedures for all special programs, including gifted programs. Schools must identify the children, make sure they are eligible, and then actually make good on a different program that works. While children's problems are complex, their special needs are often not so complicated. There are after all just so many ways of helping. Taking more time and giving more attention are two of the most common. However, when compensatory education combines with and adds to schools' bureaucracies, the result can bring out the worst. The push toward efficiency through specialization and the search for scientific methods produces a maze of special diagnoses, labels, and prescriptions. This maze can obscure the obvious: all some children need is more time, attention, and tolerance.

We offer two caveats to guide this overview of how schools deal with children who have special needs. First, we are critical of many special programs. The programs have unintended consequences and sometimes do less for the child than the regular program. However, our criticism here often addresses problems of schools generally, not just special programs. We intend no criticism of those who work in the special programs for the disabled. They often have no more power to effect needed changes than anyone else working in schools. Often they know more than their critics about the problems in special education.

We also want to caution that parents of a handicapped child will require far more information than we can provide here. Children's special needs and the programs designed to meet them vary widely. Schools, physicians, psychologists, and parents often disagree about what the needs are and how to help. Specific and detailed information about help for a particular problem is sometimes hard to find or understand. Most districts, if not individual schools, have a special education coordinator. And there are energetic support organizations and advocacy groups that provide independent information and lobby for children's rights at school.

CHILDREN WITH DISABILITIES

Physical Disabilities

Parents and doctors may not notice less obvious physical problems until children go to school. Sometimes a school nurse is the first to call attention to vision and hearing problems. However, many problems do not show up in routine screening. Some mild physical disabilities don't appear until children have difficulty in classrooms. For example, a teacher may first notice a dysfunction in fine motor skills when a child has trouble controlling a pencil or crayons. A child's hearing deficit may become noticeable only when the teacher observes that the child continuously shouts at classmates or frequently loses attention. Sometimes a vision problem does not come to adults' attention until a child makes many errors while reading from the board.

It may take children's misbehavior for the teacher to start searching for a physical disability. Children who seem unable to pay attention are often the first to capture the teacher's notice. Children who fidget and squirm, run around the room, or doze off during a film are hard to ignore. Adults' first inclination, in the absence of causes they can *see*, is to assign the misbehavior to social development. They may think that the child just never learned how to act in a classroom or pay attention. Perhaps her parents never disciplined her or taught her to mind adults. Sometimes the teacher will attribute a child's difficulty to emotional conditions. Possibly the child feels insecure, or there is family disruption. These explanations are often accurate and point to helpful responses. Finally, it is important to acknowledge that schools often demand that children behave in ways that are developmentally inappropriate. Young children are not well suited for the particular kinds of inactivity and quiet attention that much of classroom life requires.

The behavior problems we have just described are arguably the most frustrating, disabling, and inexplicable condition children can experience. The chronic inability to pay attention, sit still, be quiet, and act cooperatively can be a serious disability. These children are unable to concentrate on their studies and fall behind academically. They are often shunned by other children. And they can hardly escape the effects of disapproving and exasperated teachers. Complicating matters is that social and emotional problems are always difficult to distinguish from other— possibly physical—causes. Most families experience some disruption when children have severe difficulties in the classroom. If children have similar difficulties getting along at home, there will certainly be some disabling emotional responses.

Children who do not respond to obvious classroom adjustments and friendly, informal counseling are candidates for a thorough physical evaluation. The school nurse and other specialists can conduct hearing and vision assessments. However, most families will also want to consult their family physician or, if serious problems persist, other medical specialists. Children's inability to pay attention and other behavior concerns can be symptoms of a whole range of minor physical problems. Food allergies, normal growth spurts, or the need for eyeglasses can explain some serious problems at school. On the other hand, much more serious illnesses can cause both significant and minor classroom problems. Biochemical depression, cancer, and some infectious diseases, though infrequent, are causes of school problems. They are serious enough to consider even as remote possibilities.

Some view hyperactivity as a discrete diagnosis for the out-of-control child. Others see it as a catchall label for the behaviors described above. Everyone should be cautious about using the term as if it implied a single disability with a single cause. In fact, no one knows for certain what causes this condition or how to cure it. Many speculate that children's consistent inability to pay attention results from either a chemical imbalance or minimal brain dysfunction. There have been some treatment successes with drug therapy and diet changes, and many disappointments. The positive responses to medication and diet indicate at least an association with physical causes.

We caution against complete reliance on behavioral or counseling treatments without ruling out physical causes. A promising development is the emerging specialization of bio-psychiatry. Important treatments, some still experimental, are on the horizon for childhood and adolescent depression along with other mood disorders. However, even the most successful medications do not work for everyone. All require careful monitoring of side effects and often months of experimenting with dosages.

The Range of Learning Disabilities

Most people view learning handicaps according to a traditional medical model: as a disease or illness, with a cure. The researchers Gaea Leinhardt and William Bickel have investigated how this medical model shapes schools' thinking about learning problems. The medical view holds that a child's problem stems from his or her deficiency. The medical model leads schools to use diagnosis and prescription to solve learning problems. And, as with medicine, schools formalize a wide range of diagnoses, prescribing a specialized treatment tailored to each disorder. Another view—one that considers the school culture—is that school problems result from mismatches between the school and the child's different but healthy way of learning. Some researchers go so far as to assert that close to 90 percent of the children identified as mildly learning-handicapped have no real disabilities at all. Schools would do well to temper the first view with the second.

Identified learning disabilities range from quite mild to severely debilitating. Schools typically call milder problems *learning disabilities* and more serious ones *mental retardation*. Each category contains a variety of subdiagnoses. Some children with the same disability may experience different problems at school. Others with different diagnoses respond to the same treatments.

Parents and schools need to be extremely cautious when thinking about, communicating, and acting on learning handicaps. Schools have developed processes for identifying the many kinds of learning disabilities only in the last two decades. The categories lack precision, and we have little solid knowledge about causes and treatments. Once the disabilities have been diagnosed, schools have few refined tools to help children overcome them. The few proven interventions that help most are often quite simple. On the other hand, they often require the most costly of school resources—a teacher's time. Tutoring, allowing more time to complete a test, or having a child repeat directions aloud are examples. Children who get a little extra help can function much better than those who have none. Yet some children require help that goes far beyond these simple classroom accommodations.

Learning Disabilities It is not at all unusual for normal children to lag behind in some school skills. Even very bright and highly verbal children can be slow to start reading and writing. In most cases this lag is within the normal range of individual developmental differences. A few children of normal intelligence have unusual and specific disabilities, perhaps resulting from the brain's inability to process information with the same efficiency as in those without the handicap.

These children, try as they may, accomplish certain skills only with great effort. Copying correctly, spelling accurately, reading fast, or memorizing details might be painfully difficult for a mildly disabled child. This same child may be skilled at expressing ideas orally or in writing. Many children who stumble over details and rules of language and mathematics are knowledgeable about the important concepts. They are sometimes skilled at problem solving as long as they can refer to details without memorizing them. Study habits that succeed for most are frustratingly unproductive for these children. They benefit most from a teacher who is flexible, who allows more time and permits the children to refer to resources. Children with mild disabilities benefit from doing larger, skill-encompassing projects rather than learning skills and knowledge outside a context.

Amy suffered from a mild handicap. From her first years in school she had great difficulty copying lists of words and learning basic math facts. Even with hours of practice, as a third and fourth grader she just couldn't recall the multiplication tables, and her spelling was atrocious. Yet Amy was an avid reader and a nimble problem solver, abilities that saved her reputation at school. Only in junior high did her teachers suspect that Amy might have a learning disability, rather than simply being smart and careless. Her parents, however, argued to keep Amy away from special education programs—knowing that they were likely to be filled with the skill and drill activities that Amy found so difficult. Because she read so well, the school was convinced that Amy could remain in college-preparatory classes.

By sixteen, however, Amy had had enough. She took a state proficiency exam, passed, and left high school with a certificate instead of a diploma. Her parents consented to this plan only because Amy agreed to try the local community college. There she discovered political science, philosophy, art criticism, and a host of other subjects in which her thinking skills counted for more than her ability to memorize and recall facts and details. With the aid of a personal computer and a good spelling checker, Amy took off. After two years, she transferred to the university and graduated with a bachelor of arts degree in philosophy. Sure, passing exams in basic required courses like geology took an enormous amount of effort. But her success in other courses finally proved to Amy that she was smart enough and that her hard work would pay off.

Other children have more serious problems. Some don't learn to read (a problem called dyslexia). Some fail to develop arithmetic-reasoning or writing skills (dyscalculia and disgraphia). Some disabilities appear to cause broad difficulties with language, others with short-term memory, and others with visual perception. The names and categories may mean little since schools often have only limited responses. What matters is first identifying what children can actually do and what they need help with. Then they need to get that help without suffering the disadvantages of isolation.

Mental Retardation Mentally retarded children are those who score substantially below the normal range on intelligence tests. Their disability so restricts their intellectual functioning that they will never reach adult levels. The term itself is offensive to many because it implies a ceiling on ability. Retardation can be caused by genetic problems (Down's syndrome, for example) or environmental problems (physical or intellectual deprivation, traumas during pregnancy, and so on). Like learning-disabled children, those identified as retarded differ widely. Specific intellectual capabilities can differ markedly among children with the same IQ scores. Some retarded children develop strong social skills which enable them to get along and even learn far better than others who test higher.

Identifying Learning Disabilities

Children who continually perform poorly in class are candidates for a systematic assessment of whether or not they have learning disabilities. Often it is a teacher who refers the child to a counselor or school psychologist. Typically, the psychologist will administer a battery of achievement, intelligence, psychological, and perceptual tests. Other specialists, particularly those with a background in speech and language development, frequently participate. The psychologist and others will consider the test results along with interviews, observations, and reports of classroom performance. Ideally, family doctors, school and outside specialists, and parents participate in identifying the problem and planning a course of action.

Often the key to identifying a learning disability is not so much how a child performs in any one area or on any one test as the discrepancies among different areas of performance. A child might remember very well what he hears or sees. But if he remembers little of what he reads he may have a disability that requires attention.

Schools base the diagnosis of mental retardation almost exclusively on intelligence-test scores. Categories of retardation range from borderline or slow (IQs between 70 and 85) to severely and profoundly retarded (IQs below 40 to under 25).

Problems with Assessment The weaknesses of standardized testing become particularly important when schools use the tests to diagnose a learning disability. For example, one common guideline for identifying a child's learning disability is if her achievement lags two years behind her grade level. Schools use achievement tests, school performance, or both to arrive at an achievement score. If her IQ scores show that her intelligence is normal, a discrepancy would indicate a learning disability. (If the child has a low achievement score *and* a low IQ she may not qualify for some special programs. The reasoning is that she is performing at the anticipated level for a child with low IQ and that special attention would not help her.)

Achievement tests that claim to give a grade-level score are extremely imprecise. So is the concept of grade-level itself. One or two answers can sometimes raise or lower a grade-level score by a whole year. Moreover, all standardized tests have a margin of error. This means that a child could take the same test on different days and have her score vary by 10 percent. That difference, too, could alter her grade-level score by as much as a year.

Like standardized achievement tests, intelligence tests have a margin of error as large as 10 or 15 IQ points. If the margins of error on the two tests are in opposite directions, the school might decide that a child with no disability has one. If the errors converge, a child with a disability might seem to be performing up to his ability. As we pointed out in chapter 2, intelligence is far more complex than previously imagined. Intelligence tests measure only a small part of human intellectual processes, and they are not very accurate even in doing that.

A further problem is that intelligence tests and/or test users claim to measure a child's innate ability to learn. Many people believe the tests measure an enduring trait—an IQ that does not change over time. However, most scholars and psychologists realize that so-called intelligence tests are really achievement tests. Mostly, they measure what children have already learned. If a child has a disability that has prevented learning, his IQ score may reflect those deficits. As a result, his IQ score may make his intelligence seem below normal. This is a particular problem as children get older and what they learn in school shapes more of their intellectual processes.

Janet's Story Janet's story illustrates the problem of schools relying too much on standardized achievement and intelligence tests to guide their responses to children. In early childhood Janet was by all observations highly bright and verbal. She had an extensive vocabulary, was exceptionally social, and caught on quickly with each new task. Yet when she started school at age 5 she had trouble reading. By age eight, she was far behind in reading and feeling more and more uncomfortable with reading instruction. When the school psychologist evaluated her, Janet scored well above normal on her IQ test. In spite of her reading problems, Janet's overall sociability and her brightness served her well. Her teachers also gave her good reports. Both the school and her parents felt reassured and decided to give her a little longer.

The following year and for several years thereafter—during which time she continued to have reading and gradually other academic problems— she was tested again and again. Steadily, her IQ dropped. By the time Janet was thirteen, and by all accounts an unsuccessful and unhappy student, her parents were frantic. They insisted that the school give Janet some special help with reading and with subjects that require reading. By this time her IQ score was in the 90s. The school did not consider her reading-ability and other achievement scores to be out of line with her low IQ. In other words, they did not think Janet was smart enough to perform better. Therefore, they felt she would not benefit from special help.

Why did her IQ score drop? Did Janet lose her innate intellectual abilities over the years? Of course not. Two things happened. First, as she got older, more and more of the IQ test items related to things she should have learned in school. Her keen ability to learn by watching and listening, which had served her so well when she was younger, no longer was enough, for the burden of school learning had gradually shifted to her ability to read. Second, she got discouraged. She had taken the test many times, yet little had changed at school. Year after year she experienced painful failures and had little incentive to do well on another test.

Fortunately, once Janet's parents insisted on her getting help, they and the school were able to devise a useful plan. The process took several meetings at the school and a consultation with a psychologist outside the school. The school personnel took one of their legal alternatives to their standard procedure for assessing learning disabilities. They took a *functional* view and certified Janet for special help on two counts. First, she had persistent (if inexplicable) trouble learning from reading. Second, her parents and her teachers at the school were eager to help her benefit from a special program. Janet was designated learning disabled and spent part of her day in special classes designed to help her succeed in academic subjects. Her special education teacher acted as a helper and advocate for Janet in the subjects that Janet took in the regular school program. It took Janet five years of hard work and lots of frustration to finish high school and receive her diploma.

It isn't easy to draw clear-cut lessons from Janet's story. It is not a story of a school's success, but it is not entirely the story of a failure. It points to the need for adults to pay attention and be flexible when they try to decide what special help a child needs and when. Janet got help later than she should have. And that help came only because of her parents' persistence. Regrettably, by the time Janet got help, nearly everyone saw her as incapable, including herself.

Schools are sometimes too *quick* to assign children to special programs. Janet's school acted in a way that might have been, up to a point, entirely proper. Until she was eight years old, a normal developmental lag might have accounted for her being a poor reader. So might have a host of social and emotional considerations. The special designation of learning-handicapped is a serious matter, with its own social and emotional consequences for the family and child. Perhaps the culprit is the all-or-nothing nature of schools' capacity to get special help to children. Some legal designations, special accounting, elaborate testing procedures, and so forth may be necessary to ensure that schools do not squander scarce resources. However, too often children are lost in the processing.

Finally, we constantly need to remind ourselves and our schools that the assessment of learning disabilities is still very crude. Tests and observations do not *prove* that a child has a disability or that he does not. At best they give an indication that a child can benefit from some extra help. Sometimes they point in the direction of special interventions that will benefit children.

Mistaking Cultural Differences for Learning Handicaps An additional hazard in identifying learning handicaps is confusing them with cultural differences. American schools follow white, largely middle-class standards in culture and language styles—and in the criteria they use to judge school performance and learning handicaps. Many poor and minority children have difficulty adapting to expectations for behavior that differ from those of their homes and neighborhoods.

In chapter 7, we pointed out that poor and minority children are the likeliest to be in low-ability classes. Schools are also more likely to identify them as learning handicapped. Several years ago the sociologist Jane Mercer found that black children are one and a half times more likely than whites to be identified as mentally retarded. Hispanic children were three times more likely to receive that classification. Despite increasing sensitivity to cultural differences, these problems persist. Standardized tests support the disproportionate identification of minorities as retarded. Scholars hypothesize that the tests do not reflect differing aptitudes. Rather, they note the compatibility of white, middle-class children's cultural experiences with the form and content of most tests. Poor black and Hispanic children (particularly those from large families) often learn to be cooperative rather than highly competitive. They relate more to people than to things, ideas, and words. They often pay more attention to the concrete context of ideas and events than to abstractions. These and other subtle differences probably work against them when they take tests.

Teachers also mistake cultural and language differences for learning problems. Children from some cultural groups are reluctant to speak up or to outshine other students in the classroom. Other children may be more physical than verbal in the classroom or on the playground. Schools may mistake the language and dialect differences of Hispanic and black children for poor language skills, conceptual misunderstandings, or even bad attitudes.

The misidentification problem is serious enough that the legal system now sets some standards for identifying children as learning-disabled. At both federal and state levels, courts require that potentially handicapped children receive due process. In a far-reaching decision the California courts ruled (*Larry P. v. Riles*) that schools can no longer use intelligence tests to identify minority children as handicapped. Some big-city districts that enroll large percentages of minority children (Chicago, for example) have given up the practice voluntarily.

SPECIAL EDUCATION: HOW SCHOOLS HELP DISABLED CHILDREN

Once schools collect information, there is no way to predict how they will use it to prescribe special help. The general rule, however, follows from legal requirements Congress established in 1975 in the Education for All Handicapped Children Act (PL 94-142). The law requires that schools provide a "free and appropriate" education to all children regardless of their handicap. Children with mental retardation, learning disability, impaired hearing, vision, or speech, emotional or physical difficulties are all protected by the law. A key provision is that the most appropriate education will take place in the "least restrictive environment." And that is a setting that isolates a disabled child from his normal peers as little as possible.

The law also provides funding to states and local school districts for special programs and services for handicapped children. Most states and school districts now offer a wide variety of services differing according to the nature and severity of children's disabilities. We give some general descriptions of these programs below. However, categories of handicaps and program guidelines vary among states and within states and also from year to year. Some children with mild handicaps may have to wait until space is available in a particular program. Yet many states do set time limits for how long children can wait before they start receiving help. Most children with serious learning and physical problems get attention right away because education cannot begin until they do. On the other hand, highly specialized programs may also have waiting lists. These, too, can take a long time. The programs may be costly, and the diagnosing and qualifying may be slower and more rigorous.

In all, the process of discovering a problem, identifying it, and deciding what to do is a complex and emotionally wrenching experience for any parent. Parents who are poor, not native English speakers, or cautious about public institutions face additional obstacles. They are the least likely to be active advocates for their children. As a result, their children may not receive services of as high quality as the children of white, middle-class parents.

The Individual Educational Plan

Once school personnel determine that a child qualifies for special help, the school is required by law to develop a written Individual Educational Plan (IEP). During this process, the school will confer with parents and often with outside consultants. They will try to match the child's needs to particular programs and instructional approaches. They may consider the advantages of services available in a special classroom or a special school. Transportation may be a factor. In cases where the school district itself cannot provide a necessary service, state law may require contracting for help elsewhere. Help for the entire family may be available through the school or outside social service agencies. Parent-support organizations can help by providing specific information about the available programs and a family's legal rights to them. These groups often advocate for the child or mediate between the family and the school at times of important decision making. Designing or interpreting the success of an IEP is certainly one of those important times.

When parents and the school agree, the IEP should clearly state the child's needs and outline specific learning goals. It should detail the special help the child will receive. Ideally, children themselves are in some ways involved in this process, especially if their cooperation is needed. If special commitments on the part of parents are a factor, the IEP needs to state these as well.

The IEP is a mixed blessing. A statement of goals is certainly necessary to translate learning problems into specific learning strategies. Schools and parents need to keep track of successful interventions and those that need changing. On the other hand, there is a risk that a child's IEP will focus on narrowly described *behavioral* objectives, presenting lists of easy-to-check skills and bits of knowledge while neglecting the kinds of rich and complex knowledge described in chapters 4 and 5. Parents should compare their child's IEP with his grade-level curriculum. An IEP should describe how special help will enable the child to learn the same knowledge that other children of his age learn. If this is clearly not possible, the IEP should have an individualized standard of success for the child. This standard should apply to a curriculum that is as close as possible to the mainstream curriculum. Parents and teachers can hold the child himself accountable for realistic achievements. Such an IEP makes it harder for children and adults to find excuses for children's achieving less.

The Least Restrictive Environment

As both a rule of thumb and a legal requirement, the principle of the least restrictive environment should guide the help we give to children, regardless of the type, label, or seriousness of their problems. The rule attempts to counter the unintended consequences of separate programs for children, especially those with mild handicaps. In the past the special help children received often did more damage than the original problem. The biggest culprit was the frequent practice of publicly labeling children and then isolating them. Separate instruction made it predictable that their teachers would underestimate how much regular education they could benefit from. Isolation called further attention to the children's problems and embarrassed the children and their families. Children felt ashamed. They lacked the stimulating programs and academic opportunities of the regular classrooms and more capable peers. And they fell further behind.

Least restrictive environment means that if a child can function in a regular classroom, that is where he should get his education, even though he may have to function differently from his classmates and meet a different set of standards for success. A child who can manage the regular classroom for only part of the day or for some subjects should take those classes. Schools call these practices mainstreaming because, to the extent possible, they keep children with special needs in the mainstream of school life. Given the least restrictive principle, one might think that adaptations and special supports within the regular classroom would be the general rule. However, the proliferation of special programs has abated only slightly since this ruling.

With mainstreaming, much help is given routinely in the regular classroom. There the teacher makes no particular distinction among children who have an identified disability and others who need extra attention (many children need extra attention). Even if the child requires no special accommodations, the teacher and special-education specialist should keep in touch regarding the child. Schools often omit this step. Sometimes they merely identify the child via a memo to the teacher—sometimes, not even that. Usually, only minor adjustments in instruction are necessary. Again, they include a powerful if limited repertoire of special interventions. These include closer observation, a heightened sensitivity to the child's difficulty with particular tasks, and the allowing of extra time. Many teachers provide extra explanations of directions or allow children to explain or repeat the directions aloud. Such practices do not publicly distinguish between skilled, extra-careful children and children with mild disabilities. The teacher can also grade a child's work on the basis of his particular IEP standards rather than on the classroom norms.

More significant adjustments that can occur in mainstream classes are of the sort we noted in chapter 3. These involve changes in the class structure. Cooperative groups, fewer public comparisons, larger tasks, and evaluations better suited to instruction are features that help all children. Children with learning problems benefit especially.

Some "pull-out" programs and "resource classrooms" can also be fairly low in their restrictiveness. A pull-out program allows a child to spend some time with a specialist while his classmates are learning elsewhere. However, there are many problems with pull-out programs. Students who receive special help from reading or speech or hearing specialists, for example, run the risk that others will notice their absence. They may also miss out on valuable activities that take place while they are gone from class. In reading or arithmetic, they may have to grapple with two separate sets of learning activities, one in class and one in the pull-out program—a circumstance that can compound their difficulties. These problems are not inevitable. However, two conditions are critical. First, the goal of special help should be the child's success in his regular classroom work. Special help (such as speech therapy) or remedial work, no matter how useful, should not replace the regular valued schoolwork or add an unconnected curriculum to it. Second, schools should be careful to treat a child's absence and any special treatment matter-of-factly, so that both the handicapped child and his peers will learn that a routine condition of life is that some people get special help. No big deal!

"Resource classrooms" are places where children with special needs may spend a class period or more. These may be very small groups in which students receive special tutoring. Or they may provide a class for children with no mainstreaming options. The quality of the educational experience here varies. Students can benefit enormously from the extra boost of a teacher who may be among the best-trained professionals at the school. Such a teacher can help ensure the child's success in the regular program. Margaret Wang's studies of special education students in the regular classroom show that the special-education teachers help not only the child, but also his other teachers learn to accommodate a wider range of individual differences.

But there is also a dark side to resource-room programs. Often children receive coursework composed of the basic bits-and-pieces approach we have criticized elsewhere. They miss the regular, valued curriculum. Classroom teachers falsely assume that all special needs are taken care of elsewhere and make fewer efforts to tailor instruction to the individual learning needs that all children have. Sometimes other children identify the resource classroom as a low-status place and label the students they see walking in and out as children with problems—though their description is usually crueler than that. Identification by others and lack of contact with peers in normal settings contribute to a lower self-concept for these children. Often, the resource teachers are not subject-matter specialists but focus on study skills or adjustment, putting further distance between regular and special education. Sometimes a specialist supervises a cadre of nonteacher aides and has little direct contact with children.

Some children require the services of specialists outside the regular classroom or school. Hearing- or vision-disabled students, for example, may require help and equipment that typical classrooms can't offer. Children with speech and language problems may need one-to-one instruction provided outside the classroom. Some more severely learning-disabled children need to spend all or nearly all day in a special classroom. While they might join other students for physical education or some electives, for the most part they are taught separately. Some children's disabilities are so profound that their needs cannot be met in a school setting. Children with long-range illnesses might receive teaching at home or in a hospital. In some cases schools provide or pay for instruction at medical or psychiatric facilities or at institutions for legal offenders. Large school districts often support their own schools for the severely mentally retarded and for the vision- and hearing-impaired. Small school districts may contract with such centers and provide transportation. Again, there is the potential for both outstanding educational opportunities and damaging ones.

Physical or medical problems are in some ways less difficult for schools to accommodate than learning problems. Some such problems require little more than additional sensitivity and occasional teaching adjustments. Even when a disability is very serious, such as leukemia, a heart condition, or AIDS, only slight educational adjustments may be necessary. Some accommodations will be technical (that is, adjustments in the schedule of assignments to allow for absences, ramp access for a wheelchair, and so forth). Others will be social (that is, discussing a problem so class-mates can be comfortable and sensitive to a child's disability).

CONSISTENT BEHAVIOR PROBLEMS

All children experience occasional mild behavior problems. Some, though, are consistently at odds with their peers and with adults. Some states label such children socio-emotionally disabled. Though not a handicap in the usual sense, behavior problems sometimes accompany learning difficulties, especially when these are undetected. Problems may also result from a mismatch between the behavior standards in class and those of a child's home or playgroup. They may result from physical conditions that sometimes respond to medication. Misbehavior can stem from the complete range of emotional/psychological conditions that affect children.

Most school districts offer a special high school program for seriously alienated and/or disruptive older children. These students usually have at least average academic ability but are unable to conform to the pressures or routines at the regular school. Often, all they need to succeed are the smaller size and more personal attention available at these opportunity or continuation schools. Some such schools combine a vocational emphasis with the coursework students need to complete graduation requirements. These schools rarely offer the advanced courses necessary for admission to many four-year colleges. However, they do issue high school diplomas and make it possible for students who might otherwise have dropped out to graduate from high school.

These schools have some disadvantages. Their existence as alternatives makes it tempting for some regular programs to "ship out" their problem students. They will often do this before exhausting all efforts to help them in the regular program. Some students transfer back to their regular school after a semester or two. However, most do not and remain in the special school until they graduate or drop out. This sort of alternative program can be an educational salvation for certain students. It also has the potential for the kind of damage one would expect from collecting on one campus many children who have serious problems. Transfer to such a program is always a serious step.

Intermediate between a special school and the regular classroom is a temporary class (often called an opportunity class), which children attend until a behavior crisis passes. Sometimes special counseling and tutoring are available. However, even with these advantages, such classes often offer more punishment than serious help. At best, they are a temporary way for the school to cope with problems. Important academic or social learning seldom takes place in these classes.

PROGRAMS FOR DISADVANTAGED CHILDREN

Most states and school districts have special programs for poor and non-English-speaking children. Their intent is to compensate for the educational obstacles these children usually face in regular classrooms.

Special Help for Poor Children

In 1964 the federal government passed the Economic Opportunity Act and in 1965 the Elementary and Secondary Education Act, the first to provide federal funding for the education of poor children. A number of studies, including the famous Coleman Report, inspired these laws by establishing a clear relationship between poverty and unsatisfactory school performance. The laws targeted funds to help children overcome educational disadvantages stemming from their home conditions. Combined with nutrition and health programs, federal aid for boosting the school achievement of poor chidlren became the centerpiece of the War on Poverty. Most inner-city and impoverished rural schools offered Head Start programs for preschoolers and remedial programs in reading and mathematics. At the same time desegregation policies attacked the social, psychological, and academic consequences of racially segregated schools. These three efforts—nutrition and health, Head Start and remediation, and desegregation—had their greatest impact on urban school districts.

The level of funding for these programs decreased during the Reagan administration in the 1980s. Even so, federally supported extra help continues. Most schools serving low-income families get some federal help, now called Chapter 1 money. The process of determining which children should receive such help can be complicated and time-consuming. Also, many are concerned that the government's and school's repeated inquiries invade children's and their family's privacy. However, some sound administrative and educational practices result from attempts to mitigate these concerns. The federal government ties its special educational funding to guidelines that define poverty status and qualify children for free or reduced-price lunches—directing money to schools with large concentrations of poor children. Once a school qualifies, *any* child attending that school (regardless of family income) can receive the program's benefits. The requirement is that, in order to receive help, the child score substantially below grade level on mathematics or reading tests. Typically schools use the funds to provide extra teachers, instructional aides, and special materials.

Like other forms of special help, Chapter 1 programs have advantages and disadvantages. The federal legislation mandates that remedial programs *supplement* regular classroom instruction in reading and mathematics. Pull-out programs have all the potential for problems noted earlier. By contrast, the most effective programs include before- or after-school tutoring.

Compensatory-education programs are the target of considerable skepticism. Much of it comes from those who oppose federal aid to education. Some early research suggested that Head Start and similar programs made little difference in the children's school success. However, the modest scope and financial base of compensatory education have limited and continue to limit its effectiveness. The programs reach only a small portion of the disadvantaged students who might benefit. Furthermore, poor design and faulty implementation have caused some programs to fail.

On the brighter side, some recent studies find quite positive short- *and* long-term effects of Head Start compensatory programs, including lower dropout rates, less trouble with the law, and less unemployment. Such evidence helps policymakers and the public understand that seemingly expensive preschool programs can prove to be a real bargain in the long run. The costs are more than offset by the savings in welfare and unemployment compensation and in the cost of maintaining offenders in jail.

Compensatory programs that provide developmentally appropriate learning experiences to very young children are especially effective. So are those that help school-aged children succeed with their regular schoolwork. In fact, the mixed results from Head Start illustrate what the sociologist Robert Merton had in mind when he observed about social interventions more generally: "Widespread, even typical, failures in planning . . . [cannot] be cited as evidence for pessimism. . . . It is the successful experiment which is decisive and not the thousand-and-one failures which preceded it. More is learned from the single success than from the multiple failures." [1]

Many observers credit compensatory programs with raising the reading and mathematics test scores of poor and black children during the past fifteen years. Data from the National Assessment of Educational Progress show that the test-score gap between children in poor, urban schools and their more advantaged counterparts has narrowed. These gains occurred

1. Robert K. Merton, as quoted by Benjamin Demott in "Rediscovering Complexity," *The Atlantic Monthly,* September 1988, p. 70.

in the face of increasing racial isolation and poverty. In sum, special efforts to help can work, but they have been much too modest in scope to meet the need. In spite of promising gains, the academic achievement of poor, black, and Hispanic students continues to fall substantially below that of others.

Desegregation Programs

Federal and state-sponsored compensatory programs overlapped the country's mandatory and voluntary efforts to desegregate schools. Supporting desegregation was research on the negative psychological and academic effects of segregation. Court cases testing segregation's constitutionality used these and other arguments to require integration of schools. The mixed evidence about the effects of desegregation on schooling has done little to inform the heated controversy surrounding it.

Over time, however, research findings have converged somewhat. They suggest that desegregation can benefit minority students' academic achievement, particularly when children start attending desegregated schools from their earliest years. Moreover, the gains of minorities are not at the expense of the achievement of white children attending integrated schools. Other findings suggest that minority students who attend desegregated schools are more likely to attend white colleges, to find work in desegregated settings, and to live in integrated communities.

The magnet schools we described in the previous chapter are not specifically designed to meet the needs of disadvantaged or racially isolated students, though many school districts use them for that purpose. Magnets have been among the more successful efforts to desegregate schools voluntarily. They often provide some of the best education in town. To the degree that poor and minority children attend them, they benefit. Unlike neighborhood schools, magnets draw children together *voluntarily*. The children and their parents choose the magnet—often on the basis of an interest they have in common with other children and parents. The programs offer attractive advantages not available elsewhere. If such schools produce what they promise—and they often do—parents object less to busing their children outside their neighborhood. Sometimes magnets supplement their regular budget by qualifying for federal desegregation money. The success of magnets should not distract concern from the fact that more minority students attend segregated schools than ever before.

Bilingual and ESL Programs

Bilingual and English as a Second Language (ESL) programs offer help to non-English-speaking children. The concern about the handicaps faced by children who don't speak English intensified in the early 1970s. This fueled support for federal and state-sponsored bilingual education. As non-English-speaking populations continue to grow, schools increasingly struggle to accommodate the special needs of these children. Because many non-English-speaking children are also poor, these programs often overlap with Chapter 1 compensatory programs. Many schools provide both.

Like federally sponsored remedial programs in basic skills, bilingual programs generate heated controversy. Part of othe controversy stems from legitimate scholarly uncertainty about the best methods of helping children. Other arguments stem from deep ideological divisions over whether immigrants should retain their native languages.

There are two broad types of interventions. *Bilingual* programs teach children in two languages. They are intended to help children retain their good speaking skills and develop literacy in their native language in addition to learning English. The theory behind such programs is that the discarding of their first language can stunt young children's language development. Furthermore, bilingual programs allow children to learn other subjects (mathematics and reading, for example) in their native language while they are learning English. That way, they are able to keep up academically with their English-speaking peers.

ESL programs typically take the form of special classes in which non-English-speaking children learn English as a foreign language. Supporters of ESL programs believe that children will do better, both academically and socially, if they use English exclusively for their schoolwork. ESL classes usually occupy one or two hours a day. For the remainder of the time, students attend regular classes and learn their other subjects in English. Schools expect students in ESL classes to switch to English without speaking their first language in the classroom. Because ESL classes focus on English, children with different native languages can learn in the same classroom.

Some schools prefer using neither bilingual nor ESL methods. They place non-English students in regular classrooms from the beginning—calling this practice *English immersion*. Some use what is called sheltered English in these classes—limiting the teachers' vocabulary to make lessons easier for limited-English speakers to understand. Essentially, however, this is the sink or swim approach.

As with other compensatory programs, poorly designed evaluations and unstable school environments make it difficult to assess the effectiveness of bilingual education. However, even though the issue is highly controversial, research increasingly suggests that bilingual programs work.

The maintaining and improving of native language skills seems to promote both overall achivement and the acquisition of English. A number of studies suggest that children in bilingual programs learn more English than children in other programs that *require* them to use English more. It appears that the younger the child, the more important it is to maintain the first language. Even for older children, the studies suggest that the transition from native language to English is most successful when it extends over a number of years.

Not surprisingly, heated opinions and politics often overpower research findings. In spite of the evidence, many worry that bilingual programs will not motivate immigrant children to learn English. Some fear even that a foreign tongue might replace English as the dominant language. Their concern is that English speakers will be in the minority and that familiar cultural values and habits will disappear. In states with large immigrant populations such as California fears like these fuel movements for English-only legislation.

The conflicts over bilingual education point to a strange phenomenon in American education. On the one hand, we want non-English-speaking children to convert to English as soon as possible. On the other hand, we lament that few English-speaking American children ever master a foreign language in school. Adding to the irony is that many colleges require foreign language study in high school and college. Truly, being bi- or multilingual is one mark of an educated person. Many believe (erroneously) that in order to learn a new language immigrant children must give up their native tongue. Schools themselves thwart those with a clear head start toward being bilingual.

A few—too few—schools with large concentrations of Spanish-speaking children have creatively combined these two concerns. They have programs in which all children (native English speakers and native Spanish speakers) learn both English and Spanish. We think these schools are on the right track. They turn an educational handicap into an educational opportunity.

The Politics of Helping Poor Children

A growing understanding of compensatory, bilingual, and desegration interventions coincided in the 1980s with diminished support for them. Even though Congress largely protected compensatory education programs, the Reagan administration reduced federal support for elementary and secondary education by 30 percent. The most drastic cuts were in programs that benefited poor children—for example, compensatory education, bilingual education, and vocational education.

White resistance in many urban districts has largely overshadowed the positive effects of desegregation. The resistance includes busing protests, school boycotts, recall elections, racial violence, and white parents transferring their children to private schools. There have been some periodic reversals in white flight, but the movement away from inner-city schools continues. The clear trend is for middle-class families to move to places where there are fewer minority children. In 1982 between 25 and 40 percent of children in Boston, Buffalo, Chicago, Cincinnati, Cleveland, Detroit, Philadelphia, Pittsburgh, Newark, and St. Louis attended private schools. More than two-thirds of these students were white. In 1988, 82 percent of the children in the Los Angeles City School District were minorities. Most minority children face as much racial isolation as ever despite efforts to desegregate schools.

There are many reasons why schools only scratch the surface of the educational problems most poor children face. The problems are enormous. There is too little money for programs of proven merit. Attending to the needs of all children equally is a relatively recent pursuit, and schools have little practice doing it. There is a widespread belief, in schools and out, that poor and minority children are unlikely to succeed. People fear that minorities and immigrants in particular are usurping scarce resources. Some resent the success they achieve. And racial prejudice taints our society. Moreover, even if all the support were in place, schools can't be expected to solve the problems of racism and poverty without parallel commitment from the rest of society.

GIFTED AND TALENTED

Gifted and talented programs exist for children whose capacity for learning and creative expression is thought to exceed the challenges that typical classrooms provide. Gifted classes are among the most visible special programs in schools. They receive extra resources and may determine the reputations of schools and entire school districts.

Who Is Gifted?

Technically, the gifted child is one who meets the state's or the school's criteria for being gifted. Even though schools make millions of "giftedness" decisions each year, there is a vigorous debate about who is gifted and who isn't. Criteria for giftedness are constantly changing and vary from place to place. What all programs share is the attempt to identify children who are especially deserving of extra opportunities.

States usually distribute funding for gifted students according to a fixed percentage of total students enrolled. Some states and school districts designate 2 percent of their students as gifted. Others choose 5 percent, and others set the figure according to the funding available. In this sense *who* is gifted may be decided in the halls of the state legislatures. Cutoff scores on intelligence or aptitude tests are the primary method for determining which children qualify. With percentage limits, states or schools adjust the cutoff scores to make the number of qualifying children match the funding.

As in identifying disabilities, problems often arise with the tests schools use to identify children for gifted programs. One problem is that intelligence tests are less accurate at the upper end of the curve. The normal variations in assessments of IQ are especially wide for bright children, so that a given child's IQ may vary from day to day, year to year. On a good day the child might be gifted. If tested on another day, he could fall short. If he moves to a different state, he may be gifted again. And if he stays where he is, next year the cutoff scores might change. California once raised its qualifying score from an IQ of 130 to 132—thereby disqualifying thousands of children who might have been considered gifted the year before.

Schools justify gifted programs and the extra funding for them by claiming that they meet children's special needs. This argument sees the gifted as a separate category of disadvantaged children, somewhat on a par with the learning-disabled or handicapped. The gifted and the handicapped are presented as bookends, between which are ordinary children, who require little special attention. The argument suggests that if an IQ of 100 is normal, a child with a score of 130 is as different from normal children as a child with a score of 70. Further, advocates of gifted programs often believe that the gifted child has as much need for special treatment as the child identified as retarded. Also supporting this reasoning is the belief that IQ points are like inches or pounds, with each unit containing an equal measure of weight or intelligence.

In fact, differences in scores at the lower IQ ranges may reflect differences in kinds of thinking ability and processes while differences in the upper ranges may measure variations in accumulated knowledge. Very high-IQ children have far more in common with children of average IQ than average children have with children whose IQs are very low. And most opportunities that suit very fast learners are well suited to average children. On the other hand, children with severe learning handicaps may require special treatment if they are to benefit from school at all. In sum, children with very high IQs do not *necessarily* require special opportunities to be very successful, but children with very low IQs may require special help to survive.

IQ scores may not be the sole criterion for giftedness. Some states and school districts include teachers' observations of leadership, creativity, or other special abilities. Some allow for assessments of academic or performance skills that are less formal than standardized tests—thus they include "talented" children in these programs. Sometimes schools attempt to have enrollments in gifted classes reflect the ethnic or economic backgrounds of all children in the school. These policies recognize that tests, observations, and prior educational experiences nearly always place the poor and non-Asian minorities at a disadvantage. Nevertheless, national statistics reveal that children identified as gifted and talented come disproportionately from white, economically and socially advantaged families. Many multiracial schools, in fact, have gifted programs that effectively exclude poor and minority children.

Most school districts fine-tune their criteria to avoid charges of unfairness and to ward off parents who want to negotiate exceptions. Parents find it especially difficult to accept schools' rejecting their children for special programs when the child barely misses a cutoff. Yet, ever-changing standards and variations in children's day-to-day performance make it difficult to have confidence in gifted criteria. So does the inability to define giftedness except by the tests themselves. Another artifact of testing is that a young child who is verbally precocious qualifies much more easily than his peers. Schools are much more likely to pass over exceptionally bright children with normal language development. Some research shows that children who are first in birth order and children from small families tend to develop language skills faster. This raises the interesting speculation that such children may be overrepresented in gifted classes.

Some parents have their children retested by a private psychologist or testing center and then submit the (higher) test score as evidence that the school has erred. Clearly, both parents and schools perceive the academic and social benefits of being in a gifted program. For many those benefits justify the costs and concern associated with the programs and the extraordinary attempts to get children in them. What are the benefits? How accurate are these perceptions? These matters warrant a closer look.

What Special Help Do Gifted Children Receive?

Gifted programs vary widely, but they all share at least some of the following characteristics:

- *Grouping Structures.* Some schools group gifted children in special classes for part or all of the day. Other programs pull out students from their regular classes for special group work with other gifted children taken from other classes. Sometimes schools cluster gifted students. They may have the gifted children who are in a regular class work together on special activities.

- *Social Identification.* Gifted students know one another, and often the other children at the school also know who is gifted. In some respects they form an elite group in the school. Many schools encourage gifted students to associate with each other. This may be purposeful or a by-product of some other activity. Often schools or parent associations distribute rosters with phone numbers to parents of gifted children. Educational meetings for parents (who are usually among the more active in the schools) further support the socializing of gifted children with one another. Simply by scheduling them in the same few classes instead of randomly assigning them throughout the school the programs encourage gifted children to prefer one another's company.

- *Curriculum and Instruction.* Lessons for gifted children are often fast-paced and designed to expose children to more content. Lessons stress critical or higher-level thinking more often than in other classes. Teachers expect these children, more than others, to do high-quality work.

- *Teachers.* Most schools select teachers for gifted classes for their special training, skill, or experience. Most schools assign gifted children to teachers who are perceived to be the best. The newest teachers, long-term substitutes, or marginal teachers rarely teach gifted classes.

- *Enrichment.* Often, at least one part of the gifted program includes activities that supplement the regular curriculum: for example, field trips to museums, plays, and so forth; special films or lectures; opportunities to do arts, crafts, or see a performance not available to other children. Sometimes the activities are purely social or only peripherally related to curriculum. For example, gifted children may spend lots of time working together to raise funds for a major, out-of-town field trip.

- *Materials.* Funding is often available to provide gifted children with special equipment, computers, books, project supplies. Many gifted programs share these materials with the regular program, but many don't. Some states make sharing illegal.

A gifted program that offered your child even some of the above advantages would be hard to pass up. One that offered these advantages to other children but not to yours might make you resentful. Our observations in chapter 7 about parents wanting their children in the top track apply here.

We can't fault the parent who does everything he can to get his child identified as gifted. Whenever high-status labels or advantaged programs exist, it's not surprising that parents want them for their chldren. But, as educational policy, it is difficult to support a structure that offers advantages to some children and not to others. This is especially so if the opportunities are ones that all children could benefit from. Moreover, with enough determination, schools, parents, and policymakers *could* make most of the advantages of gifted programs available to all children to the detriment of none.

Anyone Can Benefit

The implications of the idea that all children are able to benefit from the special treatment given to the gifted are serious. The likelihood that those not in gifted programs are at a disadvantage warrants concern. The characteristics listed above should give even the most ardent supporters of gifted classes pause for thought. For example, critical thinking is indeed important, and children need to have more opportunities to do it. But we shouldn't look at high-level critical thinking as a pedagogical bonus for exceptional children taught by exceptional teachers. There is no evidence that only very bright children can learn critical thinking skills. And they do not need separate classes to learn them.

The evidence we have suggests that the benefits of gifted programs do not result from clustering special children. Rather, gifted programs are outstanding because they marshal challenging curriculum, higher expectations, better teachers, enrichment, and so on.

Teacher A. We can compose a scenario that illustrates some of the issues gifted programs raise. Everyone at the school acknowledges that Teacher A is an outstanding teacher. She has some extra money for books and equipment. The principal encourages her to pursue her own studies on how to teach critical, high-level thinking and problem solving. She takes her students on field trips. A steady stream of specialists and members of the community come to her classes to offer enrichment activities. Her students' parents watch their children's progress carefully and supportively. This teacher designs multidimensional lessons that allow children of differing abilities to succeed and be challenged. The children in her classes include some of the most capable and creative in the school. She also has a few mainstreamed special education children. Most of her students are somewhere in between.

Teacher D. Teacher D is newly hired and has a temporary "emergency" teaching credential. He has little prior experience as a teacher. Although he majored in history, he will teach mathematics because he was a math major before he switched to history. His class sizes are somewhat larger than the school average. Because he is new to the school, he has fewer classroom materials and books at his disposal. His is a gifted class. His students are among the quickest to learn and score the highest on intelligence tests. Teacher D will try his best to follow the school district curriculum for his special charges.

Which class would you choose for your child? Is there any question?

Of course, we have had to compose this scenario because in actual practice the obvious benefits of Teacher A's class would go to gifted children. Teacher D would teach average or below-average students. No wonder parents want their children in gifted programs. Although in many schools, the extremes of teacher qualifications are not as vivid as we have painted them here, in many schools they are.

The very existence of a gifted and talented identification communicates immediately that those not so identified are not gifted. The result can be that children have unrealistically low self-concepts and schools have low expectations. Publicly identifying some children as gifted can also place unrealistic burdens on the gifted children themselves. At a reunion of participants in Quiz Kids radio and television shows, the adult alumni discussed their adjustment after they graduated from the show. Many expressed serious reservations about having been labeled a special, gifted child (*genius* was a more likely term then). They lamented being separated from their peers and recalled their shock upon discovering in college that many students were just as intelligent and capable as they.

"Gifted" is a global definition—just like "A student" or "remedial." Both children and adults mistake the labels for certification of overall ability or worth. Many see the gifted child as one who was born deserving the special status and the special advantages the school provides. For some exceptionally bright children, this perception of birthright short-circuits their discovery that effort and persistence matter more than high scores on tests.

On the other hand, research and anecdotes underscore the boredom and frustration that underchallenged children experience in regular school programs. Many observers report solving severe behavior and learning problems by placing children in gifted programs. There are even cases reported of very smart children being diagnosed as slow because they adapted so poorly to conventional classrooms. Undoubtedly, many such stories are true. Still, this does not make a case for more gifted classes. The safest conclusion to draw is that most children would do better if there were fewer labels and more challenging classes for all.

Even the advantages of gifted programs are often a mixed bag. Ironically, in many gifted programs children also do low-level, routine drill-and-practice work. They just do more of it. They memorize thirty vocabulary words instead of twenty; they do all the textbook math problems instead of the odd numbers. Sometimes their special enrichment opportunities are "creative exploration." To be sure, puppetry and field trips to cultural spots can be worthwhile activities. And they may indeed contribute to a child's education. However, they may also offer little in the way of rigorous, academic challenges from which highly able children could benefit.

All parents want the best for their children. Most are pleased to have their child identified as gifted or talented. But parents and policymakers should consider the questionable *educational* benefits of most gifted programs. They should consider the possible disadvantages to the many capable children these programs exclude. And they should consider the unfairness of giving educational opportunities from which all children could benefit to those who need them least.

Advanced Placement Programs

Many senior high schools offer advanced placement (AP) classes for exceptionally high-achieving eleventh and twelfth graders. These courses allow students to pursue college-level study in nearly all the academic subjects. The content of AP courses is similar nationwide, since a major objective is to prepare students for the Advanced Placement examinations. The Educational Testing Service designs these exams, and the College Board administers them. This is the same organization that gives the Scholastic Aptitude Test (SAT) required for admission to many colleges. Most colleges give automatic credits to students who receive high scores on AP tests and excuse them from beginning courses in those subjects.

AP classes often overlap with gifted and talented programs at the senior high level. As with gifted programs, better teachers often teach AP classes. Schools provide extra resources that often include small class sizes. However, AP programs differ from most gifted programs in some important respects. Any student with the proper academic background, whether technically gifted or not, can enroll in AP classes. Although enrollment carries with it some elite status, there is no global label assigned to students in advanced placement programs. The courses are nearly always more rigorous than ordinary classes, and they are largely confined to the last year of high school.

However, advanced placement is not without its problems. Some students complain that their instruction is too closely tied to preparing for a single test. Teachers, too, may feel that their teaching is constrained by the rigid curriculum. College professors sometimes feel that AP classes do not prepare students well for advanced college courses. Some students, for example, never take a college course in English composition because of their AP credit. Years later, they wish they had. And the existence of AP courses may influence teachers to water down courses in the same subject that don't carry the AP label.

Many high schools and colleges cooperate to allow capable high school students to enroll in college courses as seniors or even juniors. We prefer this opportunity to the AP courses. It acknowledges that some students are ready for some college work earlier than others. Yet it doesn't blur the distinction between high school and college, and it avoids some of the tracking traps that AP classes often fall into.

Of course, as we have argued throughout this book, we'd be most comfortable if all children had rich and rigorous, heterogeneous and common learning experiences from the very beginning of their school careers. That way, by the time they were sixteen or seventeen, when Advanced Placement courses or early college enrollment became available, decisions about who should participate in these programs would be far less contaminated by the tracking that has come before. Advanced learning opportunities should be available to all students who can benefit from them. We'd know far better who all such students are if all had had equal access to solid preparation for these end-of-high-school opportunities.

Judging Special Opportunities

Though we prefer that schools make regular classrooms suitable for all children, there are times when they can't. Sometimes children's special difficulties go too far beyond the scope of what most classrooms can accommodate.

A difficult decision many parents face is whether to have their children identified, labeled, and treated as special. This is not a problem just for parents of children with disabilities. Many parents of potentially gifted children also worry about the mixed advantages and disadvantages both to their own and to other children.

How can parents know if special opportunities will be truly helpful? Since programs vary widely, we can offer here only the most general guidelines. Will the program keep the child away from a cross section of peers? Or will a well-meant desire to protect lead to separation? What is the overall quality of the program itself? Evaluate more than the special services, but also look for the cultural characteristics that make for high-quality schools and classes. Which children have access to rich learning opportunities? Are there high expectations for children? Is the school staffed by professionals who feel confident and powerful enough to make a difference in children's learning? Do the classroom opportunities include those dimensions that help children feel capable and in charge of their learning? Do the adults believe that all children can learn? Are lessons filled with socially valued knowledge that is rich in meaning? Do children work cooperatively? Do evaluations promote hard work and learning? All children—gifted, retarded, physically handicapped, non-English-speaking, and poor—have needs that are best met when their schooling includes these critical characteristics.

FOR FURTHER READING

Exceptional Children. A quarterly journal reporting new research and school practices related to handicapped and learning disabled students.

K. A. Heller, W. H. Holtzman, and S. Messick (eds.), *Placing Children in Special Education: A Strategy for Equity.* Washington, DC: National Academy Press, 1982.

Stephen Krashen and Douglas Biber, *On Course: Bilingual Education's Success in California.* Sacramento: California Association for Bilingual Education, 1988.

Gaea Leinhardt and William Bickel, "Instruction's the Thing Wherein to Catch the Mind that Falls Behind," *Educational Psychologist* 22, no. 2 (1987).

Jane Mercer, *Labeling the Mentally Retarded.* Berkeley, CA: University of California Press, 1973.

Cecil Reynolds and Robert T. Brown (eds.), *Perspectives on Bias in Mental Testing.* New York: Plenum Press, 1984.

Robert Slavin, "Making Chapter 1 Make a Difference," *Phi Delta Kappan* 70, no. 2 (1987).

Christine E. Sleeter, "Why is there Learning Disabilities? A Critical Analysis of the Birth of the Field in its Social Context." In Thomas S. Popkewitz (ed.), *The Formation of School Subject Matter: The Struggle for an American Institution.* New York: Falmer Press, 1977.

L. J. Sweinhart and D. P. Weikart, "Evidence that Good Early Childhood Programs Work," *Phi Delta Kappan* 68, no. 8 (1985).

U.S. Government Accounting Office, *Bilingual Education: A New Look at the Research Evidence.* Washington, DC: GAO, 1987.

Margaret C. Wang, M. C. Reynolds, and Herbert J. Walberg (eds.), *The Handbook of Special Education: Research and Practices.* Oxford, England: Pergamon, 1988.

CHAPTER NINE

Home Support for Learning

Nearly all families—whether two-career, single-parent, or the dad-works-and-mom-stays-at-home variety—find it increasingly difficult to provide children with basic support for schooling. These supporting basics—love, supervision, a healthy environment rich in learning experiences, and so on—are largely known to all. But in the past, parents themselves were supported by a safety net of neighborhood and community. What they didn't know, couldn't observe, couldn't provide, or had doubts about, they could check with friends and family, neighbors, or the school. Likely as not, the values held in common by all these people made being a parent, if not easy, at least a partly shared task. Today, most parents work, many families are mobile and know few of their neighbors, and growing numbers of children attend schools far from home. In many communities, if values are commonly held they are only rarely shared.

Today's generation of young families is caught in transition. We have lost some of the traditional ways of supporting children's success in school (mom at home, stable, highly interacting neighborhoods, and neighborhood schools), and the replacement supports are new, untried, or inadequate. We accept the value and need for professional day care, but many can't afford it. Those who can have difficulty finding high-quality preschools and after-school care. Some well-off mothers are signing up their children for preschools as soon as they learn they are pregnant. Less well-off parents take what they can find. Some obvious solutions such as flexible work schedules and child-care facilities at the workplace have been slow to take hold.

Local, grass-roots efforts to involve schools and use their facilities after and before school for supervision and enrichment programs run into monumental legal, insurance, and bureaucratic obstacles. Still other community organizations could, but usually don't, take more active roles in helping children and their parents. And even with good child care most families are on their own—pioneering ways to juggle childrearing and careers. Few have models from their own childhood, and nearly all parents have trouble bucking social forces that are often stronger than their own knowledge and confidence.

The education researcher James Coleman has suggested that, because of economic and life style changes, our society will have to give greater support to new structures, institutions, and people who love and supervise children. Coleman and others suggest that the entire community must reassert its concern, emotional support, and willingness to supervise all the community's children. We agree. But this won't happen until there is a wider understanding of how society generally will benefit. Too many people cling to the notion that the only source of love and supervision is a caring home that conforms to the stereotype of the rapidly disappearing middle-class nuclear family, "Leave it to Beaver" style. It is unlikely that we will ever return to a society in which most children grow up in an intact nuclear family with one parent raising children full-time at home.

But the outlook is not entirely grim. Indeed, our transitional state may mean that this is a time that, although difficult and uncertain, already offers new and better ways for helping many children get the best possible education. First, considerable research on child development and parenting has established the resilience and adaptability of children to a variety of family situations. Single-parent families, stepfamilies, and nuclear families with both parents working are all viable arrangements for raising healthy, secure, and academically successful children. And even with added pressures on today's families, many parents are better equipped to help their children than in past generations. Many more parents, especially mothers, have college educations, and more parents have some knowledge of child development and child rearing. Many schools today are paying attention to the need to involve parents in order to replace the largely informal contacts of the past. Finally, let's keep in mind that even in the good old days raising children to be successful in school was no breeze—just ask your own parents.

In this chapter and the next we describe those home conditions that support children's intellectual development and success at school. While tough, all these conditions can be put into place by any determined family. In the next chapter, "Helping with Schoolwork," we discuss the specific types of adult involvement in schoolwork that students require to be successful.

Five Educational Priorities

The basics of parenting are familiar to most—love, good nutrition, enough sleep, clothing, shelter, health and safety. We won't say much about them here except to note that a growing body of research on parenting suggests that when parents provide these basics with warmth and firm direction, children are more likely to be healthy, intelligent, confident, and independent. These qualities are essential if children are to respond to guidance and sensible discipline, play well with others, and develop sound social and ethical values. The basics are not matters for great deliberation, negotiation, or family decision making; they are givens. And even though the way parents provide these basics changes considerably as children grow up, they continue to be matters of concern for both the first-time parent of a kindergartener and the experienced parents of teenagers. Even that employable, articulate, space-consuming, opinionated, and, yes, lovable seventeen-year-old needs a parent's attention to these basics.

However, the basics themselves are not enough to guarantee schoolreadiness. Children who are intellectually and socially ready to learn at school also require consistent, specific, and purposeful support for learning. But support for learning does not mean that you must charge off to your local educational bookstore or supermarket, load up on math and reading workbooks, and begin teaching your kids at home. What matters most are the priorities you set, the values you communicate, and your consistent interest and encouragement.

In the following pages we describe five home priorities that support children's school achievement: First, take advantage of every possible opportunity to help your children develop language and explore ideas. Second, provide your children with time out from structured activities and intensive interactions. Third, allow them plenty of opportunities to play, explore, and discover. Fourth, establish household routines that reinforce good learning habits. Finally, stay involved and enthusiastic about your children's learning, even as they get older.

PRIORITY 1. DEVELOPING LANGUAGE AND IDEAS

Children learn to think and use language as they listen and talk with their family and peers. Modern children learn language in fundamentally the same ways as the children in preliterate societies learn and as we all learned, whether or not our parents gave a hoot for language development or read books on child-raising or schools.

We marvel that such complex and mysterious processes take place so quickly, efficiently, and beautifully. Through the senses of sight, touch, smell, and so on, as well as revelation, inspiration, and intuition, we take in and recreate the world in ways that scientists barely understand and artists and poets reveal only in occasional glimpses. And it is not just the geniuses, the blessed, or the gifted who learn to represent the world in symbols of all kinds, including language. As we described in more detail in chapter 2, everyone learns, and the learning process begins when we are very young.

Nothing parents do influences their children's thinking and language as much as their own natural, everyday interaction with their children. Parents take tremendous pleasure in their children's earliest attempts to communicate. The simple expression of one's delight and amazement over an infant's babble, drool, gurgle, and coo is the best encouragement. The child will continue to experiment with and receive satisfaction from language. Just as a parent's enthusiastic response creates a wonderful climate for learning, so a negative response dampens it. Of course, we all have times when we are too tired, impatient, annoyed, or bored to attend to children's chatter. But if these times are very frequent, children may soon be less inclined to stretch their language and thought.

Adults Who Listen

There is evidence that children respond to their parents' conversation from their first days, and most young children, from the age of about two, enjoy nothing more than talking to their parents. Children of all ages need substantial time during which they are listened to and talked with in an essentially noncritical way. When children know that the conversation is safe—that their ideas and feelings will be listened to and accepted—they share, take risks, and experiment. As they share, they begin to dispel frightening or hurtful worries and experiences, even dreams.

By confessing bad thoughts and mistakes, they not only receive the emotional benefits of not having to hold onto those secrets, but also gain valuable firsthand experience with openness and honesty as powerful intellectual tools and problem solvers. We can assume that many of the concerns that children will voice pertain to school, and, if unexpressed can impede success there. Those concerns that have no direct bearing on school can still rob valuable energy and attention from learning activities.

But sharing isn't simply curative. Noncritical listening and sharing slowly and inexorably develop your child's sense that his intellectual and emotional responses to knowledge and experience really matter. So much of what children experience, think, and then express is new to them. If their first attempts with words or ideas are met with criticism the words might not get learned, the ideas might not mature, and the value of communicating anything but the safest and simplest concepts might go unrecognized.

Particular kinds of interactions are helpful for children's intellectual development. Ask for and listen for ideas that express relationships— comparing, finding opposites, ordering things, placing things in categories, locating things in space and time, and identifying directions. Ask about the meanings of objects, events, people, and words. Don't settle for the simplest replies; ask for speculation and interpretation. Ask children to make sense of new experiences in light of old ones: "What does that remind you of?" "How is that different from . . . ?" These are questions that elicit abstract thinking and prepare children to be curious, inquiring, and knowledge-loving youngsters who relish learning.

Ask "What's Happening?"

Kids need to talk as they are experiencing life's events. Young children especially like to comment on what is happening at the moment. Without necessarily probing for explanations or reasons, simply ask them to describe what they are doing. When children talk about their current play or concerns, they get used to allowing others into their experiences, and they learn the pleasures of spontaneous, fluent, unguarded communication. As they put their perceptions and experiences into words, they engage in important mental processes that are at the heart of learning—abstracting, predicting, categorizing, and reflecting, to name a few.

Ask "What Happened?"

Don't fall into the familiar exchange "Where did you go?" "Out." "What did you do?" "Nothing." Ask frequently for explanations of what has already happened. Telling what happened helps children make sense of their experiences and capture them for future use. Children work on their skills of memory, narration, drawing inferences, discovering significance and meaning during these recreations of the past. Sometimes younger children embellish reality. They may not distinguish between an accurate account of the facts and their own fanciful version of what took place. Within sensible bounds, don't hold them to very high degrees of accuracy. If you respond with interest, your children will push their thinking further and sometimes revise their versions toward greater accuracy as they continue the telling.

Ask "What Will Happen?"

Ask about your child's experiences before they happen. Predicting helps develop an important sense of time and sequence. Anticipating events, predicting, imagining, and guessing are highly abstract and sophisticated thinking tasks. Struggling to find the language to describe them will help your child develop those skills. "What do you think Grandma will make for lunch?" "What will it feel like to jump into the water?" "What will it be like when you try to ride the two-wheeler?" "What do you think you will do when you sleep over at your friend Sandy's house?" "What do you think will happen if you hand in your assignment late again?" "How do you think the book is going to end?" Answering such questions, the child uses available knowledge to predict results or general principles. This is the same type of thinking that schools require for writing expository compositions, doing science experiments, and deciding which math formula to use in solving a word problem. Keep in mind that looking to the future is harder for young children than describing the present or telling what happened. Even older kids can find it frustrating.

The Intellectual Family

Another essential kind of interaction—this one seems to come more easily to some parents than noncritical conversation—is a rigorous, questioning, sometimes debating, issue-raising discussion. We associate this kind of conversation with the dinner table, although it can take place whenever family members talk over the day's events and ideas. Sometimes these interactions can be less personally risky if everyone carefully keeps them in the arena of ideas that they can try out and retract. Of course, when we recommend argumentative interactions with your children, we don't mean the kind of combative pitched battle that results in hurt feelings and spoiled meals. Take care that the youngest don't consistently lose. Teenagers may ground their first forays into adult idea-based discussions on the flimsiest data—sometimes selected because it appears to conflict with or be superior to a parent's views. Parents can help by pointing out the complexity of problems and the diversity of possible views rather than trying to pin down the best resolution.

Whether interests run to world events and politics, to books read and movies watched, or to what went on in sports and in the neighborhood, discussions involve piecing together facts, analyzing the meaning of events, and challenging opinions. In these conversations children gather information. They extend their vocabularies. They stretch intellectually as they formulate their own opinions and evaluate the views of those close to them. They gain confidence and social presence. Of course, all this presumes that children at the table are allowed as much latitude to be foolish, bullheaded, and plain wrong as their parents are. Participation in vigorous discussion tempered with patience, tolerance, and a sense of humor can be among the best "homework" your child will ever get.

It's hard to imagine anything that can have a more positive impact on children's self-esteem and confidence than having an adult give time and serious attention to their thoughts and feelings. Interactions of this type will take place in your child's classroom, since teachers are often good listeners. But the mathematics of teacher–pupil ratios are not promising. Perhaps your child can get an exclusive few minutes during the hour set aside for a particular topic. Perhaps not. Schools, unfortunately, can prefer quiet to talk and short answers to long ones. Schools can be places where questions are seen as tests if asked by adults and as admissions of ignorance if asked by children.

Playing with Words

Children's language and thought develop when they are playful with words and ideas. Tricks, jokes, puns, riddles, and double meanings all help kids identify language as fun and provide opportunities for using language in new and unusual ways. Use rhymes, sing, tell riddles, try tongue twisters, recite poems. Older children as well as younger ones revel in the fun of language. They love big words and technical terms and repeat them over and over. The names of their bones and muscles and other body parts, for example, hold a particular fascination.

Word games, jokes, and puzzles are available in books and magazines for children. These "think and do" books include crosswords, word search puzzles, scrambled word games, and other kinds of brain teasers. They are wonderful treats for a child home with the flu, stuck inside on a rainy day, or on a long ride in the car. Many word and language games are available for families with older children. Keep in mind that word games such as Scrabble are not necessarily superior for developing language skills than other games that encourage lots of conversation. Finally, the many children we have asked seem to love these games, and when we ask why they don't play them more, they respond that they don't think of it. It certainly wouldn't hurt to keep a few on top of the television set as a reminder.

Educational Gifts—This Is a Present?

Too often, our first thought when we want to please our children is to offer them a treat, a change of pace, something, anything, that doesn't have to do with school. Even older children whose ideas of specialness may be circumscribed by the familiar boundaries of rock and roll, laser toys, and movies may respond well to educational trips and special events, usually listed in local newspapers. Some stores that specialize in educational toys and games have catalogs for customers outside their area. Children may not lose their taste for plastic destructo-monsters or dolls modeled on soap opera heroines, but there are many thought-provoking and skill-building toys and games that can compete.

We do offer these cautions regarding games: (1) not everything presented as educational is, and (2) many things that are perceived as being strictly entertaining are quite valuable additions to a child's education. A good rule of thumb is that if the present, trip, or treat generates lots of questions, discussion, and opportunities to solve problems or provides new ways to think about something, it can probably be considered educational.

Toy telephone and dolls promote pretend conversations in which young children practice words and ideas and try out adult talk. Small tape recorders let children talk and listen to their own words. Walkie-talkies encourage conversations full of adventure and make-believe. Remember, though, it is your child's language you want, not some machine's. Periodically, a batch of new computer software, toys, dolls, and stuffed animals is marketed with recorded phrases that one can play at the push of a button or the pull of a string. Some are purported to be "interactive," able to carry on "real conversations." We much prefer simpler toys—blocks, small cars, and dolls—that stimulate children's ideas, fantasies, and speech. These toys promote a very active kind of language development. Toys that encourage children to *speak* their imaginings bring rich language practice along with the play and fantasy, and they may help children feel less self-conscious.

Books as Possessions

Along with challenging conversation, reading helps children develop intellectually. Comfortable and pleasant associations with books, established when children are young, set the stage for pleasurable and rewarding reading. A baby's first possessions can include a soft cloth book and a plastic bathtub book. The positive regard for books that comes from owning them and being read to can ward off the tendency for children to associate books negatively with school assignments. Library cards and, by inference, all the books in the library also can be prized possessions. Libraries are warm, welcoming places. When treated as a personal resource, they will enhance children's positive attitudes toward reading and learning.

Computers

As aides to learning, computers are valuable tools. But we don't mean computers as "teachers." Much software designed specifically to be educational is low-level. Some programs provide cute animation; others offer nice bells and spoken phrases when kids get the right answers. But it will be years before computers have the interactive capability to add much to our current educational resource–mix of teachers, books, media, personal experience, and so on. Among the best computer mind-stretchers are the adventure games that rely on mystery problems, memory, and logical deduction. With time, there should be an increasing number of richly engaging simulation games that can provide important intellectual challenges and fun. However, parents should check these games, as they would check movies and television, for content that is compatible with good taste and family values.

One computer function, though, stands out as an invaluable language tool right now. Computer word processing can enable even young students to write more and better. The computer has all the advantages of a typewriter, and it can help produce work that is easier to improve and correct. It will not be long before many students own laptops—sturdy, lightweight, notebook-sized computers that they can take to their classes. We know of elementary school classes where young children already are learning typing skills in order to make use of word processing. But whatever the state of computer technology, few families need the most expensive computer with a state-of-the-art collection of software. An economical computer, the kind marketed through discount and general merchandise stores, along with a basic word-processing program will meet most needs.

Children will benefit from beginning early on computers, but there is no rule regarding how young they can start other than the usual caution to be sensitive to the child's interest in and readiness to master the task.

Write Me a Note

With or without a computer, make writing important to family communication. Write lots of notes to each other. Keep an active family chalkboard or bulletin board. Even the youngest can get involved. Take dictation of their letters to relatives, thank you notes for presents, messages for brothers and sisters, and lists of favorite foods to remember at the grocery store. Children as young as three love to see adults write down what they have said. And what a powerful language lesson it is for a child to learn that his written words have been read miles away or hours later. Stationery, diaries, and unusual pencils, pens, and erasers are inexpensive gifts that encourage children to write.

Read to Each Other

Our enthusiasm for books stops short of teaching children to read early. We agree with reading specialists who encourage parents to read to very young children, but we worry about the rash of "build-a-better-baby" books and programs on the market. Many claim that parents can raise their children's IQ by teaching reading and language very early. These programs may be harmless, although some developmental psychologists would disagree. Our concern is that if parents follow these schemes seriously, they can place too much pressure and tension on young children. These plans are like fad diets or extreme exercise programs. Most adults just can't muster the time, energy, and patience to adhere to them for long, especially since they produce so few results.

Without trying to teach reading, read to your child frequently, from the first moment he is willing to sit and listen to a few words while looking at the pictures. Many one-year-olds are not too young. Read the same stories over and over if your child wishes, and most do. Children love repetition; as they get older, they love the powerful feeling of knowing what is about to happen. Children too young to read will mimic what reading looks like. When a book becomes familiar enough, a young child will associate memorized lines with key story events or pictures. He can then pretend to read. This is the child's first step toward identifying himself as a reader, and it is an important one. Encourage pretend-reading—but just don't seize the opportunity to make it a reading lesson. "What's this word?" is a question children might ask, but parents probably shouldn't.

Be sure to include older children and adults in the house for story time.

A special reading time each day helps everyone remember and schedule other tasks to make room for reading. By reading to your older child, you emphasize that what one reads can be shared, and that the rewards of reading are not confined to our individual and private lives. An older child will also enjoy reading aloud to parents and younger siblngs if he feels comfortable about his skills. Often he will want to share with parents something he has written himself—a report or a story. Resist making technical criticisms of either the reading or what he has composed. Questions for clarification, however, will reflect your interest, and in that spirit children should welcome them. Reading aloud need not stop as children mature. A brief newspaper article, a remarkable line or two from a book, an outrageous advertisement, as well as longer readings can continue the family's discourse over reading.

PRIORITY 2. TIME OUT

Children do important mental work when they take time out from structured activities and intensive interactions. Alone, especially in quiet, safe places, they pretend, reflect, imagine, and solve problems. This is not passive stuff but often vigorous and fast-paced. And this mental activity comes from within—from children's own resources. When alone, children can mentally twist and turn, drift and shift, and sort through problems in their own ways. They have the opportunity to exercise the free-ranging, open-ended, creative thoughtfulness that may be very different from what takes place with others.

A child talking to herself in her bedroom or engrossed in playing alone with toys engages in such activities. It is in this very active quiet time that children digest the tremendous volume of information that bombards them during the rest of the day. They begin to see themselves as individuals separate from other people and things. It is an important time for making sense of the world and their experiences in it. Reading for no utilitarian purpose—the sports page, a favorite book (perhaps one read many times before), the comics, and so on; listening to music; playing a musical instrument (not practicing, but playing); and countless other activities—even watching television—can be essential moments of the effortless, largely pleasurable escape children require. A variation of this and other kinds of alone-time can occur when children are near others, especially family members. An entire family, respecting the tranquility and priorities of others, can be wonderfully "alone" in the same room while engaged in quiet play, reading, daydreaming.

Children's lives, especially in achievement-oriented families, can be highly scheduled and stressful, and providing time alone can have a low priority. The psychologist David Elkind cautions against pushing children from activity to activity and encouraging them to act (and speak and dress) in ways that call for maturity beyond their years. Elkind finds that these "hurried" children often wind up as troubled adolescents and adults. A time out can be one way to relieve stress, to slow down, to turn off attention to the tasks and pressures of being a "good child," a "smart child," a "mature child," a "sensitive child," an "achieving child," and all the other responsible things we expect kids to be.

School, preschool, and child care are all highly social, and the level of interaction is often intense. Children returning home may still be shouting as if to make themselves heard over the voices of ten or forty others. They may speak everything they think or share anything that comes to mind. Or they may shut down completely, seeking relief from all the talking of the day.

One of our own children attended a preschool program at a large university staffed by warm, caring, and talkative early-childhood specialists and interns from the psychology department. These adults wanted children to use language, and they planned activities that kept the children talking. By lunchtime our child was talked out. Even though the twenty-minute ride home seemed an ideal opportunity for a private mother-daughter chat, she remained silent. When the prodding to talk finally stopped, her relief was visible. The ride home became a precious bit of quiet time in an otherwise noisy day. And yes, she talked plenty later.

More restrictive school settings or hours alone after school may affect children in the opposite way. In a highly structured classroom a child, especially a shy one, may have little interaction for five to nine hours. This child may greet her parents with an explosion of talk, or she may require a gradual warming-up to conversation. Either response can be quite normal, and, with important exceptions, parents shouldn't attempt to alter their children's inclination toward interaction or quiet. There are also times when a parent can't handle talking to his child—perhaps the moment the parent walks in the door after work or when the whole family is getting ready to leave in the morning. Nothing we have advised means that parents must be ready to be patient listeners at an instant's notice. Parents who make good on their promise to talk or listen later are no less helpful and may serve their children better than those who drop every-thing to turn on to a child who wants to speak.

The less time parents and children are at home together, the trickier it becomes for parents to have a role in how their kids spend time. Children may drift into patterns of being mostly with others (supervised after-school programs and play groups, for example) or mostly alone (so-called latchkey children, who let themselves into their empty home and spend the afternoon or longer alone without contact with others). The quality of a child's time alone is a judgment for sensitive parents to make. School reports of "attention problems," or "talks too much," or "does not participate" may indicate that children need more or less interaction or solitude at home. Obviously, a child who would prefer to be alone nearly all the time because relating to others is painful may need some special professional help. Similarly, a child who can't bear to be alone, who seems always to crave the company of others, and who if required to be alone is likely to fall asleep may have problems that go beyond adjusting a schedule.

A good balance of solitude and companionship is essential, but we're not suggesting any particular ratio. We caution against quick, organizational decisions or master-plan schedules—for example, "4:45 to 5:15 Tuesdays and Thursdays, go to your room and be alone." They rarely work.

PRIORITY 3. EXPLORATION, DISCOVERY, AND PLAY

In chapter 2, we discussed theories of how children learn. One of the central messages was that children do their own learning. Parents teach children the names of things and how to perform simple tasks. Parents model, and they help create important learning environments. But the important *meanings* children need often cannot be taught directly.

Children's best learning takes place when they act like scientists, examining the world around them and coming to conclusions about how things work and what things mean. Exploration, discovery, and play are the work of these child scientists. What kinds of activities take place in the midst of exploration? The following suggests more specifically some of the possibilities of children's learning from their own experiences and some times for parents to limit their own involvement.

Think about how children begin to learn the meaning of such fundamental concepts as light and heavy, big and small, floating and sinking, shades of colors, numbers of things, and so on. These are not matters parents teach. We can tell a young child that something is heavy and something else is light, and we can explain the relationship between objects that are heavier or lighter. And children can repeat what we tell them. This does not mean they understand the idea of weight or the relationship between two things of different weights. Give them two new objects, and they may have no idea which is heavier and which lighter. They must experiment with many objects in many circumstances, moving them about, comparing one with another, until it dawns on them that objects have a property their parents have been calling weight, and that some objects have more of it than others. Our having taught them the words *heavy* and *light* is important, but will have little direct bearing on their grasping the concept.

An interesting experiment to "prove" this point would be to try to explain light and heavy without using words and concepts equally obscure or difficult—for example, "something that is heavy weighs more." Advice, help, instruction—they all fall short without experience. If you've ever tried to teach an eleven-year-old a new lesson about "responsibility" or show a sixteen-year-old how to drive a manual-transmission car, you know the limits of direct verbal instruction not accompanied by extensive and sometimes risky experience. Unfortunately, many parents and schools see youngsters as passive receptacles waiting to be taught about the physical world. After keeping their children occupied with lots of planned activities, some parents are disappointed when the children seem uninterested and have little curiosity or energy for learning.

We mustn't neglect another, equally essential domain of children's learning from exploration, discovery, and play—the development of their social skills and sensitivity to others. Children learn to get along by practice, watching, figuring it out—not by being told. They learn to feel confident and to give and take. They learn to stick up for themselves and be gracious about accommodating the needs of others.

Getting Out of the Way

What can you do to aid a child in her explorations, discoveries, and play? Follow your child's inclinations. Step back and watch. Let children make the first move. Let them get dirty. Give kids room. Let them out of the playpen for a chance to scoot around the floor investigating everything that is safe. A walk with a parent is less predictable than a stroller-ride, but it gives a toddler chances to touch things, to inspect them closely, to approach strangers, and to make decisions about which direction to take. Take kids places where they can be around strangers, both adults and other children. Introduce them to the full range and variety of people who enter into your life—people of all ages, occupations, and backgrounds.

In years past children may have had more opportunities for independent exploration. Older children went alone to visit neighbors. Ten-year-olds rode bicycles to the market, the library, the barber shop, or the local park. Kids took public transportation, got lost, and figured out where they were. Many of these opportunities still exist. But for increasing numbers of children, acting independently outside the home is more difficult now and the variety of experiences more limited. To recognize and encourage safe, independent activities is a difficult challenge for parents.

More and more children live in neighborhoods that don't provide easy access to "best" friends. Perhaps your child's school is out of the immediate area, or perhaps his time is split between mother's home and father's. Encourage children to have their friends sleep over. Likewise, staying with relatives and taking advantage of overnight camps and other opportunities to get off on their own will sharpen their awareness of life outside home and family and heighten their confidence to experience *on their own* things that parents are not immediately connected to. After all, that is a lot of what school and education are about.

Keeping Exploring Children Safe

Sending children out into the world makes sensible parents nervous. We all live close to real dangers. From the sharp corner of the coffee table to an entirely random meeting with a drunk driver, from the pollution in our air and food to the specter of nuclear destruction or the greenhouse effect, dangers exist, and our children must neither disregard nor be paralyzed by them.

Parents' own fears can work against children's learning that the world is an exciting and worthwhile place to explore. Kids must not be so over prepared that they view the world and their fellow humans with wariness and suspicion. We need to bring safety awareness to children without scaring the daylights out of them. One way to do that is to uncover your own sensible thoughts and motivations about how you adjust your actions to life's steady stream of potential dangers. The principle here is that many children miss much potentially good *modeling* simply because parents don't reveal their own thinking. Instead of just *acting* sensibly, call attention to it: "Let's move that lamp cord so no one trips." "It's getting foggy; I'd better slow down." "I'll wash my fruit because I'm concerned about pesticides." "We can leave to go climbing as soon as I find some safer shoes to wear." This takes some conscious effort since most of our "survival" responses are second nature. With these statements, you simply report your own practical concerns of the moment; you needn't elaborate the gory horrors of What if? Unless the child inquires, there is usually no need for further discussion. By making visible your cautious, sensible approach to life, you communicate that life's manifold dangers need not intimidate the adventurous. You also make your point better than with the easily disregarded, "Be careful."

Absolutely, children need to know some safety rules that are firm, clear, and inviolable (never go anywhere with a stranger, always be sure an adult knows where you are, don't eat or drink food unknown persons have left behind, and so on). But even ironclad rules have cracks in them, and you simply must trust children. For example, what constitutes a stranger? Someone who is not a relative? The complete answer cannot be taught directly any more than the meaning of *heavy* can.

As children outgrow parental supervision, whether by walking home from school, riding a bicycle to the shopping center, or driving the family car, they will meet situations parents cannot possibly prepare them for in any but the most general way. The safest way to raise children is to find opportunities for them to act safely in situations that call for responsible behaviors. Acknowledge every case of sound judgment you notice. Allow them to experience personally as many of the consequences of lack of responsibility as they can handle. Be available to them with reassurance and comfort when the consequences are painful. And cross your fingers. Exploration is essential for the healthy development of the intellect and the emotions. The risks are well worth taking.

PRIORITY 4. FAMILY ROUTINES THAT PROMOTE SCHOOL SUCCESS

Imagine waking up one morning and finding that you have to make decisions about all those things you normally do as a matter of routine: Will you brush your teeth? Will you wear shoes? Will you have coffee for breakfast? Go to work? Feed the cat? Even assuming that you made the correct decisions to keep your life in order, you would feel exhausted by the time you decided whether to tidy up the breakfast table or leave it for someone else. One of the toughest things about being a child is having to make decisions like those. For adults, they are mostly routine. For children, they can be energy-consuming distractions that sap their concentration and time.

Tomorrow seems much farther away to children than it does to adults. Television, play, and daydreaming offer strong competition to homework and bedtime. But routines at home can improve the odds and help children cope with their school responsibilities—partly by getting them used to regular habits.

Put School First

We know a ninth grader who had an orthodontist appointment every other Tuesday at 9 A.M. When the school counselor pointed out to his parents that they had *scheduled* the boy to miss 10 percent of his math classes, they were surprised. Over the course of the semester, a cold, chicken pox, a three-day religious retreat, a field trip with another class, and a day to make up some testing missed during the chicken pox added to the days missed so that the boy had an attendance rate of 75 percent— he missed one math class out of every four. Not one of these obligations was frivolous, and some absolutely required that he miss school. But combined, they demonstrate how easy it is for priorities other than school to stack up—even if they are important.

Overall, family routines must make it clear that schoolwork takes precedence. Resist the temptation to take children out of school so as to add an extra day to your holiday. Take the time to find an orthodontist who makes after-school appointments, or at least insist that appointment times be staggered throughout the day. Restricting television and social phone calls to after dinner and after homework makes clear the family's priority for school. Refuse to lie by writing an illness excuse for a child who was not ill—even if you want her to miss school for a reason *you* find important (such as babysitting for her sick brother) and even if the penalty for truancy seems unfair. And if you must participate in your child's missing school for questionable purposes, share your difficult decision and concern with her. Let her know it is not a choice you take lightly.

At times, however, breaking established routines *helps* send a message about school priorities. A trip to the local library after a day's work and a hurried dinner may not be your favorite way of unwinding—especially if your child could have gone there that afternoon but "forgot" about the assignment and went to her friend's house instead. But you grumble (or worse), give her a few choice words about responsibility or whatever, pack her into the car, and go to the library. Rearranging study time for a quality television program, traveling to a live performance on a school night, or accommodating your schedule to take in some other worthwhile cultural or educational event helps children to distinguish sensible exceptions to family routines from frivolous ones.

Monitor the Tube

Little can be said with absolute certainty about television's effects on children's learning. We know that some exposure to television teaches children things they wouldn't ordinarily learn and that some things they learn from television give them a head start at school. For example, children who watch "Sesame Street" and similar programs aimed at helping them learn basic reading skills may begin school with an advantage over kids who don't. For them, letters, numbers, and shapes may be "old friends" and more easily worked with at school. However, initial early advantages often disappear, and many nonwatchers catch up in the early grades.

On the negative side, there has been heavy speculation and some research evidence about how the passive nature of television watching affects children. Extensive television watching probably diminishes children's ability to be active, aggressive learners. We worry that violence on television, including that on news broadcasts, can preoccupy kids, cause sleep disturbances, and affect learning both in and out of school. In his book *The Disappearance of Childhood,* Neil Postman theorizes that television exposes children to adult "secrets" from which society formerly excluded and protected them. Postman contends that by exposing children to mature themes, including sex, violence, illness, and death, television robs them of some of their childhood. Night after night and Saturday after Saturday of commercial-filled sitcoms, game shows, and cartoons may impede children's capacity to pay attention to serious matters for more than a few minutes at a time. These programs may create expectations that worthwhile listening and watching must always be easy and that complicated problems are usually happily resolved.

Our biggest worry about television watching, however, is that it often fills up so much time that other activities—including homework—are squeezed out of the day. Children too often identify that productive sense of needing to *do* something as boredom. And boredom is too easily and unproductively cured with a flick of the television switch. And for older children, the time spent in front of the television set rather than on homework has a direct and negative effect on learning and on grades at school.

Clearly, parents should monitor television watching, and at least some watching should be a family activity. Talking about programs makes watching television a less passive and more analytic experience. Often news-based programs and occasionally dramas deal with important but potentially upsetting social issues. These are worth watching but may require a thoughtful debriefing with parents. Children can easily miss the point of programs that depict violence, environment harm, divorce, or the problems of children and teenagers.

The following questions can help a family understand its television watching. We can't say that any of these questions should be answered with an unequivocal yes or no. The "right" answers depend on a particular family's circumstances and how they answer all the questions. The picture you get of your family's television watching habits from all of the answers together is more important than any single answer.

- How are the children doing in school?
- Does the family limit their watching to favorite or high quality programs?
- Is television time an important time for the family to be together?
- Does the children's watching give mom and dad a few moments to themselves or a chance to sleep late in the morning?
- Are the kids still watching after parents have gone to bed?
- Do the kids watch in the afternoon before mom or dad arrives home?
- Is program selection an ongoing matter of discussion? And when explaining selection decisions, does anyone ever go beyond, "Because I like it"?
- Do you wait until the evening's chores are done and then select the best of what's available?
- Do the children have their own television set? If yes, is it in their own room?
- Do children have unrestricted access to programs you would not approve of? That is, do they watch programs that would offend or embarrass you to watch with them?
- Do you tend to get involved with your children's watching only when you are fed up or the kids are arguing?
- Is television used as a reward, a bribe, or a punishment?
- Are public broadcasting stations, educational channels, or cultural cable stations frequent choices?
- Are reviews and schedules used, including recommendations from parent magazines, school or PTA communications, and so on?
- Does the television set go on automatically whenever someone is at home?
- Is the television set on when no one is watching or is it used as comforting background to keep one company?
- Is the set turned off when the particular program selected is over?
- Do the children do their homework in front of the television set?

If your thinking about these questions raises concern, perhaps you can change the television-watching habits in your house. If you do so, a caution is in order. Because television is a central part of most children's lives, changes in watching habits should be the subject of ongoing discussion by everyone. Rules may be necessary, but agreements on criteria for selections are preferred.

PRIORITY 5. KEEPING INVOLVED AND ENTHUSIASTIC

There seems to be no end to the ways that young children can reach out and capture their parents' attention. As a result, most new parents thoroughly participate in their young children's learning. A baby who smiles, recognizes the family, begins to crawl, stand, and walk is almost always surrounded by an encouraging atmosphere. When a toddler says, "DaDa" to Father (rather than to the cat or the table), when he engages in creative and imaginative play, when he is helpful or concerned with others, he almost always gains enthusiastic praise and approval. This parental fascination, as instinctive as feeding and loving, eases children's learning.

As we described in earlier chapters, once children go to school, they shift from following their own learning timetables to following the school's fairly regimented learning schedule. Schools will pay less attention to their natural learning inclinations, and, for most children, offer less enthusiastic responses to their accomplishments. Success becomes more and more defined by whether children's achievements match the school's routines.

Parents of older children are no less concerned about their youngsters' achievements, but much interferes with their involvement. Many parents have little knowledge about what the school expects and little information about how their child is progressing. Some think that school learning is beyond their control or expertise. Older children tend to reach out to their parents less, and they may discourage their parents from asking questions. Also, schools treat success as more and more of a scarce commodity as children get older.

Most often only those children who get the top 10 or 25 percent of the grades are able to receive praise and enthusiasm unsullied by parental or school reservations that they should have done better. Schools allow only limited numbers of children to be truly successful. This can dampen both children's and parents' enthusiasm. Children who achieve less get fewer rewards and are thus further disinclined to talk about school.

Sometimes the same parents who were comfortable with the struggle and gradualness of their child's learning when she was young assume that, once grown older, she should be ready for any learning the school asks her to do. They may assume that any normal child who tries will be able to learn on the school's schedule. Some parents even expect their children to exceed the school's schedule. Most schools decide (usually without cause) that a few children are so advanced that they require special opportunities, labels, or classes. This invites parents' interpretation that children who are not in the top ranks are less intelligent, capable, or worthy than those who are. It is no wonder that some parents are quick to find fault with their children's "normal," on-schedule successes.

When kids come home from school struggling with new lessons, it's easy to worry that something might be wrong—that the child is lazy or unintelligent. These worries reinforce rather than diminish the child's own interpretation that success is beyond his control or reach. The result is less patient, less optimistic support at home. The perception by parents that their child is slow to learn how to read may trigger anxious reactions and presage troubles that will follow children throughout school. We have seen parents close to panic when their child had not yet caught onto reading by the middle of the first grade. Of course, schools often encourage parents to jump to the conclusion that their children are in trouble.

It may not take long for a parent to silently lower her estimate of her child's abilities and lower her expectations. When this happens, the parent is rarely able to match her earlier level of enthusiasm and involvement. Another parent may turn up the pressure and launch intensive drill and practice at home, thinking that she can push her "slow" child to keep up with or surpass other children. Neither approach is likely to help children be successful. Most often, discouraged and nervous parents create discouraged and nervous children.

Sometimes parents hold back their spontaneous pleasure at children's school accomplishments for fear of misjudging the achievement. Perhaps they feel that too much approval will result in a "swelled head" and that the child might stop trying. Others believe a response like "You did pretty well, but why did you misspell these words?" will motivate the child to do better. Sometimes children are pushed out of the nest by younger siblings who demand more immediate attention. And sometimes parents are notified by their older children that parental involvement is no longer appropriate. Once in a while the school itself gives that message. For these reasons and more, most parents gradually move from active involvement to more cautious, tentative expressions of interest in their children's learning. Despite these pressures, there are a number of ways that parents can keep involved comfortably and helpfully.

Helping Children Feel in Charge

We have emphasized the importance of children's feeling in charge. Often students who don't do well in school see their days as filled with random surprises they can't control or prepare for. They may consider high achievement fragile and precarious, determined more by luck or the actions of others ("The teacher made the test too hard." "I can't study that because it's so boring"). Unsuccessful students sometimes don't see their overall achievement as connected to their daily activities and routines: to last week's homework, to study for yesterday's exam, to today's class discussion, or to tomorrow's field trip. Our hunch is that when the parents of such students express their heartfelt concern and interest, they do so sporadically and in the context of long-range goals. They say, "What is your grade going to be?" rather than, "Let's look at your homework."

Successful students sense that their hard work and everyday attention add up to high achievement; they are capable of deriving some satisfaction from the work itself and the effort it takes. We suspect that they learn much of this as they watch and talk to their parents.

A review of your child's day enhances this important connection between achievement and effort. Kids need to organize and digest the events and wrap up the loose ends of unfinished work or lingering disappointments. Your knowledge and concern for details can ward off your child's inclination to sum up her day by saying, "Nothing much happened," or, worse, thinking it. Similarly, previewing what will happen tomorrow helps organize what happened last, and it sets the tone for a day that will be purposeful and to a degree predictable. Previewing can even alert children to pay more careful attention because they know that each incident has the potential for making an interesting story or interaction later.

Help your child attend to school matters of the moment. Listen to him as he anticipates the quiz, reports on how he thought it went as he took it, and shares his feeling about the grade or evaluation when the teacher returns it. Ask about the motivation of characters in the story he read in class today and expect to hear what he will watch for on tomorrow's field trip. These conversations help children sense that their achievement is the inescapable consequence of their effort and attention to the task at hand.

While it is reasonable for parents to want to know about their children's lessons and grades, there is much more that happens at school that children need to talk about. What time does he eat lunch? Have the new computers arrived? Is there news about who vandalized the art room? Were there any breaks from routine: assemblies, substitutes, state testing programs? Was it terribly hot and stuffy in class again? If children know you are interested, they will eagerly volunteer what interests them: the number of pushups they did in PE; the joke the biology teacher told; the progress on the "pioneers" project. Disappointments, too, complete with the details that led to them, need discussion. Finally, lessons and grades are important, and you will find out more about them if you remember that they are woven through the context of all the other details of the day.

Keeping track of the many details of the school day helps parents stay involved and children feel in charge. When parents can ask specific, relevant questions, they are much more credible as listeners and won't get brushed off so easily with superficial answers. Children who reflect on the events and concerns of the day feel more in control of them. As parents learn and remember more about their children's school experiences, the children's day will become more interesting.

Encouragement and Praise

Enthusiasm, encouragement, and praise are as necessary for older children as for younger children. The fifth or tenth grader's science lesson is as deserving of his parent's focus and energy as the infant's experiments with sounds, the toddler's first steps, and the two-or three-year-old's first thoughtful questions. In each case the most straightforward, helpful parent involvement is genuine curiosity, interest, and enthusiasm for learning achievements and for *what* the child learns, and it is best to avoid global praise for the "whole child." For example, we recently heard a parent gush, upon seeing "100%" on his daughter's spelling test, "You are the most brilliantly beautiful little girl in the whole world!" Aside from the irrelevance of beauty in the matter of spelling, it was a mistake to couple this overall judgment with specific school performance. After all, what sense might the little girl make of this hyperbole when she brings home a 70 percent? Will she be a less brilliant (or beautiful!) person?

Make your praise specific and believable—based on what a child actually does. This lets children know that they have been successful because of their own effort rather than because of their general goodness or other conditions that are essentially beyond their control (such as being naturally smart, pretty, or having an adult or authority nearby to praise them). Thomas Gordon, in his series of books on "effectiveness training," advises parents to express approval and enthusiasm without judging. Gordon would have the parent we just referred to give an "I message" to express his enthusiasm for his daughter's spelling grade—perhaps, "I am delighted with your grade, and you certainly seem pleased with having learned to spell all those words." That may sound awfully antiseptic when compared to "You are the most brilliantly beautiful . . . ," but at least it allows the parent to support his daughter's achievement without overwhelming the achievement with his own power to judge.

Finally, despite our cautions about how indiscriminate praise can cause a child to be motivated by the praise instead of intrinsic satisfaction with the task, don't second-guess your impulse to show enthusiasm. Children do not ease up on their schoolwork because parents got excited about their children's learning. Similarly, we know of no children who have been spurred on to success by discouraged, critical, or overanxious parents.

Involvement When There Is a Problem

It is hard to maintain enthusiasm when your child has trouble at school—especially when there is a pattern of difficulty rather than a few poor grades that result from temporary distractions or simply not studying. Rather than turning concern into pressure on the child or school, there are ways to reconcile the mismatch between what the school provides and what the child appears to need. Why look first to a mismatch? Many in schools would object and tell parents to look first to their child. But suppose the child is indeed ill-behaved, traumatized by events at home, or has special learning needs. In each case, it will take some accommodation by the school to go along with the child's efforts and the parents. The concept of a mismatch implies adjustment rather than blame. Consider, first, how a child's academic problem might result from a developmental mismatch rather than his personal failure or the school's insensitivity, inappropriate program, or faulty instruction. Rarely is it productive or accurate to view a problem as the school's full responsibility, as the child's or family's fault, or even "half and half." As we will discuss in more detail in chapter 11, the solving of problems usually requires that everyone—teacher, parent, and child—become involved in making small adjustments over time.

The first step is to gather all the information you can. How do the teacher, the counselor, the principal see the problem? What opportunities are there for finding out more? Will closer observation of your child or more frequent progress reports help? What additional help is available within the classroom? Does the classroom atmosphere foster your child's confidence in his ability to learn, or is her failure steadily reinforced? What steps can the school take to provide extra help without removing your child from her peers? What does the school suggest that you might do at home? Often, simply by asking these questions you signal to the school that your child warrants some special observation, help, or attention. At the same time, you can judge whether the teacher and school are working with your child in a way that fosters her academic learning and self-esteem. If the answers to these questions do not satisfy you, work with the teacher or others at school to design a specific plan that will support your child.

Communicate High Expectations

Children achieve more when parents expect more. On the other hand, parents who are pushy, overinvolved, and relentless in their demands for high achievement jeopardize both their children's education and their emotional health. Once again, the balance is not easy to achieve. We have seen bright youngsters driven by parents until they cheat, rebel, develop nervous tics, and more. And we have seen capable children who achieve little in school while cloyingly protesting that they mustn't become overachievers or get stressed out.

Expectations are least effective when someone else sets or demands them. They work best when they are subtle, pervasive elements of daily life. We don't mean that you have to be sneaky or silent about hoping your child will go to graduate school or get A's and B's. Neither do parents damage children when they implore and badger them to try harder and learn more. But expectations are really a daily matter, built in small increments that include turning off the television set, saying no to missing a day of school, adding a book to the birthday presents, and so on. Expectations flow from family values and habits that, taken together, add up to the belief that children will achieve.

Taking school and intellectual pursuits seriously is not a character trait or quirk of personality. It is a value that children learn over time. It is important to reinforce each day that you expect your child to be thoughtful about his schoolwork, reflective about the ideas he encounters, and concerned about conditions in the world. Too often the culture at school—peer pressure, lack of opportunity, competition from frivolous activities, and so on—can work against children who show concern for important ideas. Support from home can be crucial. Surely, we don't want to clobber our kids with seriousness. But children can and need to become genuinely interested in important, thought-provoking matters.

Even younger children can grapple with tough, complex questions that relate distinctly to real-life problem solving as well as to the issues and topics of the school curriculum. "What did you think when James got so angry at his mother?—What happens when kids get very angry at school?" "What do you think could be done to help countries where there is famine?—What have you talked about in social studies that could help you figure that out?" "What do you like best about our neighborhood?—What have you learned in school about things people need in order to be happy in their communities?" "Did you hear what the president said about schools?" "Do you think I should vote for the school bond issue?" "What do you think sports teams should do about athletes who take drugs?" When parents talk about important ideas that children learn about at school or are likely to have opinions about, they communicate that ideas are important and that children should take them seriously.

Children's social life at school is at least as important—serious—as their academic progress. If it is going well, schoolwork will be enhanced. If not, achievement can be impaired. Social matters also require serious discussion. Is Bobby still bothering you on the playground? Did Juanita help you with division? Do you think you will ask someone to the prom? Is everyone wearing a costume for Halloween? These discussions will keep you informed and signal that you take all of school seriously—not just school subjects.

High expectations are reinforced when parents take careful measures to be available to talk to their children. New routines that fit modern families sometimes need to be created. A good opportunity to talk about school is over the telephone. Calling Dad or Mom at work can be an important way for children to check in, unload a few problems, share a triumph or two, and focus for a while on school matters. Although it's not unusual for this to happen in an emergency, it is particularly useful as a routine and especially nice when children's calls are received cordially by whoever answers the phone at the parent's workplace. Even very short calls can cover important subjects. Besides, people tend to be a lot more efficient and get to the point faster if they know time is short. Frequent telephone contact with a parent who doesn't live with the child is a valuable way to keep up ongoing conversations.

Rewards and Punishment

Some parents try to encourage their children to do well in school by promising rewards for better grades. We've heard of everything from five dollars for each A for an elementary school child to a new car for a sixteen-year-old's modest achievement of "passing all your classes." Other parents try the reverse approach, threatening punishments for poor grades— restriction of social activities and use of the telephone are common.

Rewards and punishments are poor communicators of high expectations. They do not seem to help children learn more in school. They do not help most children get better grades (and they sometimes encourage cheating). For children, especially those who are not doing well in school, the end of the semester or year is far enough away that the reward seems out of reach and the punishment escapable. The link between daily attention to learning and the particular reward or punishment is so obscure that kids simply don't make the connection. Through rewards and punishments many children learn very quickly that it is the grade that matters and not what they learned. The intrinsic pleasure of knowledge gained or a skill mastered is replaced with a sense of pride or shame in grades alone.

Summing Up Home Support

When parents support learning at home, their children are almost guaranteed to do well at school. Children from such families are likely to attend school regularly, respect school rules and routines, take their classwork seriously, and do their homework. Even more important, when parents encourage their children to learn at home, the children are more likely to be *intellectually* ready to learn school knowledge.

Home support for learning does not require that parents become their children's teachers or take extraordinary steps to guide their development. Indeed, enthusiastic involvement with children's learning, provision of time for children to be alone to discover and play, exploration of language and ideas, and daily routines that support high expectations are consistent with most parents' inclination, intuition, common sense, and knowledge.

What really matters are the values you communicate and the consistent encouragement you provide your child. Your priorities will influence what your children think is important and, to a large extent, what they accomplish. Fortunately, all parents who value education can, regardless of their own educational background, communicate clearly that school achievement is a top priority.

FOR FURTHER READING

Bruno Bettelheim, *The Good Enough Parent.* New York: Vintage Books, 1987.
———, "The Importance of Play," *The Atlantic Monthly,* March 1987, pp. 35–46.
———, *The Uses of Enchantment.* New York: Random House, 1976.
James Comer, *Maggie's American Dream.* New York: New American Library, 1988.
David Elkind, *The Hurried Child: Growing Up Too Fast, Too Soon.* Reading, MA: Addison-Wesley, 1981.
Thomas Gordon, *Parent Effectiveness Training: The Tested New Way to Raise Responsible Children.* New York: McKay, 1970.
L. Larosa and I. Sigel, *Families as Learning Environments for Children.* New York: Plenum Press, 1982.
Eden Ross Lipson, *New York Times Parent's Guide to the Best Books for Children,* New York: Times Books, 1988.
Kenneth Marjoribanks, *Families and Their Learning Environments.* London: Routledge and Kegan Paul, 1979.

Elliot Medrich, J. Rosen, V. Rubin, and S. Buckley, *The Serious Business of Growing Up.* Berkeley, CA: University of California Press, 1982.

Neil Postman, *The Disappearance of Childhood.* New York: Delacorte, 1982.

Dorothy Rich, *Megaskills: How Families Can Help Children Succeed in School and Beyond.* Boston: Houghton Mifflin, 1988.

CHAPTER TEN

Helping with Schoolwork

Pick a class, any class. Ask the students, "Do you like homework?" Count the raised hands. None? That's what we'd all expect. Even those children who often enjoy doing some homework assignments would prefer having none. So much in our society encourages children to view learning at home and in school as an escalating misery associated with age and maturity.

There are reasons for homework's strong negative tradition: it can be repetitive, too easy, or too hard. Doing even the more enjoyable assignments can deprive children of far more attractive activities. Some teachers give perfunctory assignments, perhaps because they (along with many administrators, school boards, and parents) think that homework signals a good educational program. Other teachers assign homework simply to get students used to it—to toughen them up for later grades, when they will get lots more homework. Occasionally teachers use homework as a threat or punishment to control students' behavior. This is commonly busywork that does little to further learning.

But usually the picture is not so grim. Teachers assign homework because there are just not enough hours in the school day for children to learn all they can and should. Teachers may give homework to stretch out the learning time and allow children to relearn material presented in class. Occasionally, individually designed assignments help students with a particular learning need. Teachers design some homework—reports and projects, for example—to give students independent experiences and longer-range assignments that require a variety of tasks that can't be accomplished during the school day or within a classroom.

A great deal of recent educational research indicates that when attentive children perform well-designed homework assignments that teachers respond to, homework contributes to school success. Not surprisingly, high school students who spend more time on homework typically get better grades and score higher on achievement tests. There is equally important evidence that parents who provide academic guidance and support at home also help children—both younger children and high schoolers—be successful. Moreover, all children seem to benefit from parental involvement—even those lucky students who learn quickly and easily. This research evidence adds up to a powerful conclusion: children are more likely to succeed in school when parents offer guidance and support with homework.

In the last chapter we described ways of creating an environment at home that encourages children to be learners. We urged parents to provide children with opportunities to develop thinking and use language, establish family schedules and routines, and talk to youngsters about all of life's events, including school. All these activities help establish education as a top family priority and communicate expectations for academic accomplishments. Here, we suggest more specific ways to help children succeed with schoolwork. We offer strategies for helping children learn to study and become more proficient with the basic homework skills of reading and remembering information, completing writing assignments, doing projects, and studying for tests.

A THEORY ABOUT STUDYING

During the past few years researchers have formulated new theories about how students become proficient at directing their natural learning abilities (those processes we described in chapter 2) toward systematic studying. As a part of this work, developmental psychologists, led by John Flavell, have refined the notion of *metacognition* to describe the way students notice and then take charge of their own learning processes.

Metacognition consists of four basic components that work together to improve children's ability to learn new information and skills. The first component, *action*, includes specific tactics for learning something new: using memory tricks, taking notes, outlining, and so forth. The second, *goals*, is the ability to recognize what they want to learn. The third component is *metacognitive experiences*, or opportunities to become aware of how effectively the learning was accomplished. Finally, *metacognitive knowledge* is the store of information a student develops about when and how to use various learning tactics for the best results. More simply, in order to study effectively, children must have a repertoire of strategies to accomplish learning tasks; they must identify what they are supposed to learn and monitor both their learning processes and the results. We cannot train children to be skilled at these metacognitive components easily, quickly, or directly. Rather, they gradually develop the skills over time if they have guidance along with ample opportunity to experiment and practice.

All of the suggestions that follow about helping children learn to study and complete homework assignments fit this theory of metacognition. Notice that the theory is firmly grounded in the belief that learners themselves must be in charge of these studying processes. Consequently, parents can help most by creating an environment conducive to study, teaching their children specific learning techniques, encouraging them to try out various strategies as they study, and initiating discussions that allow them to reflect on their learning. Only children can actually learn and accumulate their own metacognitive knowledge. The most important goal for parents helping with schoolwork, then, is to encourage their children to be independent and proficient learners.

Getting Started

Despite their protests, most children are more relaxed about homework if their energy can be spent on getting the job done rather than avoiding it. An established study routine relieves children from some of the burden of deciding whether, when, and how to do homework. Parents can help by setting a regular time and place for studying, by getting assignments off to a good start, and by showing children some ways to concentrate.

Regular Study Time

No one time for study is best suited for all families and all children, but there are some good guidelines:

- Set aside a *regular* time for studying. How much time depends on how efficiently your child works and how old she is. A half hour may be enough for a child in primary grades, while older ones will need an increasing amount as they tackle more difficult subjects. It is often un-productive to tell children they can play or talk on the phone as soon as they finish their work. The children's goal too easily becomes getting finished rather than doing a good job. It's difficult, but try to establish that study time is for more than just getting assignments done. It is a time to review other subjects that might be causing trouble, a time to go beyond the minimum assignment, a time to write in a journal, do some work for extra credit, or read for fun.

- Schedule time when adults are nearby. When children are on their own, the temptation to procrastinate or avoid studying altogether is usually too great, even for serious and responsible children. Having an adult around also helps avoid the inevitable tension that arises when parents try to check up later on what was accomplished in their absence. Parents will often find something that could be improved, and even if a suggestion is well received, no child likes to go back and fix something he thought he had finished. Also, parents need a chance to observe how their children study and to suggest strategies for getting the job done.
  In many families the schedule just doesn't allow homework to wait for adults and children to be at home together. Children can often work part way through their assignments by themselves and save the finishing touches—the last draft of a composition, a couple of math problems, a final review for a test,—for the time when their parents are at home.
- Consider establishing a "family study-time." Plan your own reading or some other quiet activity while children are studying. This gives families who are away from home all day time to be together in an atmosphere conducive to study. A scheduled time helps parents model some impor-tant study behaviors like sitting still, telling a phone caller that you will return the call, adjusting the light, turning off the stereo, working at a computer, using a dictionary or another reference, and so on. Nothing may be harder for a child than trying to concentrate on homework when parents or siblings are watching television or playing noisily nearby.
- Allow ample time in the morning—but not for studying. Children who rely on this time feel too much last-minute pressure. One useful last-minute activity, though, may be a cursory preview of what your child expects to happen that day—in much the same way that a business executive would check her calendar first thing in the morning. This an-ticipation can help give the day a more manageable feeling. It's also a good time to remember the map left on the table, the parent permission slip for the field trip, gym shorts in the dryer, and so forth.
- Sometimes it helps to schedule other activities as well as studying, in-

cluding visiting with friends, spending time with games and sports, and watching television. Through scheduling children can include much in addition to study in their day or evening.

Space for Learning

Children don't need a well-appointed study or home library. But they do need a special place for studying. If space is in short supply, the best location for study might be the table where meals are served. If this is the case, that space needs to be reserved and protected for a sufficient amount of study time during the day. A nice bit of "power" to give a child is the privilege of claiming his right to study at the table, even if it means that adults who wish to linger over coffee must relocate.

Many children have their own rooms. Some of these rooms have a well-lighted, well-stocked desk, but they also have a phone, a television set, posters screaming from the walls, a stereo turned "not that loud," and various other amenities. Sending a child to such a room to concentrate on homework is like sending a fox to study in a chicken coop. Reconsider the kitchen table.

A Productive Start: What Do You Need to Learn?

A central component of metacognitive theory is that the ability to learn is linked to identifying what one is supposed to learn. It's a simple and obvious enough premise, but amazingly, children are often unaware of what they are supposed to learn. Few realize the distinction between learning and doing, and their teachers sometimes don't make the point clear. A youngster will bring home an assignment that reads, "Do exercise 3," or "Write a paragraph about . . ." and assume that simply completing the task is what the assignment is about. Even with the very best homework assignments children are unlikely to learn what is intended unless they identify what they are supposed to *learn* as well as what they are supposed to *do*.

When you ask your child, "What homework do you have tonight?" listen carefully for evidence that he has considered what he should learn. Below, we have listed some typical child-responses to the parent's question, "What's for homework?" After each exploratory comment a parent might make there follows an example of a response showing that the child understands what he's supposed to learn.

CHILD: I have to write three paragraphs about the best gift I ever got.
PARENT: What is something your teacher wants you to learn?

CHILD: She wants us to be sure we remember to give reasons for our choice.

CHILD: I have to bring a current event.
PARENT: I wonder why kids in history classes are always asked for current events.
CHILD: It's because we're supposed to figure out why things happen in the world.

CHILD: He's making us write all our vocabulary words in sentences.
PARENT: Why?
CHILD: He says we learn the meaning better than if we just memorize the definitions.

CHILD: We got to bring home our reading books today.
PARENT: What would be the purpose for that?
CHILD: We're just supposed to read for fun.

CHILD: We have to find out where all our family members come from and make a map.
PARENT: What for?
CHILD: We're studying immigration. I think the teacher wants us to see how far spread-out everybody's ancestors were.

CHILD: Sixteen long-division problems.
PARENT: Why?
CHILD: Practice.

CHILD: She told us to read the chapter on Lewis and Clark and answer the questions at the end.
PARENT: What are you supposed to learn?
CHILD: I don't know; I guess I could read the questions.

Of course, we have collapsed these conversations into brief exchanges. In reality these answers may not be so easy to get—at least when children are asked these kinds of What's-the-purpose? questions. You might have to ask a number of questions to help your child identify what he is supposed to learn: Why do you think your teacher thought you should do this? What did the teacher say when she made this assignment? What have you been learning in class that relates to this? In some instances, you may realize that the teacher has said very little about the purpose of a homework assignment. In this case, you can make the best of a bad situation as the two of you look over the work and puzzle, "What *can* be learned from doing this assignment?" With patience, your child can probably figure it out on his own. Gradually, and ideally, children who expect to be asked for reasons will begin looking and listening for these reasons when instruction is taking place and assignments are given.

Don't Worry, You Can Do It

Children often feel overwhelmed by the sheer volume of work and the length of time they think assignments will take. They may get discouraged soon after opening their books. "This will take forever!" At some time, all children need reassurance that it really won't. Often children become scattered; they start one assignment, switch to another, find it difficult and go back to the first, or on to a third. An hour later, they have little to show for their efforts. That hopeless feeling sets in, and parents may begin to hear some explanations that rarely tell the whole story: "I'm done." "I'm too dumb." "The teacher is confusing." "It's okay if we don't finish, she'll explain it in class."

These feelings are really not so different from what most adults experience from time to time, and the best help parents can give is to share the techniques they use to manage their own time productively. Start by helping the child list what he needs to accomplish (to learn, as well as to do). The child can estimate the time he needs, determine priorities, and select a few strategies for accomplishing the tasks. These are tactics adults use all the time, in keeping a daily calendar, writing an estimate, designing a proposal, planning a meeting or a party, going shopping, even running errands; all require thought, organizing, planning, time, and materials. Whether in a simple list or an elaborate outline, adults who work efficiently give thought to the purposes, the steps, the materials, and the time the job will take. Children don't just "naturally" figure these things out. And they are not often taught to do it in school.

You also need to gently remind your child that she is not necessarily supposed to understand the work before studying it. Children often feel that the only work they should do is what they already know how to do, and they need assurance that one's first attempts at anything can be frustrating.

Concentrating

A serious study problem, especially for younger children, is keeping attention focused on the task at hand. Learning to concentrate takes years of normal development and lots of practice. It isn't easy to separate what to focus on from what to ignore. Not until their midteens are children able to concentrate as well as adults, and there is no guarantee that they will be skilled even then. Improved concentration must be a

long-range goal, but there are things you can do to help your child make
the most of whatever powers of concentration he already has.

Distractions Concentration is an internal, mental state of recep-
tiveness that is easily disrupted. Your child will concentrate best with
fewer external distractions (conversation, television); a minimum of body
distractions (fatigue, hunger) and a minimum of emotional distractions
(worry, excitement). Parents can have some influence over these distractions. Teenagers especially may argue that they can concentrate just as
well in front of the television set or with only a few hours' sleep. This is
just not so. Certainly, children can become habituated to working with
loud music. They can experience real agitation if they are suddenly required to read in a quiet place if they have always done their work with the
television set on. The child may feel that she will never be able to get used
to quiet study. But she will.

Practicing Concentration Children who, from their earliest
years, have ample time alone and lots of opportunities to explore and discover the world have practiced concentration. The language and play activities we described in the last chapter help children establish a habit of
concentrating on activities that they initiate, sustain, and complete. These
early experiences are the basis for concentrating on schoolwork.

All children concentrate on activities they are interested in—when they
really want to solve a problem, finish a project, or develop a high level of
skill in, say, riding a bike, styling their hair, or remembering friends'
phone numbers. The broader their range of experiences, the more open
they are to finding new interests. The more curious they are, the better
their concentration skills are likely to be. Schoolwork, unfortunately,
often includes activities that do not arouse even the most curious child's
keen interest, and here is where most of the problems lie. While it is definitely the school's responsibility to make learning interesting, children
themselves must fill the interest gap when lessons fall short. If parents
allow children to "cop out" to the claim "it doesn't interest me," children
cultivate a sense of powerlessness. Their enthusiasm for schoolwork becomes subject to circumstances outside their control—"French is too
dull." "The teacher is boring." "I can't get into algebra."

Parents can acknowledge the lack of interest and call children's attention to some specific techniques. One of the best is to limit the length of
time spent on a boring task at any one time. If the estimated time it takes
to read the chapter or memorize the vocabulary words is one hour, chil-

dren might schedule four increments of fifteen minutes each. It is much easier to marshal one's attention if the task doesn't seem endless.

Describe How You Concentrate You can show your child how you keep your attention focused on tasks you must complete. No, you can't model the actual concentration (though a humorous picture comes to mind of furrowed brows, narrowed eyes, and an intense stare). But you can describe what you do when you are determined to pay attention. For example, some people help themselves concentrate and keep organized by talking to themselves, to direct attention to the task at hand. Children talk aloud to themselves at an early age but are soon socialized (embarrassed) into not speaking their thoughts. You can encourage this thinking out loud—actually give permission for it to continue—by doing it yourself. Most helpful are positive, encouraging comments, organizing questions, and goal-setting statements: "I am really making progress on this letter." "I've paid close attention for twenty minutes." "I'm going to spend the next fifteen minutes trying to balance the checkbook." "Now I've got the checks added." "Let's see, on the way to work, I have to stop at the post office, drop by the . . ."

Visual images are also useful attention holders. A child studying the Old West, for example, will keep interested longer and more intently by imagining what the people and places being studied looked like and picturing their actions. Geometry problems can be visualized as well. When your child is trying to recall or memorize, suggest that she close her eyes and picture the word, the problem, or the narrative. Outlines and a special way to organize main ideas called mapping are especially helpful because they lend themselves to being pictured. When working with complex ideas, your child might find it helpful to write all the important parts of the idea on a single sheet of paper (a large section of butcher paper is useful) and label the relationships between ideas.

Some children find that these techniques come quite naturally. Others resist the idea that mental games like these will help them do better in school. Whatever your child's disposition toward learning techniques, it pays to start early with the *idea* that conscious plans to concentrate and memorize are truly helpful. (We caution that younger children who do not take to a particular kind of organizing might not be developmentally ready to make sense out of the categories or other organizing plans that occur to their parents.)

Of course, no parent can control a child's thoughts, but you can encourage him to try these and the other strategies we suggest in this chapter.

Mention that athletes use concentration strategies to achieve their best performances. So do actors, musicians, and others whose work requires that they concentrate intently for long periods of time. We'll even toss in a reminder of the maligned absent-minded professor mumbling around his office. Yes, he may forget that his glasses are perched on his forehead, but, by talking to himself, he won't forget his writing, his formulas, or his research.

Using Resources

Given the limits of our minds and our experiences the measure of our intellectual development is not the knowledge we have memorized but the knowledge we can get when we need it. Further, we would be severely limited if we couldn't go beyond what others have told us to know. For this reason the most important study habit may be asking the questions "How can I find out more?" "How can I be sure this is accurate?" and "How can I think about this differently?" In each case it is not the resource that is the key but the inquiring mind, the need to know, and the value that says, "Let's find out" rather than "Oh, forget it."

In the normal course of going through the grades, children learn about the dictionary, the thesaurus, the atlas, and so on. They will do exercises with these reference works and be able, when required, to find a definition, a synonym, a country, and so on. Students will also "do research" and extend their range of reference works to magazines, books, experts, interviews, libraries, letters, family members, all of which become part of their expanding world of resources. But even then, many view resources as little more than tiresome obstacles. Children will ask, "Why don't they just tell me what they want me to know and I'll learn it?"

Unfortunately, much schoolwork that requires sources other than the teacher or textbook has the research or reference skill as its sole purpose: "Why do we have to look up these words?" "Because it's important to learn how to use the dictionary." Skills taught in the context of doing exercises instead of solving a real problem usually miss the point of research. When a real question arises, too few children can connect the research lesson to the new situation.

At home, parents can take advantage of children's genuine interest in information for its own sake: "Let's look it up" is the best response to many children's questions. The concept of research is slow to develop in children, and it takes a while for them to see the relationship between knowing information and going to the sources of that information. Often children neglect the most obvious resource that many skilled students use all the time, calling a friend. Children need to watch adults satisfy their own information needs ("I think I'll look that up in the encyclopedia"). They need to hear parents make explicit their research thinking ("Sure, I can help you with the question. Let's see, the first thing I'd do is look for 'Boston Tea Party' in the index"). Children must usually witness these processes of inquiry over a period of years before they begin to develop the same habit.

Very young children can learn that the public library is an extension of home and school resources and that libraries are not mysterious places. Especially with increased use of computerized cataloging, children can learn that finding information in the library is a breeze. To the extent that you understand how to get information in the library, go ahead and show your child. But another fine lesson is for parents to gather their confidence to ask the librarian, even if the question "sounds stupid." Children, especially adolescents, would often rather go home empty-handed than ask a question. Modeling can be powerful. Watching a parent ask a vague or ill-formed question and then be well received and helped by a librarian can pave the way for children to raise their own questions in the future.

Let Your Child Teach You

Teaching someone else is so sound and reliable a technique for learning and remembering that a serious student can hardly avoid it. Teaching requires that you review and remember not only the facts and conclusions but the logic, the transitions, and the "story" of the new knowledge. In the process of teaching we put the new knowledge in our own words, we link it to our previously acquired knowledge, we consider the knowledge of our pupil. All of these steps push us closer toward mastering that which used to be only familiar. By teaching someone else children gain important metacognitive experience and knowledge. As they teach, they will inevitably reflect on how well they have learned the material themselves. And, with a little encouragement, they can assess the effectiveness of the learning strategies they employed as they suggest some for you to try.

You can support this study habit in your child by valuing it so highly that it takes precedence in the time the family spends together. View your "being taught" as your most prized connection to the child's learning. It is an activity that supports mastery of the school curriculum, and it is as important a study habit as memorizing or taking notes. There are no special tricks to having your child teach you. Our suggestions in the last chapter for talking about concepts and skills include several ways for you to elicit your children's best thinking and to be a helpful student.

Parents help children most with schoolwork when they provide an environment that is conducive for studying at home and give their children support for tackling hard assignments and sticking with them until they finish. They also help when they show their children general strategies for accomplishing academic work, including techniques to improve concentration and skills for using resources and references. Parents help when they let their children teach them. These strategies apply regardless of the child's age or the particular homework assignment. But there are more specific ways to help your child become skillful at particular kinds of schoolwork. We turn to these in the following sections.

READING FOR HOMEWORK

No single activity or skill carries greater weight and significance for successful schoolwork than a child's facility with reading. Reading is a basic homework skill, and children can complete few assignments if they have trouble reading the directions. Because reading is so central to success at school, we urge parents to be especially sensitive when their child has reading to do. At no time are parents more likely to feel tense and apply pressure than when children have reading homework.

As we noted in chapter 4, reading, like learning itself, takes on a life of its own once it gets started. Children who have a good foundation and who follow their own developmental clocks will probably learn to be good readers. Troubles with reading tend to come when children are hurried or pressured, identify themselves as reading failures, miss key reading instructions, or when they have missed out on early pleasures of reading—such as being read to when they were young. In this section, we suggest some ways to help young children with reading homework and to help older children read for information.

Young Children

Young children often bring home basal readers or other books for homework. Most often, teachers hope that parents and children will take the time to sit down and read together. In the best cases, they want younger children to enjoy reading and discover that it helps them "find out." The suggestions in the previous chapter about families reading together apply here too. If you have established habits of reading to your child and if you listen to him read in a friendly, encouraging way—which may include helping out with unfamiliar words—you may avoid adding to the pressures of learning to read. You especially want to avoid making every reading experience into a lesson. Whether at school or at home, the best reading practice is to read enjoyable, accessible books under pleasant circumstances. Helping achieve that is the best homework help parents can give young schoolchildren.

Your child may also bring home worksheets that ask him to practice such reading skills as matching letter sounds or words to pictures, finding words that begin with the same sounds, and so forth. If a child is struggling with a particular reading worksheet, often a friendly question or two will be enough to help him figure things out. However, it is usually best to let children work on these assignments alone, and leave the actual systematic reading instruction to teachers. If he is truly baffled over a period of several assignments, that is a good sign that you and the teacher need to talk about the trouble.

Purposes and Expectations

When an older child has homework that requires reading for information (rather than to develop reading skills), he needs to pay attention to why he is reading and let that determine how he will read: Is he reading the chapter in his social studies text in order to answer questions at the end? A novel for a book report on the theme? A worksheet prepared by the teacher for a detailed test on biology terms? A scene from Shakespeare for class discussion? Math directions to learn how to do the exercises? A newspaper article for a current event in health? Whatever the case, the purpose for reading should shape how the child reads the material. Many children get discouraged and may jump to the conclusion that they are stupid if they don't "get it" when they read. They need assurance that a first-time reading for facts and information is very demanding and that having difficulty—if not overwhelming—should not be a cause for distress.

A quick conversation about the selection, the purpose of reading it, and the expected ease or difficulty of the reading can help make your child a better reader. Often children are unaware that reading difficulties can be perfectly normal and are to be expected. For example, your ninth grader is not *supposed* to find *Romeo and Juliet* easy reading. He is not supposed to read it as if it were a teenage novel. But he may not know that. Let him hear you agree that this can be tough reading. He may not know that most readers and watchers of Shakespeare's work are already at least roughly familiar with the plot. Does he know that college students of literature sometimes read a summary of the play before the play itself without anyone's thinking they were cheating?

Ask your child why he is reading chapter 4 in his social studies book. What does he think he should know? Big ideas? Small details? Does he think the reading should be easy? very difficult? Will he have a test? Can he explain what he already knows? What is the single most interesting part? Without such prompting, children may not give a moment's thought to either the purposes of the reading or the ease with which they expect to accomplish it.

READING STRATEGIES

Beyond reassurance and conversation, there are a number of reading strategies that parents can, with the utmost caution, discretion, and tact, share with their children. Why are we so tentative about these specific strategies? All parents are well aware that teaching their own children can require great patience and diplomacy. Children, like most adults we know, are not about to put helpful hints into practice simply because a concerned parent suggests them.

Review to Establish a Context Have your child look over the previous chapters or recall main ideas that might lead to the current ones. Before he reads, help him recall the class discussions. Ask to see his notes if the teacher has encouraged note taking. Your goal is to help him see the value in previewing and finding the context and framework for understanding new information.

Preview What Is to Be Read The child should quickly scan new material before reading it carefully, paying attention to all the section headings and boldface type. He should skim any summary sections and read questions scattered throughout the material or at the end to predict the main ideas. Previewing gives students an idea of where they are headed and the broad outlines of what they will meet along the way. It helps prevent getting lost or hopelessly sidetracked somewhere in the middle.

If your child is given the familiar "read the chapter and answer the questions" assignment, he should read the questions *before* reading the chapter, and then read the chapter *before* answering the questions. Many children will have successful experiences reading the question and then hunting for the answer. But you can point out that this method takes almost as long as the preferred way and is a lot less interesting than reading the chapter start to finish.

Read Actively When your child reads unfamiliar information, he will understand and remember it more easily if he makes a few speculations or inferences as he goes along. For example, if he is reading about climate in various parts of the country, he might think about how his home climate would be different if there were a range of mountains to the east or a large lake to the west, or how that might affect the people and products of the area. If he's reading about the Civil War he might imagine how America would be different if the South had won. He could imagine how it felt to be a slave or to fight in a battle against one's relatives.

Relating and comparing new ideas to familiar things also can make reading easier. A child reading about how a species of wild animals rears its young might compare this information to what he already knows about how humans raise their children. The internal-combustion engine might be compared with human digestion. All stories and literature of value can be related to events, emotions, and ideas that your child has personally experienced. Children at first will not generate these questions and speculations, which require a kind of curiosity, speculation, and creativity. But with the encouragement and guidance of their teacher, classmates, and parents, they can learn it.

Reading fast is often overvalued. Speculating, comparing new information with old, and classifying ideas are active processes that slow children down as they chew over information to make it more understandable and easier to remember. Later, when children need to recall or apply what they have read, they will have many more associations with the categories they invented and with the speculations and comparisons they have worked through. That is what having learned is all about.

Notes and Outlines When information is new it is hard to distinguish between essential ideas and interesting details. Children don't naturally arrive at this separation when they read. Older students can quickly catch on to making outlines or diagrams of new information that show which ideas are most important and which are subordinate. Younger children can search for the "big idea" and jot it down. Note taking and outlining require children to make decisions about what's important to remember. They also come in handy when it's time to prepare for tests and review for what comes next. Note taking or outlining can be a good bridge to writing assignments. Teachers also may use these activities to determine if children have read the assignment. Whatever the reason, children may need help to avoid getting caught up in outlines or notes as ends in themselves. The broader and much more important goal of *making sense* out of what they read is harder for them to keep in mind.

Review What Has Just Been Read When your child finishes a reading assignment, be available to help her with a systematic review. Together scan headings and summaries and ask her to connect all the pieces of information. Children frequently do not understand ideas encountered at the start of a selection until they reach the end, and the review will help your child see that the material as a whole consists of interrelated parts.

As an experiment, try sitting down with a watch and timing this review process. Children are often so much in a hurry to wrap it up after finishing the last word that they resist this extra review step. They may be shocked to find that an entire review can take five minutes or less. Considering the benefits, even children who are ready to head for the ballfield or the television set may see the value.

Self-Tests A last step is for your child to quiz himself. Sometimes questions are a part of the assignment. Notes can be used to make up questions. Suggest that he list the main ideas without looking at his notes. Self-quizzes provide important confidence-building closure. This is also an appropriate time for the child to reflect on how well he learned what he read and how useful his learning strategies turned out to be. When finished, children will be able to say, we hope, "I've learned it" in addition to "I'm done."

When a Child Has Trouble

Some reading is difficult because the information is complicated or poorly explained. Prior knowledge and interest play a major role. Comprehension is not a straightforward matter of being able to sound out all the words or even knowing the meanings of individual words. Students with a strong background in math will have less difficulty with their algebra instructions than better readers who are poor math students; a child who loves airplanes may get through material written on that subject even if the vocabulary otherwise would be too difficult. You can reassure your child when he is having trouble understanding directions or a difficult chapter that he is not necessarily expected to "get it" with a casual or even strenuous first-time reading.

If encouragement is not enough, a brief explanation can sometimes give enough clues to help the child get through difficult reading. Under some circumstances you might actually read to your child to let him hear the ideas. There is absolutely no educationally sound purpose served by making a child struggle with, or perhaps miss entirely, concepts and skills simply because he cannot read them. That will only compound his difficulties at school and generate bad feelings about himself.

If your child frequently has a hard time reading his homework, you probably need to talk to his teacher and discuss a plan for more systematic help. Children with ongoing reading problems can feel hopeless and defeated if their reading is a barrier to other kinds of learning. Once a child is older than eight or nine, reading problems rarely take care of themselves. Some schools have special programs that provide encouragement and specific help with reading skills from trained reading specialists. If your school has such a program, check to see that it provides serious study and high expectations for genuine improvement. Also make sure that it will not take your child away from other valued classroom experiences. If it meets these criteria, the school program may provide the help that is needed. If not, investigate the resources at a local college or university that trains teachers. You might also ask for a recommendation of a private reading clinic in your community. Also be aware that children with reading problems often benefit from counseling along with specific reading help. Sometimes children have reading problems because they have other educational or emotional troubles. Finally, reading difficulties can cause children to develop bad feelings about themselves generally, and counseling may help.

WRITING FOR HOMEWORK

"Want to hear what I wrote?"

Your child has a page or two in his hand. The assignment is to write a story or an essay. You've seen some corrected papers he has written recently, and you found the low grades generous. Words were misspelled. Sentences rambled on. Topics seemed to change in midparagraph. Some of the handwriting was illegible.

"I think I'd like to read it," you reply.

"No, I want to read it to you." You sit back to listen. With the expression, presence, style, and tone of an experienced orator, your child delivers a credible composition. Sure, it has its flaws, but on the whole, it sounds good. So why does it look so bad? We can't analyze your child's writing, but we can suggest some general things you can do at home to help his writing sound and look better.

Help When Invited

The first step is to realize that your help must be by invitation only. If your child, for whatever reason, doesn't want your help, you can probably make no useful contribution. And once you've been invited, it won't take much in the way of criticism, correction, or suggestion to have the invitation withdrawn. The child above relished the chance to read his paper to his parent but wouldn't let the parent read it. Many children are unwilling to do either. Children are cautious about how criticism will make them feel when they express and expose their feelings, ideas, and skills.

Strategies for Helping

Discuss Ideas before Writing Children who won't allow their parents to read their writing are usually less reluctant to share their ideas. You can ask your child what ideas he plans to include in his composition before he writes it. Many problems of composition stem from not having thought through the ideas; a talk beforehand does more to generate a good composition than correcting the writing afterward. Ask him what he *thinks* and urge him to elaborate as he talks about the topic. The following remarks are likely to push his thinking beyond his initial thoughts: "Tell me more." "Can you give me an example of that?" "What is the reason you have for saying that?" "I think it would be great if you could describe what you mean in detail." "Could you describe what that looks like?" These questions relate to your interest rather than to your intent to correct, improve, or take control of the composition.

Offer to Proofread Parents should limit their efforts to edit their children's writing. It's worse than useless to impose corrections; you will succeed only in cutting off future opportunities to help. But you can offer to proofread. We suggest that you start by making a specific limited offer: "Would you like me to check your spelling? I could put a light pencil mark over the misspelled word, and I'll write the correct spelling on a piece of scratch paper." Don't be surprised if even this generous offer is rejected at first. Just remember, the key to being helpful is having your child *value* your help.

Try to offer your help in the early stages of writing, rather than waiting until your child thinks he is finished. Although most of the resistance children have to getting help is related to interpersonal issues and risks, a substantial amount is very pragmatic. After children think they have given their composition their best shot, they want to be done with it. If Dad finds a mistake or an omission or some bit of foolishness, the child will have to copy the whole thing over. About all you can do with your child's final composition is appreciate it. At this point children have little interest in proofreading, editing, correcting, and so forth. Your offer to proofread the first draft may be received more positively.

A child's resistance to parental correcting, revising, and improving of his writing is not nearly so great if these things can be done neatly and quickly. Keeping erasable pens, correcting fluids, and lots of extra paper around can help a little. A word-processing program for the family's personal computer can help a lot. We have watched some of our children and students move from near-complete resistance to revision to a genuine willingness to rewrite once they were facile with the word processor.

Don't be shocked, however, if the school discourages use of a word processor. Just as slide rules, calculators, ballpoint pens, correction fluid, and so on were all at one time forbidden technological shortcuts, some schools will resist word processors to the bitter end. "Her handwriting will never develop" is a complaint you may hear. "He won't learn how to spell if his computer has a spelling checker" is another. We have no evidence that either fear is warranted.

Type What the Child Composes Parents can be helpful, by typing children's compositions but typing requires a parent's careful judgment. Start with children who are too young to write at all. Thinking, composing, organizing, finding appropriate words, forming meaningful sequences, feeling confident, and so on are all essentials of writing. There is no reason for children to delay practicing these skills until they can write with a pencil or strike appropriate keys on a keyboard. One of the greatest motivators for children to work hard at writing can be seeing their own expressions neatly printed. They will value their writing more, and they will value learning to type as soon as they have the skills and opportunity. Furthermore, some young children's best *reading* experiences involve reading their own words and ideas. This practice forms an essential element of one of the preferred approaches to teaching reading at school, the "whole language" approach we described in chapter 4.

DOING PROJECTS

Projects are long-term assignments that involve more than simply reading and writing. Habits that children develop as they manage these large-scale endeavors carry over to major reading and writing assignments such as term or research papers in high school and college. Typically, young children will build, draw, grow, or experiment in an area related to what they are learning at school. Most teachers want students to read about the subject of their project as they work on it and write a summary or report about what they have done. Some favorite project assignments include designing a book jacket, advertisement, or poster to accompany or serve as a book report; drawing a diagram that traces family origins; growing and observing plants, animals, mold, and other living things; interviewing or asking others to complete questionnaires about current issues and problems; and building models or three-dimensional scenes depicting book settings, inventions, or historic events. The variety will be limited only by teachers' and students' imaginations. Expect almost anything!

The Project Trap

Projects can be deceptively frustrating family experiences. Usually, teachers assign projects far in advance of when they are due. Teachers almost always hope for elaborate and creative project-work and want to allow students plenty of time. Children greet the project assignment enthusiastically. Few schoolwork activities allow for so much imaginative problem solving, and for a day or two children will talk animatedly about their grandiose plans. These plans are often stimulated by the elaborate, mind-boggling "best" projects the teacher has saved over the years.

Once the child makes a topic decision (usually insufficiently narrowed and at least slightly impractical) the project moves to the mental back burner and waits to be worked on until all of the pressing day-to-day assignments are finished. Unfortunately, for a busy schoolchild, that time rarely comes around. Even the best-intentioned students may procrastinate until a few days before the project is due. Contributing to the delay is the realization that some hard work is required before the exciting part of the project—presenting it to an admiring audience—can be achieved.

Eventually, there is a mad scramble to get the project done and turned in on time. By this point more may be required than the time and materials on hand allow. Good ideas and intentions turn into compromises. Parents may feel compelled to bail out a panicky child. They end up exasperated and impatient with their children as they do more of the project themselves than they or their children intended. Both students and teacher end up disappointed.

Planning for Projects

Parents can avoid this sad and sloppy end and foster the independent and sustained learning that projects make possible. Often projects require far more planning and consistent attention than children can anticipate or are capable of mustering on their own. Without taking over the project, parents can help their children attend to it in step-by-step, manageable pieces. Here's a plan of action that may help:

Get All the Details at the Start Children need to make all the details public when they receive their project assignments. The project may take four, eight, or maybe twenty or more hours. An event of this magnitude is bound to have an impact on the rest of the child's schedule and on the family as a whole. The parameters, guidelines, and due dates belong on the family calendar.

Gather Materials Early Choosing the project materials early helps focus and define the finished product. Having materials on hand also sustains interest during some less exciting phases of the work. The praise, glory, and acclaim that children anticipate for their spectacular finished project (remember the best projects the teacher kept and saved as models for future classes) are closely linked to its materials. The poster board, lettering, glue, paints, wires, bolts, and so on are what initially distinguishes this assignment from the ordinary.

By choosing and gathering materials early parents and children help keep the project costs within reason. Materials can be expensive, especially when the student is working against the clock. Eleventh-hour stops at the hardware store, the art supply store, and the nursery, grocery, and variety store can leave parent and child gasping at the bill. Early decisions allow the project to be designed with a budget. Families who plan early might devote a corner of a garage or closet to projects and keep it routinely stocked with scavenged and surplus materials known to be useful. When the current finished project comes home from school it goes back in the closet to be recycled. Don't be surprised if children, having materials handy, start inventing experiments and projects on their own just for fun.

Keep the Project on Schedule Help plan a schedule for the project. Then make it a matter of daily discussion. This ensures that the content and display will be adequately conceptualized for both the child's learning and the viewer's understanding. A useful lesson behind all projects—perhaps the most important lesson of all—is that a good job on a large endeavor does not suddenly appear in "full bloom." It grows, changes, and gets modified. There are some dead ends. Sometimes substantial work has to be abandoned for a new start. Finally, the challenge for parents is to provide all this *guidance* without becoming a coparticipant. The project must remain the child's.

PREPARING FOR TESTS

Tests are to be studied for. As noted throughout this book, tests have consequences that go far beyond simple checks on learning. Grades are based on test results, as are decisions about students' future school opportunities. And, at least as significant, grades report other important information back to the student herself. The child's self-concept as a learner is colored by the grades she receives. Rarely does a child with a 72 on a test say, "Now I must go learn the 28% I didn't know." More likely she will think, "I did about average. That's the sort of student I am."

Test Anxiety

Tests *should* create some tension in students. A little anxiety prods children to study the material before the test and to learn more than is possible from just class activities and homework. And a little anxiety sharpens the child's attention during the test and helps make sure that he doesn't skip over anything too lightly. But too much anxiety has the opposite effect. An overanxious student may want to study but finds that his worry crowds out the information he is trying to learn. Instead of learning the causes of the Civil War, he worries that he will never be able to remember them all. In the actual test situation, too much anxiety can cause words to blur on the page and ideas to disappear. Worry focuses the child's attention on answers rather than understanding. Cheating, if it is not practiced, is often considered.

Test anxiety takes many forms as children try to cope with their discomfort and protect their self-concept and dignity. Those who can readily admit and share their worries are the easiest to help. But for many, admitting worries is too risky. They are more likely to say they don't care about an upcoming test. You can assume that "I don't care" nearly always covers up the anxious feelings of children who do care. Another "cover," especially if "not caring" is clearly not acceptable in the family, is for children to insist that they are prepared, that they have studied extensively, that the test will be very easy for them. That these views are entirely unsupported (you know your child could not have prepared sufficiently) does not mean that he is insincere. He may be convinced that he is prepared to the extent that preparation will help—so strong is his doubt that he can turn his study efforts into a good grade. The following suggestions for test-preparation can give parents something tangible to offer their children as they study for tests.

Starting early is one cure for test anxiety. Find out when the test will be given and what it will cover. As soon as the child learns of an upcoming test, he should make a brief list of what he should know and a plan for how he intends to prepare. If either isn't clear, he needs to check with his teacher the following day. Teachers are usually happy to clarify what will be on the test. Children who ask a few extra questions about the test wind up understanding the subject better. Just formulating the questions is helpful. Listing the content, planning how to study, and double-checking with the teacher helps make the test seem more manageable and a lot less scary. Further, a check with the teacher (if not overdone) establishes the child in the teacher's mind as a student who is serious about doing well.

If the test is important (a weekly spelling quiz can be very important if the results on the last ones were poor) it, too, deserves a spot on the family calendar. This establishes its importance, keeps the event in the family consciousness, and diffuses some of the anxiety as concern and study are spread over a longer period.

Three Study and Test-Preparation Strategies

You can help your child by working with three well kown but widely neglected techniques for test preparation: flash cards, mnemonic devices, and outlining. The key here is not so much the technique itself (most children learn about them at an early age), but ensuring that it makes sense to children. For example, children must understand that flash cards are efficient time-savers. You will know that they make sense when children use them on their own. Again, remember that a technique like outlining may involve fairly sophisticated mental operations, and young children may not be ready for it.

Flash cards are useful aids to memorization. Examples are vocabulary definitions (English, foreign language, science terms), spelling words, arithmetic facts (like multiplication tables), formulas (if they don't have to be derived), rules and definitions (grammar and social studies), and names and dates (important people, treaties). Flash cards are useful to separate quickly what the child already knows from what he needs to study more. Much of the learning happens simply by writing out the flash cards. Afterwards, they form a convenient package the child can refer to often for brief study sessions. The practice is useful because rote learning is quickly forgotten and needs to be relearned frequently before it is permanent. We know students who saved their high school vocabulary flash cards and used them for an efficient SAT review. Flash cards, because the student herself prepares them, make it easy for parents or friends to quiz her in a neutral but helpful way that is less threatening than other methods of being quizzed.

Mnemonic devices are memory tricks. Not only do they help study, they can be fun in their own right and add a creative challenge to spice up a lesson. A familiar example is "Every good boy does fine"—used by music students to remember the lines on the treble clef: E, G, B, D, F.

Trigonometry students are served by SOHCAHTOA, pronounced sock-uh-toe-uh: sine (S) equals opposite (O) divided by hypotenuse (H): cosine (C) equals adjacent (A) divided by hypotenuse (H): and tangent (T) equals opposite (O) divided by adjacent (A). Singing facts to a familiar tune and conjuring up images ("picturing" maps) are other methods.

Mnemonic devices work because they give a meaningful structure to seemingly unrelated bits of information. The child recalls the familiar, and then the information associated with it comes to mind. Like flash cards, this kind of learning may not last long because it is not grounded in understanding or meaning. We don't recommend it as a substitute for making sense of complex ideas. But, if lots of facts need to be memorized for a test, it is a useful way to accomplish that.

Outlining is a good way to organize and study a topic that has an inter-related structure of large concepts, major ideas, and subpoints. If the child can remember enough pieces of the outline, these pieces can suggest the rest and call forth many of the minor details. Sometimes the child remembers a minor detail or a particularly vivid example on the outline, and these suggest the major points. Outlining helps students understand how related ideas fit together as a whole. And once the student grasps the larger ideas it is harder to forget the important parts. Also, the outlining *process,* as distinguished from the outline itself, gets to the very heart of learning—manipulating ideas, forming categories, and creating meaning out of new information and experiences.

Mapping is a less linear, more pictorial version of outlining. Using circles, labeled arrows, and clusters of ideas, the child can represent multiple relationships without repeating the same words in many different categories. The map adds a degree of visual representation missing from typical outlines. Novak and Gowin, in their book *Learning to Learn,* explain mapping techniques and why they are compatible with a cognitive view of learning.

More Strategies for the Test-Wise

There is simply no good substitute for understanding the material, but, even so, some children have more trouble taking tests than others whose command of the material may not be as strong. Taking tests is a skill in itself, quite apart from whatever is being tested. Encourage your child to use the following strategies. Parents might review this list or similar ones before each test:

- Anticipate the test. A day or two or the night before the test try to guess questions that will be on it.

- Look over the entire test. How many questions are there? How much is each worth? Estimate how much time to spend on each section if it seems as though time could be a problem.

- If directions have been a problem in the past, double-check your understanding. Teachers are usually willing to clarify directions during the test. Sometimes they help a student figure out one answer as a starter. Ask—it's worth a try.

- Go through the test and answer all the easy questions first. Make marks in the margin beside the hard questions and return to them if there is time.

- Make quick notes about essay questions. First scribble a few notes or even an outline in the margin of the test or on scratch paper. Setting your ideas down quickly at the beginning prevents you from forgetting important points while writing. Refer to the notes while you are writing for a more complete and better organized essay. If you find yourself running out of time, outline the remainder of your answer or list the important information for possible partial credit. Most teachers will allow a few extra minutes to finish. Again, it's worth asking.

- Guess. Very few teachers penalize for guesses. They just count the correct answers. Children often think they're guessing when they're not. Often what they consider a guess is knowledge that they lack confidence in. Some children wrongly think that guessing is like cheating. On the other hand, when you're writing an essay, don't fabricate answers out of thin air. Teachers rarely appreciate or are amused by creative but totally off-base answers.

- Don't cheat. Cheating is always wrong. Always dishonest. Always serious. Sometimes looking in the direction of another's paper—perhaps to see if that student is farther along—is not meant as cheating, but the teacher can't tell that. Possibly the admonition should be, "Do not cheat and do not give even the *appearance* of cheating." That way the child's intention and momentary ethical posture is not brought into question, and accusations and denials can be avoided. ("I was just stretching." "These are notes I studied from. I didn't realize they had fallen out of my notebook.")

A few of the major standardized tests—the Scholastic Aptitude Test, for example—penalize guessing by subtracting points or partial points from the student's score for each wrong answer. Questions left blank have no such penalty. On such tests strong hunches warrant an answer, but wild guessing is not a good idea. If students can eliminate one or two choices on these multiple-choice questions it pays to guess.

For the SAT and other nationally administered admissions tests there is a burgeoning industry of test-preparation courses, books, and computer study programs. For years the publishers of such tests vigorously denied that students could raise their scores by preparing for the tests, but now it is widely recognized that preparation can help in two ways. First, preparation familiarizes students with the type of questions and directions they will encounter, resulting, perhaps, in fewer surprises, less anxiety, and a saving of precious moments. Second, since studying specific information that will likely be on the test can indeed raise scores, preparation courses and books can structure students' study time. In each case it is the time and effort the student spends, not the particular book or course, that seem to make the difference.

We find that children are quite open to suggestions about how to be test-wise, whether a full-scale course or handy hints. They regard strategies like these as tricks that help them outsmart the test. However, children require years of developing confidence and commitment to take test preparation seriously. It is truly difficult to account for why some children will and some won't study the extra hours to gain a slight edge or a few points on tests.

TAKING HOMEWORK BACK TO SCHOOL

Every experienced teacher has heard dozens of variations, each more preposterous than the last, on the old "the cat ate my homework" story. And, indeed, sometimes cats do eat homework. So do dogs. And hamsters. And sisters. But consider this: A teacher of seventh graders may have more than 150 students in a single day. These students may receive as many as four homework assignments in a week. The teacher can be amused and forgiving with individual homework problems and excuses, but after all, she may have to pay some attention to over six hundred samples of student work in a week. Not surprisingly, a teacher's sense of humor and charity can be stretched thin by excuses about homework.

Now consider children. Even some second and third graders—but definitely older students—may have four or five homework subject-areas to keep track of. If they received a few homework assignments in each subject each week, they would have a sizable number of papers and due dates to remember, not to mention the hard work of actually doing them. Students need skills for producing on schedule large amounts of work that meet the exacting standards of teachers who have little patience for exceptions and problems. The work, all of it, must be neat, complete, correct, and on time. It's easy to see what children need from parents: Help!

The best way to get a sense of a child's homework habits is to take a look at his notebook. It should have several divisions for the various school subjects. Some system is necessary to organize the mass of papers he will collect and should save. A quick check after homework is done at night will tell parents if the homework is completely and neatly done and if the child is likely to find it when he sits down in class (instead of spending ten minutes shuffling through a mess of papers looking for it). Children who are not used to this kind of scrutiny of their homework won't like it one bit. They will fuss and fume and insist that the parent has no right to look, that they are not trusted, that their schoolwork is their business. Our advice is to be patient—but check the homework.

It is quite possible that after trying all the work on a particular assignment, the child will have some incomplete or skipped problems. Help him jot down some notes for specific questions he should ask in class. Sometimes just writing the question reveals clues to the answer itself. (Sometimes children are too quick to decide that a problem is too difficult and needs to be skipped until the teacher can explain it.) In addition to jogging the child's memory, the note indicates to the teacher that the child takes the difficulty or omission seriously. Assignments to read or "study" are harder for parents to get a cursory sense about. Here, we suggest a brief conversation about the main ideas as a way to help both parent and child assess whether the assignment is indeed finished.

SOME CAUTIONS ABOUT HELPING

Now, after pages of suggestions about how to help your child with homework, we'd like to repeat some important cautions about helping and offer a few new ones. Helping children with homework, like all schooling activities, should be firmly grounded in the view that learning depends most on what the child does, not on what the parent or teacher does. As we have emphasized throughout, the foundation of this view is the principle that new knowledge, to be understood and remembered, must be related to existing knowledge and experience. A second principle is that the learner must do the relating himself. Teachers or parents can guide, but they cannot do it for him. The child must be an active learner who tests, checks, connects, questions, and probes new knowledge and experiences, rather than a passive learner who receives answers, parrots information, and stays within familiar boundaries. Specifically, the child must recognize what he needs to learn, decide which learning strategies to use, and monitor the effectiveness of his own learning.

Moreover, since successful students feel responsible for their own learning and believe that success results from their own efforts, children need homework that demonstrates how they can accomplish learning without the immediate direction of an older and probably more knowledgeable person. When parents cross the line between guiding and doing, children can lose this independence.

The parent who provides answers, rewrites a poorly done composition, or does a large part of a project makes his child feel helpless, dependent, even stupid. Parents should avoid nightly help with the actual content of homework assignments. They should leave routine homework to children and their teachers. A parent's nightly involvement in the details of homework may communicate anxiety and lack of confidence about his child's ability to do well. Children sense their parent's insecurity and can lose confidence in themselves. Other children with overly involved parents often use homework as a battleground for conflicts unrelated to homework. It's not unusual for children of ambitious parents to use homework as a focus for rebellion. For some children, needing help with homework is a favorite way to capture large chunks of their parent's time and undivided attention. Competent children who claim they don't understand or can't do their work by themselves when other signs indicate they can may need time and attention in areas other than homework.

Finally, there will be times when you and your child may share an interest in an assignment and take genuine pleasure in working side by side. Cooperative efforts on schoolwork—especially project assignments—can be valuable opportunities both for learning and for your relationship. The feeling here is that you participate for *your* sake as a "guest" because you enjoy it. An obvious but easily forgotten caution is that ownership, leadership, and final decision making must rest with your child.

When Children Have Trouble

All children are stumped by their homework from time to time, and they will turn to a friendly parent for help. So help. If your child is in the middle of a composition and needs to know how to spell a word, no great purpose is served by making her look it up. Quick bits of helpful information, if they are asked for and graciously accepted, can be given freely. Often when children ask for help, what they want and need is the answer: quickly, cleanly, and without a big deal being made. Go ahead and answer unless the answer is the main point of the lesson. In that case direct the child to a way of figuring it out.

Some children's difficulties are far more serious, however, and some who do poorly in classes will benefit from nightly help and review with parents. Theirs may be less an issue of independent learning and more an issue of survival—success or failure. We do not suggest that parents sit back and allow their children to learn by failing a class. Just avoid some approches we know don't work. Too often tension about schoolwork problems leads to badgering and belittling children who are not as responsible, punctual, neat, or quick to learn their schoolwork as we would like them to be. All frustrated adults succumb to feeling, if not saying, "If I've told you once . . . ," "You never . . . ," "How can you be so . . . ," and "When will you ever learn . . . ?" Even the most nurturing, forgiving, and encouraging adults can slip a bit when it comes to offering support in the face of school tensions. Too often, when a child comes home with a school problem, he leaves the next day with a school problem *and a parent problem.*

Parents' responses to school troubles signal to children whether schooling generally will bring them support and comfort or tension and further problems. Helping children be positive about school may depend on the ability of important adults to express support in the midst of the frustration and confusion that trouble with schoolwork inevitably brings.

THE HOMEWORK DILEMMA

Homework brings together a potent mixture of schooling elements: family work-habits, environment, and learning values; learning theory; school curriculum; teaching practices; and, of course, the school culture. And no other activity is so ripe for conflict. Before we conclude this chapter on homework, consider a situation which, while not routine, will sound familiar to most parents.

It's Tuesday. Your son's science project, assigned weeks ago, is due on Friday. The experiment has been to subject potted plants to different environmental conditions and keep careful records of the results. What remains is to chart the daily growth on a poster and draw conclusions about the experiment—a task requiring some artistic skills, some routine recording skills, some heavy thinking, and lots of time. You have been involved in the project in part because of your interest and in part because the logistics of getting plants established and finding space and materials for the experiment initially were too much for your child to handle. The project is clearly your child's—you haven't taken over—but you worry that the approaching deadline will draw you in to spending more time on it than you consider appropriate.

Also, he has an assignment for social studies that requires him to memorize the names of the presidents and vice-presidents since the Civil War; there will be a quiz on Thursday. You have some trouble with the assignment itself. "What's the value?" you wonder. The teacher has previously explained to the class that the mind is like a muscle; it needs to be exercised. You sharply reject this physical comparison to learning, intelligence, and the mind. You're also put off by the motivation for the assignment—punishment of the entire class for being too noisy. This is not the first time you have considered either complaining to the school or telling your child just to forget the assignment. But then again, there are consequences.

Furthermore, due tomorrow are drill and practice exercises in math and English: sixteen prealgebra problems and a worksheet on identifying simple, complex, and compound sentences. Your child, quite conscientious about keeping up, is now immobilized and feeling hopeless. The pizza dinner on Wednesday to present trophies to the league-winning softball team complicates matters. And to make things worse, he had the flu last week and isn't entirely recovered.

Clearly there is no easy solution to this dilemma that would suit everyone. A respectable goal for such a Tuesday evening would be to approach the problem as a large but manageable inconvenience rather than as an occasion for defeat. We think that parents who have a good understanding of what homework is about—in terms of what the teacher expects and what the child stands to gain or lose—are in a good position to help children out of such a homework crisis.

You need to help your child decide what *must* be done carefully and attentively because of the learning investment already made and the weight given to the work (probably finishing the potted plant project). Maybe the intimidating or embarrassing consequences of showing up at school without some work is of greatest concern (favoring the worksheets, but maybe the presidents). Could the child skip the pizza and just show up for the trophy? Eat the pizza and run? Could Thursday be a stay-up-late night? There are countless possibilities—none entirely satisfactory. We know for certain that a plan is essential, and it needs the cooperation and support of the whole family. Knowledgeable families whose relationships over homework are in good standing will do fine.

FOR FURTHER READING

Richard Anderson and others, *Becoming a Nation of Readers: A Report of the Commission on Reading.* Washington, DC: U.S. Department of Education, 1985.

Benjamin Bloom, *All Our Children Learning*. New York: McGraw-Hill, 1980.

D. K. Detterman and Robert J. Sternberg (eds.), *How and How Much Can Intelligence Be Increased?* Norwood, NJ: ABLEX Publishing, 1982.

John Flavell, "Metacognition and Cognitive Monitoring," *American Psychologist* 34 (1979): 906–11.

Robert M. Gagne, *The Conditions of Learning*. New York: Holt, Rinehart and Winston, 1985.

Richard Mayer, *Thinking, Problem Solving, Cognition*. New York: W. H. Freeman, 1983.

Joseph D. Novak and D. Bob Gowin, *Learning How to Learn*. New York: Cambridge University Press, 1984.

Robert J. Sternberg (ed.), *Handbook of Human Intelligence*. New York: Cambridge University Press, 1982.

CHAPTER ELEVEN

Getting Involved at School: The Trouble Worth Taking

"It's already December, and he hasn't even *started* to read."

"Yes, a 3.5 grade-point average is good. It's very good. But it's not good enough for Berkeley."

"Sometimes that child has no self-discipline."

"She failed the proficiency test! Can't they do something besides making her repeat the entire year?"

"The school called. They think she might have a learning disability. What are we supposed to do?"

"Let me get this straight. You have three classes. Then you're an attendance office aide. Then you're done . . . ?"

"The counselor told me that she's doing okay, but *I* know she doesn't come even close to realizing her potential."

"Of course you're smart enough to take algebra and go to college!"

"I know that having students memorize lists of vocabulary words hasn't much educational value. Even so, it sure improves their SAT scores."

Such challenges and frustrations capture parents' attention year after year. They elicit fundamental concerns about academic success, good teaching, adequate schooling resources, and children's day-to-day welfare. They represent clashes between children's needs and the culture of schools. The time has passed when schools had the unquestioned trust or acquiescence of parents. We think that's good. Schools and individual children benefit enormously when knowledgeable parents seek information and express their concerns. They also benefit when parents and schools work for compromises that challenge the regularities of schools.

Every child's school career brings problems, frequent or rare, that call for more than help at home. A parent's advice to his son or daughter won't suffice. A minor problem may arise that simply needs an easily reached accommodation among the school, parent, and child. Other problems take considerably more work. These require parents and schools to try to see eye to eye and act in the child's best interest. Still other problems can be so serious that no amount of working together can fix them.

Schools and policymakers increasingly call for home/school partnerships. Everyone likes the idea, but few schools and parents accomplish it. Most schools tend to go about their business with parents watching from the sidelines. Most parents have their hands full just raising their own children and responding to the needs and crises of the moment.

The terms *home/school partnerships* and *parent involvement* usually mean organized parent participation in school decision making or classroom instruction. Such organized involvement can be useful. And a few successful models prove that large numbers of parents can productively engage in decision making and instruction at schools. Parents can help their own children and the whole school by volunteering, keeping informed, and supporting good programs and teaching. Absent widespread community support, parents are sometimes shocked to find that a vocal minority succeeded in getting a good program dropped, or that the school district has suddenly cut its funding. Without organized involvement, individual parents usually feel powerless to insist on changes in programs that don't serve children well. Visible, assertive parent organizations can often save good programs and insist that bad ones be done away with. Not surprisingly, many schools feel ambivalent about nurturing a cadre of involved, empowered parents. Many administrators are not adept at drumming up parent support and often prefer to keep a low profile. They don't want to risk stirring up a band of frequent objectors. So, many schools keep parent contacts to a minimum. They may confine parent involvement to a carefully orchestrated open house and to phone calls home—usually triggered by teachers' exasperation with disruptive behavior. Nevertheless, some schools work hard to involve parents. And some parents are knowledgeable and confident enough to intervene. When parents and the school do work together, children benefit.

Earlier chapters offer perspectives about how schools can be better. In each chapter, we have tried to explain what we think is wrong with schools and how they got that way. These perspectives make clear why parents have to get involved and why frustration often results when they do. In the next chapter we will outline some promising reforms that go to the heart of the school culture. These reforms challenge the regularities that work against children's opportunities and keep parents distant from schools. But reform that attacks root causes of school problems is a long-range prospect at best. And there are no guarantees that such reform will actually take place. Besides, talk of school reform gives little comfort to a parent whose child must go back to school tomorrow morning.

We recommend that all parents become involved in partnerships and school-based parent-involvement programs. Through these, parents can exercise leverage over school practice and influence school reform. Nevertheless, we focus in this chapter on more immediate concerns: how individual parents can act on behalf of their own children in the schools we've got today.

STEP IN WITH CONFIDENCE AND KNOWLEDGE

Mismatches between what children need and what schools do may require tricky negotiations. Parents should neither anticipate a quick and friendly response nor accept "We're sorry" as a final answer. In most cases they should expect both the school and themselves to compromise. In other cases schools and parents can't negotiate problems satisfactorily. As a last resort, parents may have to capitulate to the school and try to meet their child's needs in another way. If the alternative is available, parents may choose to find another school where conditions are better.

Confident parents usually prefer to avoid either giving up or getting out. But it's easy to see why many parents approach schools timidly. They want to be trusting and supportive. Or they worry about seeming too pushy, asking presumptuous questions, or creating the impression that they seek an advantage their child doesn't deserve. Everyone recognizes that an aggressive, steamrolling parent makes things worse for his child and makes a shambles of his own reputation at the school.

Sometimes parents need to risk offending. It may be the only route to getting information and action on their child's behalf. Children need advocates at school, and most often they need their parents to perform that role. About all we can guarantee is that parents will surely make mistakes. However, risking mistakes is usually better than not acting and waiting to see what happens.

Since being confident is so difficult, it helps to stick with a few convictions supported throughout this book. These convictions can help parents frame their questions and clarify their objectives:

- Your child is a capable learner. Under the right conditions, he can accomplish almost anything the school expects him to. When he meets with difficulty, the *least likely* reason is that he is not smart enough.
- Your child wants to do well at school, academically and socially. If her behavior seems otherwise, it's not because she wants to do poorly or get into trouble. Trust her wishes for success, even when she misjudges how to act on them.
- What is true of your own child is also true of others. Often actions that improve conditions for your child will benefit his classmates. Similarly, actions on behalf of other children will often benefit your child.

These convictions are easy enough to hang onto when things are going well. The real test comes when worrisome, hurtful, disappointing, or embarrassing events occur. Few parents can maintain confidence when school regularities and ignorance conspire to act against the interests of their children. The school may marshal evidence that the child is *not* intelligent enough or actually *prefers* to do poorly. It may insist that he *is* so different from others that he deserves different opportunities.

Moreover, sometimes acting on behalf of one's own child may not, at the moment, benefit others. Outstanding teachers, special programs, computers, or whatever else might help your child may be scarce. At such times parents face a difficult ethical as well as personal conflict: Should I try to get for my child what some other children won't have? This is a dilemma we can't resolve with a clear conscience. Since schools don't now provide enough of the best for all children, parents must hope that pursuing what's good for their own child will push schools to be better for all children. They might even tell the schools that is what they hope will happen.

Some children fare quite well in fundamentally flawed schools, even without their parents' intervention. The presence of a critical mass of parent involvement may be a factor in their success. Many children have advantages at school in part because there is a knowledgeable parental presence that the school can't ignore. By means of this presence (most often found in prosperous communities) most children benefit. However, in schools without this critical mass or without well-informed community pressure, parents must seek allies for their children on their own. Parents in even the most discouraging schools stand a good chance of finding some adults who will keep a special eye on their child. However, it takes patience, a knowledge of schools, and a willingness to listen and compromise when possible.

WHAT'S THE PROBLEM?

It's hard to imagine a school problem that wouldn't be easier to solve if the parent and school had acted sooner. It's hard to imagine a parent who hasn't wondered, "What did I miss?" The first hints of problems often come from children, but children may be unreliable, obfuscating sources of information. Schools, of course, let parents know of problems, but they often wait until they are manifest as serious behavior or academic trouble.

When Children Complain

The following statements reflect problems. They *may* be serious, maybe not. Parents should listen to them carefully and ask questions. If parents choose not to act on these statements immediately, they should not forget them either.

"I don't understand."
"The teacher picks on me."
"I did that work last year."
"Mr. Jones's class is four chapters ahead of us."
"I don't have anyone to eat lunch with."
"Some of the kids smoke dope in the parking lot."
"Allan took my potato chips again."
"I'm in the class with the dumb kids."
"Teacher won't let me go to the bathroom."
"Somebody broke into my locker."
"All we do is watch videos and do worksheets."
"All the black kids are in the same reading group."
"Some kids got to go on a special trip."
"I fell asleep in class again."

These statements indicate an individual problem for a child and possibly a widespread problem at the school. But children are not always so straightforward. Sometimes they express their fears rather than tell what actually happened ("Everyone hates me"). Sometimes they try to deflect attention from their own responsibility ("The teacher tries to get me into trouble." "She only calls on me when I don't have my homework"). Even complaints that are blatantly off the mark deserve attention. There could be a more serious problem lurking beneath the surface.

Many students quickly grow accustomed to school problems. They get blasé about events that ought to shock them and probably did the first few times they occurred. Children soon stop noticing some commonplace problems. ("Oh, yeah, nobody walks by that building unless they want to lose their lunch money." "I can skip the homework for that class; she never checks it." "Lots of kids eat alone. I like it").

When in Doubt, Check It Out

When do you call the school? If you have been asking that question for a few days, you have your answer. Call now. Contact the school whenever you suspect a problem. Most schools welcome calls that express concern as distinguished from calls that express complaints. Parents can safely assume that a child who is unhappy at school also presents a problem for the school. At the very least the child creates some tension around himself. Children who get D's and F's; children who are socially awkward; those who look sad much of the time—they all cause teachers' concern. The teacher may not initiate action but will probably respond positively to a parent's worry.

Each school has its own procedures for channeling parent inquiries. Most school offices are congested and understaffed. At junior and senior highs, students often answer the phone—with varying degrees of competence. You should try to speak directly to the teacher, but you probably won't reach him with the first call. You may need to ask for the teacher's preparation time and leave a message for him to call you back. If teachers don't return calls, parents should try again—soon.

The first task is to find out more about the problem from the teacher's perspective. Few things can cause parents to feel so foolish as angrily jumping to a child's defense ("Why did you refuse to allow my son to take a makeup test?") before gathering the facts. The teacher may clear matters up with a simple explanation ("Why didn't you tell me the teacher said you could take a makeup test at lunch?"). Only as a last resort should parents cross the thin line between expressing worry and accusing or complaining. Educators, like everyone else, nearly always respond defensively if they think a parent has already made a negative judgment, and they will probably be less amenable to cooperation if they think you will settle for only one solution. Instead, phrase your concern in a way that will elicit information:

"My child seems worried about his progress in class."

"My child feels she is unpopular."

"My child thinks you are displeased with her."

"My child has been ill, has asthma, has a hearing problem, etc."

"There has been a death (accident, divorce, or other trauma) in our family."

"I am concerned about a poor grade."

"My child tells me that he has no homework."

"My child worries about a bully."

"My child is often upset when she comes home, and we can't figure out why."

"I sense that my child 'gets by' but doesn't really try to excel."

Parents need the teacher's view to find out just how well-founded their worries are. Does the child have fewer friends than other children? Is her behavior displeasing to the teacher? Are her homework efforts inconsistent? Do her recent poor grades suggest that she is seriously behind or having a temporary lapse in understanding or effort?

Older students have several teachers, and it can be difficult to contact each of them. A general concern that affects all classes (an illness of more than a couple of days, for example) warrants a call to the school counselor, who will pass the word along. If parents do speak to more than one teacher, they should mention the names of the other teachers they have contacted so that the teachers can check their perceptions with one another, ask advice, or share concerns. When so many people touch upon a child's well-being, they can all help solve important problems.

When the School Raises a Concern

"He hasn't brought his books to class or turned in a single homework assignment for two weeks."

"Since she is having so much trouble reading, we're considering having her repeat first grade."

"Sharon was late to history class five times last month. She dawdles in the hallway, talking to her friends."

"Henry just doesn't seem ready for prealgebra. I think he should enroll in basic math next year."

"Three times this week Kevin was fighting during the lunch period."

"We would like your permission to test Robbie for a possible learning disability."

"She was smoking in the bathroom."

"When I handed Daniel his paper, he was practically in tears."

We couldn't possibly catalog all the academic and behavioral problems that cause schools to contact parents. However, few teachers and counselors have time to call about any but the most serious problems. Additionally, calling or sending a note home nearly always generates some unhappy feelings, so most schools are more likely to err on the side of waiting for things to get worse. A child's consistent forgetting to bring materials, failure to do homework, or poor academic performance should always trigger a contact from the school. So should consistent behavior problems in class or on the playground. Most parents wouldn't want anything less. But that doesn't always happen. When the school does call, it's probably serious.

Earlier we suggested some confidence-building guidelines that parents would do well to remember and schools ought to promote. Each child is capable and wants to do well, and improving conditions for one's own child usually benefits all children. Here we can suggest two additional rules of thumb to help when schools alert parents about difficult problems.

No One Deserves Trouble Problems at school don't mean that children are "looking for trouble" or deserve it. Sometimes problems reflect temporary academic setbacks or minor lapses in good work habits. Some result from upsetting events at home or with friends. Others stem from serious health or learning impairments. Still others are inexplicable, and parents and schools are hard-pressed to figure out just what is going on.

No child's problems should disqualify him from the school's care and attention. Some children seem to be purposefully obnoxious. Some can be provocative to the point that any institution or adult who has to deal with them deserves sympathy. However, no child deserves problems. A child with an organic or medical reason for being out of his seat and "overactive" merits special consideration. But so does the one whose unruly behavior no one can explain. The withdrawn and uninvolved child warrants as much concern as the disruptive one. Language styles, personal appearance, and choice of friends can upset adults as much as blatant rule violations like cutting school, swearing, and disobedience. Some children act out their difficulties in ways that make adults angry. Others engender sympathy. All of these children deserve concern and wise treatment at school.

Problems Occur in the Context of the School Culture Children have school problems to the degree that they are out of sync with the school's academic and social norms and regularities. This is not to suggest that the school culture causes all problems, or that children never bring a problem to school. Nonetheless, once he is at school, we cannot separate the child's problem from the school.

If schools were different, many children who now have problems wouldn't, and schools would recognize some problems they now overlook. For instance, most schools find some degree of failure inevitable, even acceptable. While educators want all students to do well, most don't believe that all of them can or will. They usually don't recognize that many students who are low achievers have serious and correctable problems.

For example, Henry, a seventh grader, was having trouble with math. At the end of the year Henry's counselor scheduled him to take basic math—a remedial course. However, the school did not think Henry had a serious problem. His previous teacher thought that if Henry tried harder he might catch on. True, like many others, Henry didn't try very hard. The school saw Henry's lack of success as his own fault—stemming from his decision not to work hard. The teacher and counselor reasoned that not everyone is cut out to excel in mathematics. Besides, they offered a course to match Henry's poor skills and low interest—basic math.

This school responded to Henry in a typical way. First, they saw his low achievement as part of an expected larger pattern: not all children will do well. The school structure supported this pattern with tracked math classes. Second, since some children do well in math, the school assumed that those who don't either lack the ability or don't try. The school culture made sense of Henry's low achievement in a way that was consistent with the school's beliefs, traditions, and organization.

Henry was at a schooling crossroads. If his parents looked at his problem the way the school did, they would accept the school's decision. Henry's path most likely would lead to mediocre high school math performance and second-rate, postgraduation opportunities. On the other hand, his parents could try to understand Henry in the context of a school culture ill-suited to help children recover once they fall behind. By doing so, they could possibly change Henry's future path. But it wouldn't be easy.

Fortunately, Henry's parents asked questions. As they listened to the answers, they discovered that the "year of extra practice to help Henry brush up on his skills" looked like a very bad deal. The parents assured the counselor that Henry did indeed want to go to college. (Henry had told the counselor earlier that he "didn't really know.") Then they found out that most college-bound students enroll in prealgebra in the eighth grade. After prealgebra, these students take algebra I, geometry, algebra II, and a course in advanced mathematics—often trigonometry and calculus. Students who fall behind in this sequence wind up taking less mathematics in high school, or they take a variety of basic, remedial, consumer, or applied math courses instead of the college-preparatory sequence.

Henry's parents got enough information to understand the consequences of his math placement. And they felt confident enough to ask more questions. Throughout, they were clear about their goal: they would insist that Henry, at the age of twelve, not begin a path that would lead to fewer opportunities. They wanted to know exactly what skills Henry lacked. Was the basic class likely to help him learn them? How many children actually moved from the basic class into the college-preparatory math sequence? Did the school ever change its placement decisions? What if the parents agreed to provide a tutor to give Henry extra help at home while he takes prealgebra? Was there a summer school math class that could help Henry get up to speed?

Henry's parents concluded their meeting by stating that they wanted Henry to start the college-preparatory sequence. The counselor said he would schedule Henry with a well-qualified prealgebra teacher who was willing to work with students who were having difficulty. The counselor thought that a tutor would be a good idea at the first sign that Henry was falling behind. The teacher had noted that Henry frequently did not turn in his homework, so the counselor also asked Henry's parents to guarantee that Henry would do his work. They agreed.

Henry's parents did not start by blaming the school. Naturally enough, they looked first to Henry. Why didn't he work harder? Then they looked at themselves. Could they have kept after Henry to do his homework? to study before tests? And they wished there were better alternatives. Neither holding Henry back (risking his falling farther behind) nor pushing him ahead (with skills that might be inadequate) seemed the ideal solution.

As we described in chapter 4, schools rarely provide alternative routes to success in math. However, many math educators believe that more children would be successful if schools were not so firmly wedded to the typical mathematics sequence. Others suggest that students don't need a complete mastery of computation skills before they begin algebra. They hold that many students can learn algebra concepts at the same time that they improve their skills. Similarly, many children could find success in geometry if schools didn't require success in algebra I as a condition of enrollment. The two subjects bear little relation to one another. More students could succeed if schools routinely provided extra tutoring help to those who fall behind. Schools might encourage some students who fall behind in their college-prep math courses to repeat courses without penalties or take two math courses simultaneously. None of these options was available to Henry.

CONSENSUS, COMPROMISE, AND CAPITULATION: FINDING A SOLUTION

- A child regularly comes home cranky. He says he doesn't want to go to school in the morning. His parent calls the teacher, who reports that the child is shy and has made few friends in class. The teacher offers to change the child's work group. And she gives the parent the name of a new student in that group who also knows few children. Parent and teacher agree to observe the child and to encourage the new friendship.
- A parent, worried because her child never brings schoolwork home, checks with the teacher. She finds out that there is at least some homework each night. She also learns that some children finish it at school. The teacher mentions that the child makes careless mistakes, rushing through the assignments in an attempt to keep up with those who finish early. The mother decides to ask her son to bring home all his assignments for a few weeks, even if he claims he finished them at school.
- A sixth grader rarely comes to class with homework or materials. She disrupts the class—drawing quite a lot of negative attention to herself. The counselor arranges a meeting with the parent, the child, and the teacher. All agree that they will work toward some immediate improvement, but a year-long plan is also needed. Each selects a special part he or she can fulfill. The child will do homework after school and before playing in the afternoon. The parent will check the assignment sheet and homework after work and before dinner. Each week the teacher will check the child's assignment sheet for accuracy and comment on her work, scores, and behavior. The teacher will also help the child find a "homework buddy." The pair will meet with the teacher each week to discuss "the hardest thing they learned." The counselor will contact the parent if the need arises. He will relay calls from the parent

to the teacher if they have trouble connecting. Additionally, he will schedule two more meetings during the school year to follow up.

- A high school senior wants to enroll in the advanced-placement English class. Unfortunately, she fell below the cutoff score on the department placement exam. Her record is good, and her previous teacher agrees that she probably could do well in the class if she works very hard. Her parent learns from the principal that the school maintains rigorous entrance requirements to protect students. The principal worries about students who might "get in over their heads" and fail to keep up with the demanding reading assignments. In the past, a number of marginally qualified students have switched back to the regular English classes. Their transfers left the advanced-placement classes with low enrollment and made the regular classes too large. But the parent persists. Would the promise of strong support at home—and possibly a tutor—assuage the school's concern? Yes, it would. The principal suggests that the child discuss the class with the advanced-placement teacher. He also recommends that she talk with current students about the kinds of assignments they have and the workload. Further, the student should discuss her findings with her parents. With these agreements in place, the principal will bend the guidelines for the class and admit the student.

None of the above is a trivial problem. Each has a strong prospect for a good resolution. However, each could have escalated into a pitched home–school battle. In each case the parent feels that he has compromised nothing of what is best for his child. The school people have the satisfaction of a professionally handled job. In each case the parent will probably adopt a more comfortable, supportive attitude toward the school. The school will probably welcome the parent's future inquiries and requests and have heightened awareness of the child's progress. This kind of consensus is a real achievement. At best, when parents and schools arrive at a consensus, they can't distinguish their self-interest from their sense of what's best for all. The resolution may not be anyone's first choice, but all who join in believe they have made the best possible decision. If the school communicates a begrudging, "We'll make an exception in your case," or if a parent feels he had better go along with a suggestion, or if a child thinks, "What choice do I have?" that's not consensus. A consensus emerges when individual parents and educators have good social skills and quickly communicate respect and confidence. Of course, parents who have the time, knowledge, and finesse to make themselves known to the school stand a better chance of reaching consensus than parents who don't.

Solutions by consensus may differ from parents' preconceived ideas, and they may depart from the school's standard practices. This means that schools must be able to shake the inertia of their own routines. And they must gain the trust and tolerance of those who are suspicious of changes and exceptions. Also, since consensus (and the trust and respect required for it) usually requires repeated contacts and effort, a single let's-get-this-straight-once-and-for-all meeting rarely works. Families who move frequently, those in which both parents work, or speak little English, find it hard to establish a consensus-supporting relationship. And schools with revolving-door administrators and high-turnover faculties may have little commitment to long-range consensus-building.

Striking a Compromise:
When Consensus Is Not Possible

Assume that a parent can find time during the workday to attend a conference at school. Assume that she has lived in the community for several years and has a thorough understanding of her child's school. Even under these optimal conditions, the barriers to reaching consensus can still be imposing. Without these conditions, consensus may be impossible. Given most schools' unquestioned cultural regularities, even reasonable adults who care deeply for children will find it hard to achieve consensus about everything.

Suppose you don't like the curriculum or the way it's being taught. Perhaps you think the classwork is too abstract or too trivial. You may not like the tracking system, the standardized tests, or the criteria for promoting a child from one grade to the next. You may think children need more free time or that the teacher is wasting instructional time when he shows slides of his vacation. You may want more supervision on the playground. You may worry that classes are too large or that the only students who get encouragement in sports, math, art, drama, or music are the dozen or so top performers. Most likely, the teachers, the principal, and even the superintendent also recognize these problems. Their lists are probably longer! Does this means that the prospects for consensus around these concerns are good? Not at all.

We cross the line from consensus to compromise when we feel we have accomplished the best we can, even though the resolution is not ideal. Like banks, hospitals, the telephone company, and other large institutions, schools are not well suited for consensus building. We want our telephone repaired, but it doesn't happen the way we would like. ("It will take four days." "But that's too long!" "We'll do it in three days."

"Okay.") We want to know what happened to the check we deposited two days ago. ("We're sorry, the computer was down. Your check was misplaced, but it has been found." "Can't you guys take responsibility for a mistake?" "We're sorry, the computer was down." "Do you know how many hours it has taken me to straighten this out?" "We're sorry, the computer was down.") With schools as well, we observe, we trust, and we sometimes settle for the best we can get. Compromise with schools is defined by the limits of what the school is willing and able to do and by what parents are willing to settle for.

Let's look at two fairly common school problems and consider some compromises—none of them ideal, even if all are improvements over doing nothing. We have chosen especially sensitive and complex problems that any parent might encounter and that most schools do not handle well. Parents first need to feel comfortable in bringing their concern to the school's attention. Only then can they compromise on options.

Compromising about Giftedness Suppose your third grader comes home one day and announces, "I'm not gifted." He has learned this from some classmates on the playground who reported that they are gifted. Your first reaction probably includes questions and maybe anger. Is the child merely repeating a classmate's playground taunt? If so, a wise parent will carefully reassure him of his capabilities and worth. But he will also keep an ear tuned for evidence that the school pays excessive attention to giftedness. Perhaps the child talks about an official school event—a special activity for the gifted—that he and many others did not attend. Possibly the school screened some children for a gifted program or class. Maybe no one has said a thing, but a clever child (even though "not gifted") has figured out his own category.

At this point, a parent recognizes a problem that may be confined to her own child's perception. It may rest with how the school enacts a policy, or it may stem from the policy itself. Once again, parents will gain little by quickly forming an opinion or fixing on a single solution. If the parent doesn't know all the facts or gets only a trickle of new information, he must investigate further. He may start by asking the teacher to explain the meaning of the child's remarks. He may ask about the particular policies and guidelines that govern the gifted program and about the assessment practices the school follows. Having obtained the teacher's explanation, he could consult the principal, gifted coordinator, or school district personnel for additional details.

If it turns out that some children have enrichment activities that his child and others could benefit from, a compromise may be worth pursuing. At this point the most practical step is a philosophical one. Equipped with the facts, parents must confront their own beliefs and values. Some parents feel so strongly about the potential destructiveness of gifted programs that they refuse to allow their children to participate, even if they could wangle their child's admission—even if the child has already been labeled gifted. They would like such programs dissolved, or at least kept away from the mainstream of school activity. Other parents value the specialness of the program and the gifted label so highly that they're willing to take extreme measures to persuade the schools to include their children. Many parents worry about the consequences of exclusion from such programs, even though they oppose them in principle; they choose to try to "join 'em" if they can't "fight 'em." All of these parents might seek compromises with the school.

However, even the most efficacious parents may feel timid about challenging the school on such issues. Many schools discourage a parent's request for anything other than superficial information. They can be especially unfriendly when parents challenge school regularities. For example, schools will marshal powerful arguments to defend the legitimacy and evenhandedness of their special programs. They may dismiss a request for special consideration as inappropriate lobbying. They may write off complaints as sour grapes.

Many educators—perhaps the majority—are quietly ambivalent about many school practices, including special programs. They worry, for example, that the effect of gifted programs goes beyond the denial of special opportunities to all children. They often regret the unspoken (and sometimes spoken) message that some children are worthy of special opportunities and others are not. Most educators recognize that such messages can lead children to conclude that they have less capacity for success in school than other children and that they should expect less of themselves. They know that such messages can also lead teachers to expect less of nongifted children than of gifted.

Many educators would like to alter school regularities on behalf of parents and children, but state mandates, parent lobbies, and special-interest groups within education—as well as the self-sustaining power and momentum of the culture—pose formidable barriers to change. For example, many teachers and specialists view gifted classes as rewards for excellent teaching or for seniority.

Parents are often surprised to find educators who are allies. Also surprising is the extent of the compromises that schools are willing to make. Although some schools publicly advertise the alternatives available for children, others allow the news of exceptions to spread through the parent grapevine. Many schools give parents what they want—sometimes because parents find allies on the staff, and sometimes because they are especially persistent, persuasive, or helpful and supportive in other school-related matters.

For example, some parents can get a school to retest a child who just missed the cutoff score for the gifted program. Some schools permit parents to choose different tests on which the child might do better. Some schools will accept the results of privately administered tests by a licensed psychologist, as long as the parent foots the bill. Some schools make special exceptions that allow high achievers or talented students to participate in gifted programs even if they don't meet the cutoff score. Black and Hispanic children or children with primary languages other than English can sometimes qualify according to separate criteria that place less importance on IQ so as to ensure more diverse representation in the special opportunities.

Compromises about Grade Retention Consider another example of a school practice that some parents simply accept—if grudgingly—and others challenge. Each year thousands of parents confront policies that prevent their child's promotion from one grade to the next (or to middle school or high school) because of low performance on a basic competencies test. Many schools begin testing in kindergarten and use measures of reading and math "readiness" to determine whether children will go on to first grade. As with the issue of giftedness, parents need to act confidently and knowledgeably—not easy in the midst of an upsetting, tension-filled event that can have long-range consequences.

Retention, like gifted placements, school safety, or a child's general dissatisfaction with school, generates fundamental questions for parents: Will my child have access to all the high-quality educational experiences from which she could benefit? Will the school exclude her from some? Will she not attempt others? We cannot state that no child benefits from repeating a grade, but we are certain that retention damages more children than it benefits. Parents should resist efforts to have a child repeat a grade unless the school is very persuasive in explaining how the child is an exception to research findings. Schools can provide many satisfactory alternatives to holding children back. For example, tutoring programs can be effective in helping children keep up. Multidimensional classrooms, though difficult to put into place in the typical school, allow children with diverse capabilities to succeed in the same classes.

Parents who want to ask questions about grade retention at their school, like those inquiring about gifted programs, need the support that our earlier research-based reminder provides: Your child and all the children at his school are capable and want to do well. The responses parents receive from the school may not reflect a knowledge of research—especially if the school policy itself runs contrary to research findings. Schools that retain children are not likely to be forthcoming with the research evidence showing that holding children back a grade ill serves most children. Parents cannot be expected to cite chapter and verse of the latest educational research that supports a particular change of school policy. Even if they could, schools are slow—incredibly slow—to respond to research evidence that their practices need changing. However, by understanding the tenor of research that supports the general principles presented at the beginning of this chapter and elsewhere in this book parents can be emboldened to act on their best instincts.

At the very least, parents should seek advice from two or more professionals who may have different educational perspectives on their child's or even the whole school's problems. Teachers, counselors, administrators, specialists, school district personnel, private psychologists, pediatricians, and university consultants can be helpful. So can the references at the end of the chapters in this book.

Parents can't predict the next surprise or prepare for all contingencies that school might bring. However, awareness of research, adherence to solid principles about children's learning and capability, persistence, and a focus on your own values can fortify you. With these in your repertoire, you're likely to get beyond well-meaning school explanations like "It's best for the child." And you'll probably work out a compromise that everyone can live with.

Compromises that Don't Compromise Others

Nearly every school offers special opportunities for selected students. Often schools give these opportunities to children whose parents are the most vocal and visible. As we pointed out in chapter 7, we cannot fault the parent who identifies a class, teacher, or program that is clearly superior and then makes reasonable efforts to have his child enrolled. We find nothing out of line when a parent asks for special consideration to meet the needs of his child. But the presence of special opportunities raises perplexing questions: When do you act to obtain some advantage for your child that is not routinely afforded to everyone?

This dilemma is everpresent when one wants the best for his child in a system that presumes that children get what they deserve or earn. For example, you know that your child would learn more if the principal moved him to a more stimulating class. But how can you express this knowledge without conveying that you think *your* child deserves an exception to the professional judgments (or luck of the draw) of the school? We are not sure you can avoid the appearance of seeking special favors. It may be worthwhile to run that risk. It may not. One thing you can be sure of: if your child isn't getting the best the school has to offer, there are many other children also at this disadvantage. For example, if school policies routinely retain children and maintain rigid cutoffs or other standards for special programs, then there will be many children who stand no chance to qualify and many others who could benefit but will "just miss."

One way to try to live with, if not solve, the dilemma is to ask, whenever you see any child denied the best opportunities, "Why is that necessary?" You won't harm your child's chances for a good education by looking out for other children as well. If you are a parent who cares for all children, the school will probably treat you and your child well, certainly better than if you are someone working only from self-interest. By routinely speaking out on behalf of all children you can protect yourself from seeming to seek special privileges for your own child. In particular, schools need parents of the children who do qualify for special advantages to speak for those who don't. You won't please everyone, but your motives will be clear.

Taking this approach, you might be surprised at what you can accomplish. We know a mother who expressed concern about the day-after-day dull and repetitive math lessons in her child's second-grade class. As a result, the principal offered her child a spot in the gifted math program. The program featured lots of problem solving and hands-on activities that allowed children to apply math to real-world problems. Of course she took it. The child loved the class and began to shine at math.

But this mother's efforts didn't stop there. She was aware that her child was not necessarily smarter, the class was just better. So she shared information about her child's newfound success with other parents. She pointed to the clear advantages of the activities and materials in the new class. In conveying her appreciation to the principal, she asked (a number of times) what the school could do to share this special program with all of the second graders. Her credibility among parents and teachers was especially strong since her focus was on extending a high-quality opportunity to all children. Spurred by parents' enthusiasm, the exemplary math opportunities began to make inroads into other math classes. After one year, the school was pointing proudly, not to its special class, but to its outstanding math program.

Capitulation: No Satisfactory Solution in Sight

Consensus and compromise should be an involved parent's primary goal. However, the troubled state of most schools forces many parents to a third, less satisfying alternative—capitulation. When parents or the school identify a problem as unsolvable, when one or the other will not acknowledge that a serious problem exists, or when both insist upon dramatically different solutions, it may be time to throw in the towel. Capitulation is essentially giving up—either passively, by doing nothing, or actively, by taking some strong action that forecloses cooperation or compromise. There are times when nothing should be done—times when a parent or school person finds it truly sensible to lie low, wait for the trouble to pass, ignore an irritation. Sometimes the only sensible way to follow one's conscience or avoid serious damage may be to phone the superintendent, see a lawyer, or find another school. Most parents would rather avoid all of these courses. Each seems like a defeat.

Unfortunately, some parents and schools capitulate as a first option. The school may surrender by actively suspending, transferring, or expelling troublemakers, or they may react passively and ignore problems. Schools may figure it isn't worth the effort to fight regulations from above. They may lack the gumption to stand up to the demands of a determined, pushy parent. They may give in to following comfortable routines, even if they know that the practices can be harmful.

Parents frequently feel impotent when dealing with schools. Justifiably or not, their experiences in dealing with other large institutions—the bank, the welfare department, the health insurance company—spill over. Many have been worn down by daily encounters with excuses, delays, and buck-passing.

Most parents resort to capitulation only after attempts at easy agreement and negotiated compromise have failed. Recall the cheery anecdote about our friend who got her own child into a better math class and was able to change the entire math program. That story has a less than satisfactory end. Three years later, when our friend's younger child entered the second grade, she was surprised to find that the school was back to only one exemplary and challenging math class. Even though the school district had sent math experts to the school to train all the teachers in the newer math approaches, the time was too short and the support was superficial. In the second year of the program the school district offered little additional follow-up. Teachers could get help from one another only during the time they could steal from lunch or after school.

These teachers had confidence in their tried and true methods and materials and felt insecure about methods and skills that the most highly qualified teachers of mathematics had taken years to develop. Some argued, perhaps correctly, that the old focus on drill and practice in computation was better preparation for the district math test. As time went on, the teachers, one by one, slipped back into the old regularities of math instruction. The old textbooks came out of the closets. Teachers began xeroxing pages of practice problems. They once again started giving timed tests to check the children's proficiency with simple math facts.

Our friend gave up. The school, the parents, and the teachers were unable to sustain the energy, vigilance, and resources needed to make the new math curriculum stick. Tired of the struggle, uncertain of the opportunities her child would get, and having had a glimpse of quality math instruction, she looked elsewhere. Luckily, she found a magnet school in her district that emphasized science and math. The school attracted the most qualified math teachers from the surrounding area (possibly a reason that exemplary math instruction had so hard a time taking hold in her previous school). With further luck, her child was selected from hundreds on the waiting list.

At best, this is a bittersweet conclusion. True, our friend, or any parent, who has the energy and knowledge to pursue high-quality opportunities for her child can often find them. But we would prefer schools where the best is offered to every child.

CHAPTER TWELVE

What's Next?
A Cultural Shift in Schools

Across the nation, most schools offer children far less than they could. Many schools provide mediocrity rather than excellence for mainstream middle-class youth. The most privileged and successful students have far too few rich and compelling learning experiences that stretch their enthusiasm and intellect. And schools fail to improve the life chances of less privileged students by giving them the knowledge and skills to overcome the tremendous social and economic obstacles they face.

Schools must do better. Throughout this book we have pointed to barriers that keep schools from providing high-quality education. We have also pointed to promising research-based changes that schools might make. We may have much to learn about how to educate all students well, but we know enough to get started. To do so, however, parents, policymakers, and educators must combine this knowledge with the courage to act in dramatic ways.

Throughout, we have suggested that schools suffer from a malaise not likely to be remedied by small-scale changes or tinkering. We have pointed to schooling regularities that erect barriers to all children's learning. These barriers call for policy initiatives that depart from the conventional. Such changes will not simply do better for poor and minority children (although that is a critical goal). The barriers we've identified work against the learning of all children, even if their effects are less obvious among white, middle-class children. All children and the whole community gain when we remove barriers to making the best of schools.

In the short term, new school policies can mobilize public commitment. They can alter state and local regulations that limit teaching and learning and create incentives for schools to change themselves. They can marshal federal, state, and community resources and technical assistance to help schools improve. But at every turn, the vigor and energy of these initiatives are threatened by unquestioned traditions and habits of schooling. No reform will survive unless parents, policymakers, and educators work together over the long term to alter firmly entrenched beliefs, as well as the practices that follow from them.

What follows are policy categories and specific recommendations. They are areas of concern and ways of organizing the public effort to separate practice from the grip of the school culture by changing the culture itself. Three premises, elaborated throughout this book, underlie these policy recommendations:

All schools need help. Public policy must work to improve all schools since nearly all schools are not very good. Even those schools we acknowledge as the best could be far better if they were fundamentally different.

Some schools need more help than others. Public policy needs to direct special concern and resources to schools serving children who do not have (for whatever reason—poverty, neglect, health, it doesn't matter) adequate preparation before and guidance throughout their schooling. Within all schools, the opportunities provided to minorities, the poor, girls, and students with individual disabilities may need serious reconsideration. Schools may need to supplement equal access with extra help that enables children to make use of schooling opportunities.

Good schools help all children.

REFORM MANAGEMENT THAT INHIBITS TEACHER PROFESSIONALISM AND SCHOOL IMPROVEMENT

Outmoded, top-down management structures and rigid bureaucratic school organization frustrate schools' and teachers' responsiveness to change. Nearly everywhere standardization is preferred over innovation, and efficiency counts more than excellence. Conformity to traditional assumptions and expectations about education is valued more highly than experimentation and risk taking. These conditions limit policymakers and educators to tinkering around the edges of educational practice rather than allowing them to reform it.

Top-down authority structures maintain teachers' status as skilled workers who have little control over resources, program organization, content, and methods. Prompted in the past by the feminization of teaching, these structures continue to distance teachers from professional, knowledge-based decision making. In the wake of expanding opportunities for women, we now face a shortage of qualified teachers—most critically in schools serving the most disadvantaged children. Moreover, teachers receive inadequate training and preparation and low pay. Their working conditions keep them isolated from one another. While individual teachers remain responsible for children, isolation and specialization keep them from affecting children beyond the confines of their individual classrooms. Teachers don't talk or plan together, and they have few chances to learn from one another. Such conditions cannot attract, prepare, empower, or retain a cadre of teachers committed and able to help all students learn.

Upgrade Teaching and Increase the Access of Students to Highly Qualified Teachers

Rigorous teacher education programs can improve the overall quality of the field. Substantial changes in working conditions and rewards for teachers can help solve the general problems of teacher supply and quality. Policies must also provide incentives to attract and retain high-quality teachers in schools with the most disadvantaged populations.

Policies will need to alter the prevalent practice of assigning the most qualified teachers to schools and classes that serve the most advantaged students. Undoubtedly, such changes will require the participation and cooperation of teacher unions. Such policies are likely to prevent or limit teacher choice of initial assignments and transfer rights based on seniority. However, policymakers can assume that most teachers will commit themselves to help the disadvantaged if they feel that their personal and career well-being is not jeopardized. Union/school district agreements in Rochester, New York, and a number of other urban districts give evidence that such productive compromises are possible.

As in Rochester, innovative teacher-assignment policies can also create incentives for highly skilled teachers to teach in impacted schools. For example, policymakers might begin by concentrating resources that upgrade the quality of teachers' work lives in the neediest schools. Such incentives might include extra pay for developing new school programs and instructional strategies in these settings or for training new teachers in schools that serve disadvantaged students. Other incentives might be lower student–teacher ratios, less instructional and more planning time, enhanced facilities, and special equipment and materials.

Deregulate Schools and Give Them the Power to Improve

Mounting evidence about effective school change and improvement makes it clear that all schools must be reorganized and renewed individually. Many of the current disincentives to teacher professionalism and high-quality educational programs flow from the overregulation and standardization of school organization, content, instructional processes, and teacher evaluation. State and district policies can mandate site-based management and program development. Policies can alter the roles of state and central-office administration. Instead of handing down prescriptions for curriculum and school organization, as they have traditionally done, district-level administrators can build the local school's capacity for improvement. School staffs require time, material resources, central-office support and technical assistance, staff-development opportunities at the site level, and permission to redesign schools. District-level resources can be distributed to local schools to help the process. District administrators can negotiate policies with unions that ensure staff stability and provide an established union voice in school-improvement plans. Such negotiations can smooth the way for teacher participation beyond what union contracts usually specify.

Ken Sirotnik, a researcher at the University of Washington, argues persuasively that an essential part of capacity building lies in providing educators with access to information about what goes on in their own schools and classrooms. If teachers are to feel committed to changes, they must reflect on the courses they offer and who teaches and takes them, and why. They must think critically about how students spend classroom time; how teachers organize learning activities; what curriculum materials they use; and what attitudes prevail. Questions such as those raised throughout this book can be the starting point for school-based deliberations about what practices support and inhibit student access and results. For example: Do teachers believe that all children can succeed? Does the school culture press all children to work hard and take school seriously? What assumptions are made about teachers who work with bright and slow children?

CHANGE ASSUMPTIONS ABOUT LEARNING
THAT RESTRICT CURRICULUM

Obsolete but widely held assumptions about learning lead to classroom instruction that is often out of sync with how children learn and develop. When curriculum developers and teachers construct lessons from a behavioral or training perspective, low-level skills, fragmented knowledge, and easily tested facts dominate. Telling and lecturing, along with the monitoring of seatwork, characterize teaching. Studies of cognition make clear that a variety of instructional modes and activities is necessary for all children to learn well. By skillfully varying instructional strategies, teachers could meet a wider range of children's aptitudes, interests, and development than they do now. Unfortunately, most teachers lack the knowledge or power or both to use a variety of teaching techniques. Coaching, demonstrating, tutoring, symbolically representing, role playing, cooperative learning, and hands-on activities are rare as compared with lecturing and the monitoring of seatwork. Although most teachers reject the notion that students are passive receptacles for the teacher's knowledge, most conduct class as if children were just that.

Misconceptions of how children learn combine with the assembly-line mentality of schools to fragment knowledge into isolated, abstract chunks. Educators have too few opportunities to consider what is most worth knowing—what it means to have an education. As a result few schools offer core curricula that integrate rich and complex knowledge from a variety of disciplines.

Disconnected coursework, a lack of coherence in core subjects, and an approach to curriculum based on narrow objectives cheapen knowledge and make it largely irrelevant. Ironically, some recent efforts to make schools more academically rigorous have increased rather than diminished fragmentation. For example, many large school districts have recently developed specific grade-level learning objectives in academic subjects. First, curriculum specialists analyze the topics and skills included in state or standardized tests of basic skills at each grade level. Then they develop curriculum objectives and units of instruction that match them. The intent is to be sure that students learn the academic material that is on the test. Such test-driven curricula give students little opportunity to integrate ideas and connect what they learn at school to the rest of their lives. The abstraction and disconnectedness of school knowledge fly in the face of cognitive perspectives on how children learn. Such approaches particularly disadvantage poor, black, and Hispanic students while adding nothing to the opportunities of middle-class and advantaged youngsters.

Provide Rich, Integrated Curricula and Instructional Strategies

A rigorous curriculum shaped by knowledge of children's cognitive processes will be rich in meaning and easier to master and remember. Such lessons feature large-scale assignments, problem-solving approaches to knowledge, classics of literature, activities in democratic participation, and so forth. California's new model curriculum frameworks, supported by the state's efforts to upgrade textbooks, are examples that include a cognitive perspective on learning and aim at providing greater access to knowledge for all students.

New policies must tread the line between a rich common curriculum and responsiveness to both individual and cultural differences—not an easy task. We must develop educational materials and teaching practices to allow for the differences among children without consigning them to an inferior or low-status curriculum. This speaks again to the importance of leaving the specifics of curriculum and instruction design to the building level—albeit with plenty of technical assistance and accountability for student learning.

Knowledge from education researchers, cultural anthropologists, and sociolinguists exists on which to base the development of new approaches to curriculum and instruction that may be especially appropriate for inner-city students. For example, particularly effective reading strategies have been developed for poor Hawaiian children in the Kamehameha Early Education Project. Cooperative learning strategies specifically designed for teaching high-level science concepts in bilingual classrooms have led to some dramatic achievement gains. And in a number of places, special math and science interventions for minority youngsters and girls have reversed their typical inclination to drop out of these subjects.

Federal policies can provide support for research into appropriate avenues to such curriculum development. States with large education departments can help develop model (not mandated) curriculum and teaching strategies and provide technical assistance to local schools. State departments can exercise considerable leverage over the content of textbooks. Some are trying to direct textbooks away from what a National Academy of Sciences panel recently called collections of "factlets" and "beautifully illustrated dictionaries." Moves to have textbooks support a few large, important concepts will help equalize opportunities for all students to learn those concepts. Of course, states must also work explicitly to remove biased instructional materials that misrepresent the lives of many Americans and create false impressions about peoples' diverse values and experiences.

REMOVE INCENTIVES FOR COMPARING AND LABELING STUDENTS

Popular views of intelligence and ability, as well as perceptions about the distribution of talent, lead to evaluations that emphasize how students compare with others. For the most part, tests and grades are instrumental in the processes of ranking students, separating and segregating them, and sorting them for future social participation. Schools use such evaluation to select a few students for enriched educational opportunities and slate others for low-level participation.

Because few educators understand how intelligence is complex, multi-dimensional, and changeable, they have not rethought the role of schooling in developing children's potential. Too few see the possibility that all students are capable of using complex knowledge to solve problems. As a result schools neglect the nurturing and developing of students' intelligence. Many educators do not consider how standardized tests can be abused, and they fail to apply reasonable safeguards when using them. The psychologist Asa Hilliard suggests that tests be judged by the following criterion: "Can something be learned . . . to affect and improve the validity of instructional strategies?" Schools rarely use tests for this purpose.

In order to hold schools accountable for special funding, states and federal agencies often rely on standardized achievement or intelligence tests to be sure that the money goes to the proper categories of children. This identification process can work against the best interests of both special and mainstream students. Such policies have the unintended effect of directing educators' attention to children's personal characteristics, such as race, social class, or disabilities. In doing so, the policies often ignore instruction, testing, tracking, textbooks, age-grading, and other alterable school practices that help create children's social and academic attributes. Testing practices often sustain misperceptions about the learning potential of high-risk students.

These practices can limit the opportunities of most children. Nearly every school consigns all but the top scorers to average (that is, mediocre) labels, classes, and achievements. To protect these children, schools should halt the proliferation of high-status labels that knock all other students down one more notch. When one California educator heard that a new magnet school for the Highly Gifted was to be established in addition to a nearby school for the merely Gifted, he proposed (with tongue in cheek) starting a new program for the Severely Gifted. Less ironic, but only because it really happens, is the creation of "accelerated" classes to bridge the perceived gap between honors and regular classes.

Use New Forms of Assessment

Current research in cognitive psychology challenges the traditional forms and uses of evaluation—mental measurement in particular. The best evidence suggests there is an abundance of cognitive processes that go unmeasured, that children learn to be intelligent, and that it is possible for schools to nurture mental growth and produce significant gains in intellectual development. What is needed are evaluations and tests that reveal learning and thinking processes, so that educators can look at how students are functioning mentally, rather than simply note the products of that functioning—for example, an IQ or an achievement score. This is a significant distinction. Assessments that tell how students make sense of instruction (and how they have difficulty) can enable educators to help students develop thinking ability—not just learn more facts.

When diagnostic assessments of students' cognitive functioning are needed to guide remedial efforts, policies can direct educators to use less global assessment tools. For example, some new techniques (dynamic assessment is one) provide information about specific aspects of mental functioning and point to specific strategies to overcome weaknesses. Such policies can discourage the use of traditional tests that give educators little more than global labels that follow children throughout school.

The removal of labeling can cut some of the bureaucratic requirements that gobble up teacher and administrative time. Record keeping, budgeting, and other paperwork just don't translate into improved instruction.

Promote School and Classroom Practices in Which Students Learn Together

As schools reduce labeling, tracking, pull-out programs, and unidimensional classrooms that segregate students and restrict access to knowledge, they must replace them with practices that allow children to work together on a common core of learnings without watering down the curriculum for any child. Team teaching, multigrade classrooms, and cooperative small-group learning are examples of such practices. Additionally these practices can diminish the different school outcomes associated with race and class.

Perhaps by age sixteen it may become appropriate for children to diverge in their courses of study. By then some know they are bound for careers in professions that require years of higher education. Others are ready to prepare for entry into work or short-term technical preparation. However, when careers and future education choices reflect students' race, economic standing, or gender, it casts doubt on the fairness of the earlier schooling on which they base career and college choices. In addition it raises serious concerns about the talent being lost to society. To prevent such distortions, policies should provide for careful monitoring of school guidance and student choices.

Curriculum models, teacher training, and text adoptions are also policy-relevant avenues to encourage schools to have children learn together. For example, textbook adoption policies in California have mandated that mathematics texts include lessons appropriate for children working together on tasks.

Students with special needs do require extra resources and technical assistance. However, without the altering of the social and instructional context of schools that currently requires identifying and sorting, students miss the full benefit of extra help. One strategy (currently being proposed as the "regular education initiative") is to integrate specialists into the regular classroom. Together with regular classroom teachers, they would share the responsibility for helping children with special needs. Teams of teachers could develop curriculum and instructional strategies to accommodate the needs of the diverse group of children in the class. In the process, many of the typically neglected "regular" children would have access to help when they need it and would benefit from the watchful eye and help of additional resource teachers. Other approaches might avoid the labeling of children altogether, but simply identify schools with high rates of children from high-risk groups. Shifting departmentalized junior highs to middle schools with teaching teams responsible for groups of students can promote an environment more caring and tolerant of individual and social differences.

CONNECT SCHOOL AND HOME

Without romanticizing the good old days, we think it safe to say that schools once occupied a more central, familiar spot in family life—

like the neighborhood grocer, the mailman, or the family next door. Families, particularly those who had high educational aspirations for their children but were not necessarily educated (or English-speaking) themselves, could more easily say to their children, "Go to school and learn." Many could rely on broad community support for seeing that that happened. Today, schools occupy a place in society more like the telephone company or the bank. They are there to serve, and we wouldn't do without them. Nonetheless, most people would prefer to have less rather than more contact with schools. Like other large service corporations, schools can be particularly forbidding and inhospitable to the poor, minorities, and non-English-speakers.

But the old communities are gone, and few parents are likely to be working in the neighborhood of their school or home. Even affluence offers no assurance that parents will have the time or inclination to support the school or see other parents as a community involved in the education of children. Even though most middle- and upper-class children realize that diplomas and degrees are important stepping-stones to successful and affluent adult lives, many of them consider their schoolwork as entirely separate from their lives outside of school. And poor children whose parents may have no jobs at all often question school's relevance to success and real-life rewards. In the past the promise of good jobs and increased income provided considerable motivation for the hard work school learning requires. That was because most children witnessed at firsthand both the rewards of education and the hardships that accrued to those who had none.

The problem of disconnectedness and alienation among home, community, and school has social as well as school causes; schools cannot shoulder all the blame. Nevertheless, few schools explore all the avenues for opening themselves up to and using home and community resources. Shaped by tradition and unchanged by policy, schools are not welcoming places to those on the outside.

Forge Nontraditional Alliances among Schools, Families, and Communities

While schools should probably concentrate their limited resources, technical capacity, and political clout on *educational* matters, alliances with families, community groups, social service agencies, business and industry, and universities can help schools attain academic goals. They can also help families meet children's extraeducational needs.

Schools can work with parents to establish after-school tutoring programs that provide academic support and, at the same time, provide high-quality childcare. Teachers can show parents effective ways to supplement classroom instruction. As we described in chapters 9 and 10, attention to learning at home can increase students' achievement.

Collaborative arrangements with social service agencies can help families meet a wider array of children's needs. A powerful example of collaboration between the school, parents, and social service professionals can be found in the partnership between New Haven, Connecticut, schools and Yale University. Leadership teams composed of members of these three groups help with school governance by developing a comprehensive plan to achieve academic and school climate goals. They also address the social and psychological problems of individual children. These are not parent-run schools. They operate within state and district guidelines and acknowledge the legal authority of the principal. Nevertheless, the combined knowledge and resources of the team helps the school solve many academic and social problems. The empowered parent involvement that these schools promote translates into success for even the most disadvantaged children—in part by promoting greater confidence and competence for parents.

In middle-class schools, high-quality after-school care may be all that young children need outside of school. Collaborations between schools and child care providers can ensure good care and integrate help with homework into such programs. In schools serving poor children, collaborations between schools and social service agencies can also help young children and their families get nutrition and health care services. Schools are a logical center for the delivery of services by other agencies. Secondary schools can arrange social services for teenagers—particularly those thought to be at risk for school failure and dropping out because of non-academic problems such as pregnancy, unemployment, and drug abuse. Such programs can include school-based health clinics, substance-abuse programs, and child care for teenage mothers. Other programs can provide job training and job placement services.

Businesses can contribute managerial expertise and material resources. They can help create communitywide commitment to school change. In urban areas, businesses' most promising contribution may be providing real-world job experience and the promise of college tuition assistance on which disadvantaged youth can build hope. University–school partnerships can help create more effective curriculum and instructional programs through staff development. They can also launch joint efforts to provide high-quality programs for high school students on college campuses as well as at students' home schools. Such programs can provide students with a taste of college life that may help them see higher education as a realistic option.

Collectively, volunteer efforts that support schools are valuable. However, volunteerism has proven to be a shaky foundation for building lasting school reform. Collaborative projects must be viewed as serving the interests of all parties. For example, businesses' commitment should rest on their belief that good schools will lead to a productive work force. And university faculty must be convinced that working with schools will enhance their own academic careers. Existing public and private agencies could serve children and their families better if they had easier access to children via schools.

Furthermore, the separation and frequent alienation between schools and parents is so great that simply putting out the welcome mat will not be enough to attract involvement. School districts should work aggressively to engage parents and the community in making education everyone's business. Jurisdictional jealousies, funding, public statutes, overextended agencies, insurance, bureaucracies, and paperwork are all amenable to policy intervention.

HOLD SCHOOLS ACCOUNTABLE FOR BOTH QUALITY AND EQUITY

Policies that deregulate school programs and focus on capacity building do not relieve states, local school boards, or district administrators of the responsibility for educational oversight. Policymakers can set targets for improvement and establish clear accountability mechanisms for fair access and improved results. Policymakers need to develop new modes of accountability appropriate for restructuring schools. They must recognize the limitations and misuses of current measures and acknowledge how individuals and agencies use these data to increase or depress opportunity for some students. States and districts must avoid overreliance on the results of nationally normed standardized tests and, instead, establish more valuable indicators of school quality and student performance. For example they might measure the effectiveness of a school's efforts to be more responsive to families and the community. They can ask schools to specify the curricular opportunities they provide and to identify the students who participate in them. Most effective will be policies that allow schools, districts, and states to negotiate specific local goals and improvement indicators.

States and districts can also mandate that equity be monitored by disaggregating indicator data by race, social class, gender, and disability. In this way, they can avoid a common occurrence, that of taking solace in *average* test scores inching upward while certain populations—typically poor and minorities—remain at unacceptably low levels.

KEEP SCHOOLS HIGH ON THE
PUBLIC REFORM AGENDA

The conversation in the faculty lunchroom was cynical, even bitter. In response to a self-congratulatory press release built around recent math and reading scores that had inched up a few percentage points, teachers sarcastically praised one another for "doing a fine job" and having "fixed that problem." Why that response to essentially good news? First, teachers are aware of how little these scores can reflect their really important work and how they obscure how much remains to be done. Second, teachers are aware of how surges in public attention to schools can appear and fade on the basis of quickly changing perceptions that schools are in or out of trouble. The teachers worried that such specious good news might diminish public interest. Good scores might suggest that schools were on their way to improvement—the light at the end of the tunnel—no problems—no worries.

In defense of the school district officials who wrote the press release, this public relations problem represents a central challenge for educators: how to keep the public supportive of school reform. On the one hand, it is nearly impossible to get a discouraged public to support anything but the familiar. In fact, in the absence of good news, the public, through its policymakers, tends to withhold financial support instead of "throwing good money after bad." Seemingly, school policymakers must provide a steady diet of evidence (or illusion) that they are indeed making progress. On the other hand, as reflected by the teachers' worries suggested above, the public can make a full meal out of a few crumbs of good news. If a modest increase in public support and attention produces such good results, maybe there's not that much of a problem. Thus the cycle of public interest in change begins its downward turn.

Schools suffer as much from the lack of public will as from the lack of educational know-how, and the public will is certainly transitory. The Reagan administration's successful use of "bully-pulpit" exhortations clearly demonstrated that the public can be eager for action when they have information and perceive a problem. However, the public's interest (and its attendant willingness to support reform) may be driven as much by the skillful manipulation of crises as by the real understanding of underlying problems. When that is the case, their interest is hard to sustain.

Policymakers face inevitable built-in limits. They can hardly convince the public that there is a crisis without assuming some responsibility for fixing that crisis. When solutions and cures are not quickly forthcoming the public loses confidence, interest, or both. Public imagination is more easily sparked by promises of a quick fix than by calls to commit resources for incremental change. Moreover, long-range changes may not produce effects until after a term of office has expired.

As state and local policymakers themselves better understand the scope and complexity of school needs and change, we hope they will get better at generating public support for fundamental change. We would like to see politicians inform the public rather than exhort with sound and fury but little substance. The place to start is to report information that identifies needs. The facts about school conditions and barriers to education can be startling enough to mobilize the public concern.

However, sustained public dialogue is also necessary. Otherwise, data are easy to misinterpret. For example, some state education agencies and local districts have begun to publicize the racial breakdowns of student enrollments in various courses and curriculum tracks. Such data point clearly to the differential access of minority students to advanced academic coursework. This information, accompanied by calls for increasing access of minority students to college-preparatory programs, can help generate pressure from the public and politicians for needed changes. On the other hand, facts about differential access can be counterproductive in a climate of fear or ignorance about individual differences. Thoughtlessly used, they can reinforce pernicious stereotypes.

Similarly, policymakers can educate for change by focusing less on a few essentially simplistic measures such as test scores and course enrollments. They can highlight fundamental conditions that enable high-quality and fair schooling. Public discussions of these conditions will add strength, credibility, and, not least, interest to policymakers' messages. Such discussion will also advertise that improved student performance and equity are complex goals and not responsive to simplistic changes. For example, policymakers and the public should consider all of the following essential school features:

Conditions that Facilitate Access to Knowledge
   Teacher qualifications
   Instructional time
   Course offerings

Curricular quality
Grouping practices
Materials, laboratories, equipment
Academic support programs
Enrichment activities
Parent involvement
Staff development
Faculty, policymaker, and public beliefs
Conditions that Enable Schools to Push for High Achievement
Attention to Academics
Graduation requirements
Graduation rates
Enrollment in rigorous programs
Recognition of academic accomplishments
Academic expectations for students
Quantity and type of homework
Evaluation practices that emphasize learning
Conditions that Make Professional Teaching Conditions Possible
Teacher salaries
Pupil load/class size
Teacher time for planning
Collegial work
Teacher involvement in decision making
Teacher autonomy/flexibility
Support for innovation
Clerical support

WHY THESE POLICIES?

We suggest these approaches because we believe that they can stimulate both short-term action and a longer-term dialogue among state houses, departments of education, local school districts, interested citizens, and parents. They call attention to fundamentally different problems and therefore suggest solutions to an old, but increasingly serious educational and social challenge—making the best of schools for all children in a democratic society.

Each category above suggests policies that can chip away at school barriers that inhibit children's learning. Most follow from considerable evidence of educational effectiveness. Many can be achieved with current levels of resources and technical expertise, and some will meet little resistance. Some immediate and visible progress is important because policymakers are pressed for practical strategies that are cost-effective and produce quick changes—those with lots of "bang for the buck." Such policy actions can instill confidence and hope, and they help buy time for long-range reform. Parents, too, sending children to school right now, have little time to wait. And indeed, the public has a right to see changes after it spends its money.

We would mislead, however, if we suggested that short-term policy changes can start the nation's schools on the road to the massive cultural shift that is necessary. Large-scale changes will require sustained effort over the long term, especially those that challenge schooling assumptions and taken-for-granted practices. It will require five, ten, twenty, or more years before fundamental change begins to pay off in significantly improved teacher education and a more professional teaching force. Fundamental alterations in school organization and classroom practice will have to be in place for some time before we see dramatic changes in children's learning, drop-out rates, or equitable enrollments in universities.

Throughout this book we have tried to consider the self-interest of average, concerned parents, citizens, and policymakers. We hope readers can now look at their own children and at all the children they care about and make better sense of schools. We are not shy about this appeal to self-interest, as long as it leads to actions that serve everyone's interests and everyone's children. We have argued—we hope convincingly—that the same practices that make schooling better for any one child make schooling better for all children. We believe that, in fundamentally changed school cultures, there can be enough of the best education to reach all children. However, the creation of such cultures requires strong public commitment, increased resources, widespread knowledge, and support for sensible, if dramatic, changes. These, of course, depend on courageous parents, teachers, and policymakers who are willing to provide leadership in making the best of schools.

FOR FURTHER READING

Ann Bastian and others, *Chosing Equality: The Case for Democratic Schooling*. San Francisco: Public Media Center, 1985.

James Comer, "Home, School, and Academic Learning." In John I. Goodlad and Pamela Keating (eds.), *Access to Knowledge*. New York: College Board, 1989.

Committee for Economic Development, *Investing in Our Children: Business and the Public Schools*. 1985.

Marian Wright Edleman, *Children in Crisis*. Boston: Children's Defense Fund, 1986.

John I. Goodlad and Jeannie Oakes, "We Must Offer Equal Access to Knowledge," *Educational Leadership,* February 1988, pp. 16–22.

Paul Hill and Leslie Shapiro, *Cities Mobilize to Improve Their Schools.* Santa Monica, CA: The RAND Corporation, 1988.

Asa G. Hilliard, "Testing and Misunderstanding Intelligence." In John I. Goodlad and Pamela Keating (eds.), *Access to Knowledge.* New York: College Board, 1989.

Pamela Keating and Jeannie Oakes, "Access to Knowledge: Breaking Down School Barriers that Limit Learning." Boulder, CO: Education Commission of the States, 1988.

National Coalition of Advocates for Children, *Barriers to Excellence: Our Children at Risk.* Boston: NCAC, 1985.

Jeannie Oakes, *Improving Inner-City Schools: Current Strategies in Urban School Reform,* Santa Monica, CA: The RAND Corporation, 1987.

Kenneth A. Sirotnik, "Equal Access to Quality in Public Schooling." In John I. Goodlad and Pamela Keating (eds.), *Access to Knowledge.* New York: College Board, 1989.

Suzanne Soo Hoo, "School Renewal: Taking Responsibility for Providing an Education of Value." In John I. Goodlad and Pamela Keating (eds.), *Access to Knowledge.* New York: College Board, 1989.

William Julius Wilson, *The Truly Disadvantaged.* Chicago: University of Chicago Press, 1987.

INDEX

Ability: children's perception of, 63; and tracking, 155; and labeling, 292. *See also* Children's beliefs about ability; Teacher beliefs about children's ability

Ability grouping: and opportunities to learn, 15; based on teacher expectations, 61; for reading instruction, 86; in elementary schools, 161; and gifted students, 201, 202. *See also* Tracking

Abortion. *See* Health and fitness

Academic atmosphere. *See* Expectations

Academic Decathlon. *See* Competition

Academic Preparation for College, 113–14

Accelerated classes: and tracking, 158

Accommodation. *See* Assimilation

Accountability: in cooperative lessons, 73; by testing schools and teachers, 138–39; and school-reform policy, 297–98

Active and passive learning: and cognition, 34, 42, 53; in classes, 57, 64, 68–69, 77; and curriculum, 85, 95, 106, 111, 118–20, 125; and coopera-

tion, 129; with toys and games, 214–17 passim; and television, 224; and reading, 248–50, 261

Advanced placement (AP), 204–05; and tracking, 158

After-school supervision and childcare, 207–08, 218–19; and nontraditional partnerships with schools, 295–96

Aid to Families with Dependent Children (AFDC): decline in federal support, 5

AIDS: student knowledge of, 115. *See also* Health and fitness

Amusing Ourselves to Death, 113

Artists in residence, 114–15

Arts, 109, 111–15; in science lessons, 105; time schools spend on, 110

Assembly line: management model for schools, 7. *See also* Efficiency and the factory model.

Assimilation: and accommodation, 39–41; and self-concept, 44

At risk students, 177. *See also* Disadvantaged children